THE OBLIQUE LIGHT

BOOKS BY *Robert E. Spiller*

THE AMERICAN IN ENGLAND DURING THE
FIRST HALF CENTURY OF INDEPENDENCE

FENIMORE COOPER, CRITIC OF HIS TIMES

A DESCRIPTIVE BIBLIOGRAPHY OF JAMES FENIMORE COOPER *(with P. Blackburn)*

THE CYCLE OF AMERICAN LITERATURE

EIGHT AMERICAN AUTHORS: *"Henry James"*

SIX AMERICAN NOVELISTS OF THE NINETEENTH CENTURY:
AN INTRODUCTION: *"Cooper"*

THE THIRD DIMENSION

THE OBLIQUE LIGHT

EDITED BY *Robert E. Spiller*

LITERARY HISTORY OF THE UNITED STATES *(Chairman, Editorial Board)*

THE ROOTS OF NATIONAL CULTURE *(revised by H. Blodgett)*

FENIMORE COOPER'S GLEANINGS IN EUROPE: FRANCE AND ENGLAND

AMERICAN PERSPECTIVES *(with E. Larrabee)*

CHANGING PATTERNS IN AMERICAN CIVILIZATION

SOCIAL CONTROL IN A FREE SOCIETY

EMERSON: FIVE ESSAYS ON MAN AND NATURE

THE EARLY LECTURES OF RALPH WALDO EMERSON *(co-editor)*

A TIME OF HARVEST: AMERICAN LITERATURE 1910-1960

THE AMERICAN LITERARY REVOLUTION 1783-1837

THE
OBLIQUE LIGHT

Studies in Literary History
and Biography

BY

Robert E. Spiller

THE MACMILLAN COMPANY, *NEW YORK*
COLLIER-MACMILLAN LIMITED, *LONDON*

Library of Congress Catalog Card Number: 68-20748

FIRST PRINTING

The Macmillan Company, New York
Collier-Macmillan Canada Ltd., Toronto, Ontario

Printed in the United States of America

ACKNOWLEDGMENT is made to the following for permission to use copyright materials: *Journal of The Franklin Institute*, Vol. 233, April 1942, 309-329, for "Benjamin Franklin: Student of Life" © The Franklin Institute 1942; *Proceedings*, Vol. 100, No. 4, for "Franklin on the Art of Being Human" © The American Philosophical Society 1956; Holt, Rinehart and Winston, Inc. for "Fenimore Cooper: The Critical American in England" from *The American in England*, Copyright Holt, Rinehart and Winston, Inc. 1926, 1954; The New York State Historical Association for "Second Thoughts on Cooper as a Social Critic" from *James Fenimore Cooper: A Re-Appraisal* © The New York State Historical Society 1954; *New England Quarterly*, III, 55-81 (January, 1930) for "A Case for W. E. Channing"; The Macmillan Company for "Ralph Waldo Emerson: Man Thinking" and "Henry Adams: Man of Letters," from *The Literary History of the United States*, Copyright 1946, 1947, 1948, 1953, 1963 by The Macmillan Company; Scholars' Facsimiles and Reprints for "The Private Novel of Henry Adams" from the Introduction to *Esther* © Scholars' Facsimiles and Reprints 1938; *Saturday Review*, January 7, 1948, for "Sidney Lanier: Ancestor of Anti-Realism"; *The Nation* for "The Influence of Edmund Wilson"; *Studies in Philology*, XXIII, (January 1926), 1-15, for "The English Literary Horizon: 1818-1835"; *USA in Focus*, Nordic Association for American Studies, Oslo, Norway, 1966, for "The American in Europe: Then and Now."

Contents

Preface

THE ESSAYS IN this volume were, like those in its companion *The Third Dimension* (New York: Macmillan, 1965), written at various times during almost a half century of study of American literary history. I have saved for *The Oblique Light* those which focus on individual writers and seem to have contributed to important reinterpretations by setting the artist back into what can be reconstructed of his own physical, emotional, and intellectual environments. Thus literary history can contribute to an understanding of a work of art by means of biography as well as by reconstructing its larger cultural context.

It was during the period 1920–40 that my generation first challenged the assumption that American literature is one branch of English colonial literature and attempted to demonstrate that it is rather the expression, on a new continent and under new conditions of life, of the whole tradition of Western European culture.

One of the more striking by-products of this movement has been the breakdown of a false distinction between the man of letters and the man of action. Because the culture of the United States has been, at least until very recently, a fluent and developing process, its literature has suffered more than it should from this kind of division. The American man of letters has usually been judged for his contribution to an alien and British tradition, while the American man of action has been so deeply immersed in the expanding civilization of the new continent that he could not easily think of his writing as literature. Thus Cooper was long thought of as a kind of American Scott who wrote romances of the Indians and the sea rather than as one of the most perceptive of a long line of American novelists, including Howells and Lewis, who have used fiction as an instrument of social criticism; and Henry Adams, about whom the historians raised eyebrows because of his supposed confusion of mysticism with fact and his prophesies of historical doom, turns out to be a man of letters who was the first American deliberately to use dialectic symbolism as the basis of modern American literary art. Similarly, Benjamin Franklin, the colonial amateur, becomes the American adaptation of the Renaissance Man and a master of literary satire; and Emerson, the confident seer of Concord, becomes the prose-poet and romantic searcher for a new moral imperative in a godless and empirical society. At the same time, the American image of old-world culture and the European image of the renegade American find grounds for new judgments.

Much of the biographical "de-bunking" of the twenties was pure sensationalism and has been conveniently forgotten; but it served a useful scholarly purpose. Once a stereotype was shattered, the conscientious literary historian could reexamine the facts and construct a new and probably more accurate portrait. The sum of these portraits by many hands has led to a wholly new view of American literary history. This is the story I have tried to recall in my concluding reminiscences of the movement; the other essays in this volume are some of my contributions to it during the past forty years. I have here reprinted them without change, even though they may seem far less novel today than they did when they were written. Heresy has a way of becoming gospel if it has in it a grain of truth.

Philadelphia
September, 1967

I

The Discoverers

Benjamin Franklin:
Student of Life

Read in the Hall of The Franklin Institute, Philadelphia, March 1, 1940, this was one of a series by various hands which was designed to disclose the variety of Franklin's interests and personality. It was published in the *Journal of The Franklin Institute* CXXXIII (April, 1942): 309–329, and subsequently collected into a volume entitled *Meet Dr. Franklin* (Philadelphia: Franklin Institute, 1943).

THE LIFE, THOUGHT, and works of Benjamin Franklin have been the subjects of so many special studies that there should be little left to say about him. But Franklin was first and last a human being with an unusually unified reading of life. I shall try therefore to define the point of view which seems to me to have been at the root of his many and various actions, and thereby provide one more comment on that sense of wholeness and unity of character which we all feel in his presence but which we all find so difficult to define. However many avenues of his thought and experience one follows out to their manifold expressions, the return trip brings one always to the same source. Franklin asked only one question of life and of the things in it: "Does it work?" The method of his thinking seems to me always to be pragmatic. He relies in every problem upon experience in the immediate sense as his final authority.

If this seems too simple a statement of the question and too easy an answer, my excuse is that I am not a philosopher, that I do not believe Franklin to have been one, and that I do not look to philosophy in the strict sense of the term to provide much more than some of the language of the discussion that I have undertaken. It is the habit of literary critics and historians to describe people in terms of the mainsprings of their actions and thought. Such a statement as I have made about Franklin is perhaps as much a comment upon myself and my tribe as upon him. We find ourselves constantly using such phrases as "philosophy of life," "reading of life," and "romantic and classic," to the alarm and disgust of more disciplined thinkers. Because literature involves the emotions as well as the mind, the terms which are usually applied to the definitions of thinkers are inadequate. They must either be abandoned or have their meanings stretched to include emotional attitudes as well as rational systems. When I call Franklin "pragmatic," therefore, I am attempting to describe his whole personality and the meaning of his attitude toward life. In this sense I am treating Franklin as a literary figure, which undoubtedly he is, rather than primarily as a philosopher, scientist, statesman, or social critic, even though I may give much attention to these aspects of his thought and pay little or none to the form and style of his writings.

The pigeonholing of a great man in so summary a fashion must always imply the phrase "it seems to me." If you will consent to my calling his attitude "pragmatic," I shall try to define and to illustrate what the word may mean within the limits of this discussion. If we are satisfied that the elusive sense of unity which is so obvious to most students of Franklin has been thereby defined, we may raise further questions of whether this attitude is characteristically, even though not exclusively, American, and whether it is a satisfactory philosophy of life in itself—in short, we may ask whether pragmatism works.

II

To say that Franklin was a pragmatist is not to imply that he would even understand the accusation were he alive today. As far as I know, the term has been in use in this sense for scarcely more than half a century. In 1907, William James called it "a new name for some old ways of thinking," [1] and proceeded to put it into the philosopher's everyday vocabulary as one more mystification for the layman. It is the same system of thought that has more recently been called instrumentalism because, in the words of James himself, in it "theories thus become *instruments, not answers to enigmas.*" It is little more than a point of view, "the attitude of looking away from first things, principles, 'categories,' supposed necessities, and of looking toward last things, fruits, consequences, facts." The result is that "ideas (which themselves are but parts of our experience) become true just in so far as they help us to get into satisfactory relation with other parts of our experience." [2] Ideas, then, have no intrinsic value apart from experience; they are valid only insofar as they can be proved useful in practice. They therefore cannot form a philosophy in the usual sense.

If Pragmatism is not in the full sense a philosophy today, it was even less so in Franklin's time; and Franklin, who did not even have this term by which to describe his point of view, was not a philosopher. It was customary for his contemporaries to call him one, and he himself founded a society which he called philosophical. Recent biographers have continued to use the term in describing him, but it must be remembered that the word "philosopher" in the eighteenth century often meant "natural philosopher," or what we should mean by the term "natural scientist." This was Franklin's own use of it when he named as resident members of the American Philosophical Society a physician, a botanist, a mathematician, a chemist, a mechanician, a geographer, and a general natural philosopher.[3] This last Franklin himself unquestionably was, and his membership in foreign scientific societies was fit tribute to his attainments in this field. But metaphysician or logician he was not.

The danger of attempting to explain Franklin's mind in terms of systematic philosophy is illustrated by a recent analysis of his thought by Chester Jorgenson who strives to attach him to what he calls "scientific deism," a metaphysical system based upon Newtonian physics and the rationalism of Locke. Mr. Jorgenson develops his thesis at some length and concludes: "To see the reflection of Newton and his progeny in Franklin's activities, be they economic, political, literary, or philosophical, lends a compelling unity to the several sides of his genius, heretofore seen as unrelated." His *modus operandi* is best explained "in reference to the thought pattern of scientific deism." [4] This theory is undeniably suggestive if it be used merely as an explanation of the formative period of Franklin's thought, but Mr. Jorgenson has neglected to give full weight to Franklin's emphatic rejection of the naïve system-building of his youth. His short period of philosophical inquiry, 1725–29, ended with his *Modest Inquiry into the Nature and Necessity of* [not Liberty, or God, but] *a Paper Currency.*[5]

Related in so formal a sense I do not believe that the sides of his genius were. To be sure, Franklin absorbed the spirit of inquiry and experiment from the intellectual atmosphere of his day and he may justly be thought of as a product of the eighteenth-century Enlightenment, but to assume from this that he formulated in his own mind and held to a philosophical basis for his actions is to push a half-truth too far. It would be difficult to document the statement that "Franklin was a disinterested scientist in the sense that he interrogated nature with an eye to discovering its immutable laws." [6] As far as I know, Franklin only once attempted an intellectual and systematic statement of his philosophy. This was in his early pamphlet, *A Dissertation on Liberty and Necessity, Pleasure and Pain* (1725), published when he was only nineteen. By following the logic of his own propositions through, he reached conclusions which seemed to him not to work. Among his surprising results are the statements that, "If there is no such Thing as Free-Will in Creatures, there can be neither Merit nor Demerit in Creatures," and that, "Pleasure is equal to Pain." "I printed a small Number," the old man wrote in looking back over the follies of his youth. "It occasion'd my being more consider'd by Mr. Palmer, as a young Man of some Ingenuity, tho' he seriously Expostulated with me upon the Principles of my Pamphlet which to him appear'd abominable. My printing of this pamphlet," he concludes, "was another Erratum." [7] That was the beginning and the end of the philosopher Franklin.

But another kind of sage was born at that moment, one who lived rather than formulated his thought. Fifty years later he explained to Benjamin Vaughan that "the great uncertainty I found in metaphysical reasonings disgusted me, and I quitted that kind of reading and study for others more satisfactory." [8] If we wish, therefore, to discover a "compelling organic unity" in his thought, we must seek it rather in his attitude and actions than in his expression of theories. The sense of wholeness with which he impresses us is perhaps more accurately attributed by Mr. Van Doren to the fact that "his powers were from first to last in a flexible equilibrium." [9] Where should we look for the secret of that poise?

I I I

The first and most obvious field for our inquiry is of course that of scientific experiment, which he insisted in carrying out in spite of the protests of the Good Mouse Amos, who lived, according to Robert Lawson, in Ben's fur cap.

"I shall tear the lightening from the skies," Amos quotes him as saying, "and harness it to do the bidding of man."

"Personally," said the mouse, "I think the sky's an excellent place for it." [10]

The familiar stories of the Pennsylvania fireplace, or the electric kite, or any of the other examples of Franklin's investigative mind would any of them reveal the process of thinking in which I am here interested. Apparently he read the reports of investigations being conducted elsewhere and kept up a correspondence with other experimental scientists, but of theoretical reading there is little record except in his youth. His correspondence with Collinson, Kames, Hartley, and other European thinkers is full of discussions of scientific experiments and political and economic developments, with some practical morality, and no metaphysics. Phenomena themselves first attracted him—smoky chimneys, the common cold, oil on water, lightning striking barns and steeples. Then followed a few simple experiments to determine the conditions under which each operated. When he had satisfied his curiosity on this point, he did not, as would most experimental scientists, formulate a law or hypothesis and push the problem further into theoretical regions. Rather, he turned about and sought to harness the lightning with rods and wires, make a ladder for his bookshelves, or work out a system of diet and exercise that would check the common cold. Such abstractions as atoms, calories, and vitamins would have had no interest for him. But he was tireless in the observation of phenomena. In a letter to Lord

Kames, June 2, 1765, he observes that after wearing green spectacles the page he is reading appears reddish, but draws no conclusions except that here is a relationship between green and red "not yet explained." [11] In another letter, to the Abbé Soulevie, he expresses his preference for that "method of philosophizing, which proceeds upon actual observations, makes a collection of facts, and concludes no further than those facts will warrant." [12] He disciplined his imagination to discover only observable facts and then asked to what use his findings might be put to improve the lot of man, and more particularly of Philadelphians.

It would seem that Franklin's mind ran a similar course with reference to social thinking. His fire company, his postal service, his library, and his newspapers and magazines at home and in other colonies were developed to answer the public need rather than for personal profit alone. Experience in each case pointed out a situation which needed the exercise of his ingenuity, and his solution to the problem was so obvious, once it had been put into practice, that it immediately became public habit. Often it was a scientific discovery which was turned into a social channel and the two currents of his mind flowed together. He had no consistent view of the nature of society other than that dictated by his understanding of the needs of his own country. Rousseau's Sophie, the Comtesse d'Houdetot, made him the hero of a *fête champêtre* at her house at Samois, but the social reformer Franklin seems to have shown more interest in the lady than in the theories of the social idealist Rousseau. Adam Smith's *Wealth of Nations,* which appeared in 1776, does not seem to have had much direct influence, although he had met its author in 1759 at the house of Dr. Robertson in Edinburgh. When he reached the conclusion that American independence was inevitable, he joined Jefferson in approving an agricultural economy. "There seem to be but three ways for a nation to acquire wealth," he wrote. "The first is by war, as the Romans did, in plundering their conquered neighbours. This is robbery. The second is by commerce, which is generally cheating. The third is by agriculture, the only honest way, wherein man receives a real increase of the seed thrown into the ground, in a kind of continual miracle." [13] Such a simplification of Physiocratic doctrines could only be made by a man who had his eye fixed upon the practical problems of a young and unexploited country.

In the education of youth, he revealed the same lack of concern for abstract theory, the same practical and farsighted wisdom with reference to fact. In his several tracts on educational matters, he stresses the need for the establishment of academies in the colony and outlines a pragmatic curriculum in which facility in speaking and writing, and the reading of contemporary and recent English literature, share with history and natural science the places habitually assigned to logic, theoretical mathematics, and the classics. He even urges that, with this study, excursions might be made "to the neighbouring Plantations of the best Farmers, their Methods observ'd and reason'd upon for the Improvement of Youth." [14] The modern "activity" school which has developed from John Dewey's pragmatic theories of education, with its emphasis upon the study of the immediate environment, is largely a rediscovery of practices which Franklin advocated in 1749. Higher education, with its diversified vocational schools, has followed a similar pattern. To Franklin, it was enough that America needed young men to carry forward the material welfare of the colonies and their people.

A similarly pragmatic attitude is to be discovered in his political thought. Such men as Tom Paine and Jefferson were left to absorb the theories of the French political radicals and to draft the Declaration of Independence while Franklin sat back behind his spectacles and merely helped it to do its work by writing perhaps his most stinging and famous satire, "Rules by Which a Great Empire may be Reduced." Conciliator that he had been up to this time, he was ready to add a barb to the shaft. Apparent inconsistencies in his position during the years when the revolutionary movement in the colonies was taking shape are explained when reference is made to his fact-finding approach to the problem rather than to any systematic political philosophy. Professor Verner Crane has analyzed this problem so carefully and convincingly in the last of his Colver Lectures,[15] and doubtless again in his lecture in this series, that I shall merely agree here with his main point: that Franklin's first ideal was one of federated imperialism, but that colonial loyalty led him to alter his actions in terms of developing circumstances which were beyond his control. The really significant conclusion is not whether he held to this or that political philosophy, but that in the crisis he used his farsighted understanding of men and events to lead rather than to follow colonial thinking into channels which brought the most satisfactory results, within the limits of possibility. He changed his plan for action with changing circumstances.

IV

When we turn from consideration of scientific, social, and political questions to the more subjective realms of ethics and human relationships, the problems become more difficult and more subject to misunderstanding. This is the real test of the theory I have proposed.

I once asked a loyal scholar of Franklin why he was so much interested in him, why he was willing to devote so much time to a study of him and of his ideas. The answer was immediate and spoken with firm conviction, "Because he knew how to deal with women." If I repeated my question here, I should probably receive a variety of answers, but I suspect that many of them would be variations on the theme, "Because he knew how to deal with life." We are attracted to many great figures of the past because of their ideas or their works; Franklin, I think, draws us because he so obviously worked out a rule of life which brought an unusual degree of satisfaction to him and to most people with whom he came into contact.

There are two kinds of sources which might be used in reformulating Franklin's attitude on personal experience and moral conduct: the record of his relationships with other people, and his own formulation of his ethical code. On a superficial view, the conclusions derived from one of these kinds of sources do not agree with those based on the other. There appears to many people an inconsistency between the experimenter with life and people, who emerges from a review of the biographical facts, and the dogmatic moralist of the *Autobiography, Poor Richard,* and some of the letters. So great has this inconsistency appeared to some people that poor old Ben emerges from their studies as little more than a smug hypocrite. "Although I still believe that honesty is the best policy," writes the Englishman D. H. Lawrence, "I dislike policy altogether; though it is just as well not to count your chickens before they are hatched, it's still more hateful to count them with gloating after they *are* hatched. It has taken me many years and countless smarts to get out of that barbed wire moral enclosure that Poor Richard rigged up. Here am I now in tatters and scratched to ribbons, sitting in the middle of Benjamin's America looking at the barbed wire, and the fat sheep crawling under the fence to get fat outside and the watchdogs yelling at the gate lest by chance anyone should get out by the proper exit. Oh America! Oh Benjamin! And I just utter a long loud curse against Benjamin and the American corral.

"Moral America! Most moral Benjamin. Sound, satisfied Ben!" [16]

There has never been a more wrong-headed comment made on Franklin, yet it is easy to see why this romantic, mystical Englishman, who doubtless knew no other Franklin than that he extracted from the *Autobiography* and the *Almanacks,* should rebel against what seemed to him to be a self-appointed Chief Justice of Human Nature:

"Eat not to fulness; drink not to elevation.

"Lose no time, be always employed in something useful; cut off all unnecessary action.

"Avoid extremes, forebear resenting injuries as much as you think they deserve."

Do what you want to do, but don't do too much of it—a "Do" and a "Don't" in every sentence! No wonder that Lawrence found smugness here, and tried to free himself from the inhibitions he had learned from Poor Richard!

But he completely missed the fact that these moral dogmas were not set down for him. In their first form, they were merely working guides for the young man Franklin, not a final statement of his ideal of perfection. They furnished a means of pinching himself in the arm when he found himself doing something of which he, in the long run, could not approve. And, from his own testimony such occasions were not rare. Many a good New Year's resolution would make a bad law of the land. The most that the old man Franklin hoped was that some of these little instruments of conduct might be useful to some of his descendants as well.

They had been sharpened by his own experience and were of value to him chiefly as a way of paring down his own excesses. He recorded the whole experiment with the detachment of a scientific observer, himself the student and himself the object of study. His proposed book, *The Art of Virtue,* which he never wrote, was intended, he explains, to help those who had lost the better support of Christian faith, to retain at least a working morality.[17]

The frankness of the *Autobiography* has charmed and troubled the critics from the start; charmed because, in simple Addisonian English, Franklin set to work like an honest tradesman to take an inventory of his life, its successes and failures; troubled because the tradesman included in his count the qualities of spirit which for some have an untouchable sanctity. Which is the prude: the man who can evaluate his impulses and measure their consequences or the man who looks upon his own ego as the mysterious, untouchable mystery of the eternal? The elements which make up conduct are no more exempt from Franklin's analysis than are those which control the phenomena of nature. The same scales must be used for weighing one's self that have proved their worth in the weighing of objective nature. Father Abraham's speech (*Poor Richard's Almanack* for 1758) preaches frugality and industry as practical answers to the question of high taxes.[18]

The difficulty of appraising Franklin's moral attitude lies, therefore, in this apparent inconsistency between his obviously experimental way of living and the codified system of controls which he attempts in the early pages of the *Autobiography* and which finds expression in the sayings of Poor Richard and elsewhere. In his writings, Franklin apparently states a theory of conduct first and urges others to accept and apply it to themselves; in his own actions he seems to reverse the process, to work experimentally toward an inner equilibrium of desire and control without deliberate formulation of principles until after the fact. The inconsistency is a real one if his statements on moral questions be accepted primarily as an effort to guide others. Unquestionably he is himself to blame. He played the part of the moral teacher, and gave the appearance of wishing to pass on to others his own rules of conduct; but, at the same time, this impression of Franklin as a dogmatic moralist is misleading. Before he was twenty-three he had weighed pleasure against reason in the

characters of Philocles and Horatio. The resulting rule of moderation was still his fifty years later when he wrote "The Whistle." It
was a rule of living which would always allow a pragmatic test,
always be flexible.[19] It is, therefore, important to judge him not
so much by what he seemed to be or by what he thought himself
to be, as by what he was, and I think it safe to say, even in the
face of all the moral aphorisms that dot his pages, that in his own
life he tested conduct as he did nature by the experimental
method, balancing reason and pleasure anew in each new circumstance. In this view, his proverbs, epigrams, and rules become merely the laboratory notebook of a pragmatic moralist;
not texts from a secular pulpit.

"He that falls in love with himself will have no rivals." Franklin knew that he was very much in love with himself.

"The most exquisite folly is made of wisdom spun too fine."
He had tried it himself and given it up.

"We can give advice but we cannot give conduct." He had seen
his own admonitions disregarded, as were Father Abraham's.

Such aphorisms as these have the appearance of chemical
formulae derived from the test tube. Even the moralistic passages
from the *Autobiography* may be so interpreted because Franklin is
as conscientious in reporting his failures as he is his successes in
living up to his own ideals and rules of conduct. But this interpretation of his moral attitude can scarcely be avoided when the
facts of his conduct are reviewed apart from the evidence of the
Autobiography. It is his lack of dogmatism wihch charmed in all
his personal relationships, his receptivity to the ideas of others, his
adjustability to their moods. His comment on his two old Junto
friends, Potts and Parsons, would suggest that he recognized things
in human nature which wisdom could not alter: "Parsons was a
wise man that often acted foolishly; Potts a wit that seldom acted
wisely. If *enough* were the means to make a man happy, one had
always the means of happiness without ever enjoying the thing;
the other had always the thing without ever possessing the means.
Parsons even in his prosperity always fretting; Potts in the midst
of his poverty always laughing. It seems, then, that happiness in
this life rather depends on internals than externals; and that, besides the natural effects of wisdom and virtue, vice and folly, there
is such a thing as a happy or an unhappy constitution." [20] This is

indeed an admission for one who supposedly believed so fully in the correctability of human nature.

Not unlike the misunderstanding of Lawrence is that of those recent critics who have labeled Franklin "the first civilized American," and "the apostle of Modern Times," but the error is of a contrary sort.[21] Phillips Russell and Bernard Fäy revolted, as did Lawrence, against the sanctimonious lay-preacher of the misread *Autobiography*. But instead of merely condemning him, they attempt apologies by playing up in a deplorably sensational fashion his worldliness, his cosmopolitan vices, his doubts, and his weaknesses. The resulting pictures are as distorted as that which they set out to correct. The chief value of these books, in spite of the superficiality of the one and the supposedly documented thoroughness of the other, is that they free Franklin from the clutches of Mrs. Grundy and restore him to the more congenial society of Madame Brillon. Ford[22] had allowed the latter lady's confession that she sat on the sage's lap, but other evidence even more damaging was as yet unrevealed. After the bad taste and the misrepresentation of the Russell book had opened the way, it was possible for Mr. Van Doren and others to discuss, without apology, the presence of illegitimacy in the Franklin family to the fourth generation, cut short there by untimely death. And after the Fäy book, it was easier to appreciate Franklin's life as a struggle with himself and with circumstances. The starch was washed out of the bourgeois saint.

Such revelations and interpretations are in themselves of no moment except to prove once and for all that Franklin's moral aphorisms were expressed with conviction because moderation was for him an acquired art rather than a result of prudish inhibitions. They reassure us that he was a human being who developed character and kindliness by facing life squarely and evaluating it in its various and contradictory moods as it presented itself to him. The moralizing of the old man was the summary of a life which had been richly, if not always wisely or even admirably, lived. *Poor Richard* was the notebook of a laboratory moralist.

It is hardly necessary to review for this audience the many evidences of Franklin's kindly interest in others, particularly in young people, throughout his long life. Mr. Stifler's[23] collection of his correspondence with Polly Stevenson and the Shipley girls, covering more than thirty years, is almost testimony enough. But to this may be added a list of all those young men whom he stimulated and aided to successful lives through the Junto, by means of letters of introduction as in the case of Tom Paine, and by setting them up in business for themselves after an apprenticeship with him. And if evidences of his tolerance be sought, his treatment of Arthur Lee and Silas Deane, both of whom he refused openly to condemn even when the tide of popular feeling was strong against them, might be sufficient. It may be argued that good business sense and self-interest led Franklin to set his partners up in the printing and publishing business in neighboring colonies, but no such explanation can be given for his willingness to accept the risk of public stigma rather than to denounce the weaknesses of his diplomatic associates.

These instances are taken from widely spread epochs in his life, and the later ones reveal even more patience and kindliness than do the earlier ones. Franklin verified by experience his early belief that more flies are caught by molasses than by vinegar, that a world in which people get on with each other is happier and more comfortable than one in which they do not. Perhaps this point is sufficient explanation of the change in his political philosophy from a belief in British federation to one in American independence. His moral philosophy was as pragmatic and adjustable as was his political.

V

In no sphere of experience, however, is this trial-and-error method of Franklin more dramatically revealed than in that of religion. Those who would accept his guidance for the whole of life must follow him through to this, and it is here that many of his warmest admirers are forced to stop. Because he was so nearly successful in depriving God himself of his mystery, he shocks many a potential disciple who admires his experimental approach to problems of science, society, and politics, and even those who are willing to apply with him the same methods to the problems of human conduct.

A careful analysis of Franklin's religious beliefs and practices would demand a review of eighteenth-century Deism, but once more I shall be content with a discussion of his attitude alone. Again he is more interested in a workable practice of religion than in the formulated dogmatisms and skepticisms of his age. Brought up in a society which accepted a dogmatic Calvinism, the same revolt which took him to Philadelphia carried him over spiritually to the company of the religious doubters who owed their Deistic beliefs to Newton and Locke in the first instance. His first experiments in formulating a faith of his own show the traces of both influences, but they proved unsatisfying. He soon gave up the attempt to define the nature and scope of the power of God when his reasoning brought him to the conclusion that freedom of the will was a logical impossibility but a practical necessity. A system of living founded upon such premises would not work and was therefore not for him. Yet he felt the need of a God to whom he could pray. The resulting Deity was little more than a fellow-traveler, one who stood ready with his higher authority to sanction the actions which experience taught him were best. Franklin, I believe, never defined his Deity in these words, but in all his contacts with religious sects and religious people, he asked only that whatever God they might profess would prove his goodness by directing them into the wise and virtuous ways of living. He tells us that, religiously educated a Presbyterian, he attended no services for public worship with any regularity because he became impatient with theological discussion. Nevertheless he recognized the practical virtues of the churches as agencies for the public welfare, and was willing to contribute to any sect that would serve the civil interests as well as their own. For the same reason he welcomed and supported George Whitefield when he came to Philadelphia in 1739, and his justification for joining the Masons was that God judges men more for what they do than for what they think.[24] His *Articles of Belief and Acts of Religion* (1728),[25] written at the age of twenty-two, posits a Deistic Christian God who has infinite power but is above using it arbitrarily, and a curious hierarchy of beings superior to man that is suggestive of pagan pantheism. The most important clause in this creed, however, is the statement that God is good and wise, and therefore Benjamin Franklin of Philadelphia sees every reason for making Him his friend. In this spirit of independence, he proceeds to his devotions as he would to a conversation with a superior moral adviser for whom he feels deep reverence. All of his later religious efforts, including his proposed abridgement of the *Book of Common Prayer*, were designed to make more easy and immediate the everyday intercourse between man, the superior of the animals, and God, the supreme in wisdom and judgment of all beings. But in his most religious moods, this intercourse was still in the nature of a conversation between one being and another. Surely no one has ever devised a more helpful God, but the experience of religious exultation is lacking in the relationship. It was for immediate and practical aid that he urged the Constitutional Convention of 1786 to turn to God, and the psychological effect of his suggestion was good.[26] Franklin's pragmatic attitude seems to stand this final test; he created and clung to a God who helped him discover how to live, and allowed him to make the discovery for himself. With other problems of the nature and function of the Deity he early lost interest. And when Ezra Stiles asked him a month before his death, to state his opinion on the Divinity of Christ, he replied: "It is a question I do not dogmatize upon, having never studied it, and think it needless to busy myself with it now, when I expect soon an Opportunity of knowing the Truth with less Trouble."

V I

Franklin's way of thinking and living may be distinguished from those of his European contemporaries like Voltaire and Johnson in that it was so characteristically American. The particular form which his pragmatism took was a result of his participation as a principal actor in the greatest mass movement of civilization that history records. Franklin lived at the time when the frontier culture of the eastern seaboard colonies was reaching maturity through a painful adolescence. As a result, his pragmatism has a peculiarly American flavor, a vitality and aggressiveness which the tired skepticism of contemporary European thinkers lacked. Whatever his predilections may be toward a life of contemplation and dogmatic belief, the American philosopher from the earliest days has been forced out of his assumptions and into a mold of vigorous pragmatism by the very circumstances of his life. However sound his philosophy when kept in the realm of theory, and however admirable his love of security and retirement for contemplation, the immediate need for action has always been too great to allow any system of thinking which cannot justify itself by providing swiftly the needs and the minimal comforts of life. "America was promises," sings our latest Laureate Archibald MacLeish; but the American is pragmatist. He must make some of the promises work.

I should like to ask your indulgence for perhaps too long a digression at this point because I feel that we can only appreciate Franklin's pragmatism by discovering the same trait in other Americans and seeing it as a dominant strain throughout the long history of our intellectual development.

It takes little argument to prove that the original settlers in this country were primarily concerned with practical problems. Those who were not, did not live to produce books or descendants. Even when they were motivated by religious ideals as were the Plymouth colonists and the Pennsylvania Quakers, their first acts were such common sense translations of their theories into workable practices as the *Plymouth Compact* and the classic treaty with the Indians. And even when the colonies were fairly settled, there was more debate on problems of economics and government than upon the abstractions of philosophy and the amenities of literature. In the famous *Bloudy Tenent* controversy itself, Roger Williams was protesting persecution for cause of conscience as a working principle of throttling free speech in a democracy rather than as a scholastic dogma. It was more than a century before the colonies produced in Jonathan Edwards a philosopher who is worthy to take rank among original and systematic thinkers, and almost two hundred years before that type of literature which is concerned with the pleasures and amenities of life took shape in Cooper, Irving, and Bryant. The great theorist of the Revolution, Tom Paine, had few original ideas and devoted his energies to applying the principles which he had learned in his reading to the problems which his adopted country faced in the fact.

This unusual phenomenon of a whole nation working in accord with a philosophy which it had not, in almost two centuries, had time to formulate is commented on some years later by the astute Frenchman, de Toqueville: "I think that in no country in the civilized world is less attention paid to philosophy than in the United States," he writes. "The Americans have no philosophical school of their own; and they care but little for all the schools into which Europe is divided, the very names of which are scarcely known to them. Yet it is easy to perceive that almost all the inhabitants of the United States conduct their understanding in the same manner, and govern it by the same rules. . . . Each American appeals to the individual exercise of his own understanding alone. . . . As it is on their own testimony that they are accustomed to rely, they like to discern the object which engages their attention with extreme clearness; they therefore strip off as much as possible all that covers it, they rid themselves of whatever separates them from it, they remove whatever conceals it from sight, in order to view it more closely and in the broad light of day." [27]

With this shrewd explanation of the American habit of pragmatic independence of mind, even such idealists as Emerson and Thoreau consent to fall into the pattern. Kenneth Murdock has pointed out that the Puritans themselves were men of affairs and tied their idealism closely into their daily lives.[28] By 1840, Puritanism had stripped itself of all the inhibitions and regimentations of theological dogma, and life could be defined and lived as a new testing of experience each day by each individual. Emerson came very near to formulating an ethical philosophy, even though he failed to systematize his metaphysics and aesthetics. In *The American Scholar*, in 1837, he preached an idealization of the moral code of which Franklin was, in many respects, an example. Impatience with books as books is countered by a plea for closer communion with nature and for action. Franklin's nature was of the human variety, but we can easily imagine him, granted Emerson's gift of tongues, speaking the following lines: "If it were only for a vocabulary, the scholar would be covetous of action. Life is our dictionary. Years are well spent in country labors; in towns; in the insight into trades and manufactures; in frank intercourse with many men and women; in science; in art; to the one end of mastering in all their facts a language by which to illustrate and embody our perceptions. . . . Life lies behind us as the quarry from which we get tiles and copestones for the masonry of today." [29]

I am fully aware that in calling Emerson a pragmatist, at least in some phases of his thought, I am flying in the face of much of the traditional interpretation of his attitude, although I am not alone among his recent critics in committing this crime. Frederick Ives Carpenter writes: "Emerson's philosophy may perhaps be described as a Pragmatic Mysticism. It is idealistic in that it puts the mystical experience first. It is dualistic in that it looks both ways from its position on the bridge between soul and nature. It is monistic in that it maintains that this bridge is the only reality. But it is pragmatic in that it tests all truths (including the mystical belief in the value of life) by experience.

"It remains to suggest," continues Mr. Carpenter, "that this pragmatic mysticism is essentially *the* American philosophy." [30] With this conclusion I am inclined heartily to agree although it has been pointed out convincingly that Emerson, in his more mystical moods, rejects the experimental attitude toward physical facts which is characteristic of the pragmatism of Franklin and of other more practical people from William Penn to William James. But the discovery of pragmatism in any sense in Emerson is akin to the sensational. In him, and perhaps also in Thoreau, Whitman, and other leaders of the mid-nineteenth-century renaissance of idealism in literature and life, the mystical is more important than the circumstantial experience. But if we compare these idealists with European literary men and philosophers of the same general stamp, like Coleridge, Goethe, and Kant, the horns of the Yankee tradesman appear above the all-seeing eye.

Throughout the American experience, therefore, our chief problem has been the adjustment of an extreme form of pragmatic individualism, demanded by the circumstances of our civilization, to the fundamental hunger of human nature for something higher and better than it can obtain in this world. The purer forms of idealism have seldom taken root in our soil because of the urgency of the pragmatic challenge, especially in the early days. Franklin, more successfully than any other Colonial, faced this issue and was temperamentally able to make the adjustment which the circumstances of his time and country demanded. He reduced religion to practical ethics and he tested conduct by experience. Emerson, a mystic by temperament, founded his ethics, as his Puritan forefathers had done before him, on the same pragmatic base. It was left for William James to return to the foundations which Franklin had laid by the pattern of his life and to formulate a theory which Franklin had lived without formulation. There is much reason to believe that this modern pragmatism is the characteristic American philosophy, the one which our experience has dictated from the start. We may not each of us accept it without qualifications for ourselves, but as a people we have learned it and applied it throughout our history. We may, like Emerson and many another American, feel the need for accepting the mystical experience and explaining the universe in terms of a polarity rather than of a single point of reference. But in Franklin's singleness lay his strength and his unity. It might prove a sanitive to these troubled times and to the many troubled minds living in them to return more frequently to the study of a man whose philosophy was himself, and who discovered how to make himself whole by rejecting no part of the life about him, and sane by keeping it in control. On such a foundation we may build according to our various temperaments and needs.

NOTES

1. William James delivered a series of lectures on Pragmatism at the Lowell Institute in 1906 and at Columbia University in 1907. These lectures were published in 1907 under the title, *Pragmatism: A New Name for Some Old Ways of Thinking*. Although *The New English Dictionary* gives seven earlier uses of the term, its use in philosophy was invented by C. S. Peirce in discussions with James, and its special meaning was expounded by him in an article, "How to Make Our Ideas Clear," *Popular Science Monthly* XII, (January, 1878): pp. 281-302.
2. James, *Pragmatism*, Lecture II, "What Pragmatism Means," pp. 53, 54-55.
3. "A Proposal for Promoting Useful Knowledge among the British Plantations in America," Philadelphia, 1743. *The Writings of Benjamin Franklin*, edited by A. H. Smyth (New York: Macmillan Co., 1905-7), II, 228-232. (References to the Smyth edition have been retained because it was the one I used at the time. Subsequent reference to this work will be cited as *Writings*.)
4. *Benjamin Franklin, Representative Selections*, with an Introduction, Bibliography, and Notes, by Frank Luther Mott and Chester E. Jorgenson (New York: American Book Company, 1936), p. cxli.
5. *Writings*, II, 133-154.
6. *Ibid.*, p. cxi.
7. *Autobiography. Writings*, I, 277-278.
8. Passy, November 9, 1799. *Writings*, VII, 412.
9. C. Van Doren, *Benjamin Franklin* (New York: Viking Press, 1928), p. 782.
10. R. Lawson, *Ben and Me* (Boston: Little, Brown and Co., 1939), p. 41.

11. *Writings*, IV, 380.
12. *Ibid.*, VIII, 601.
13. *Ibid.*, V, 202.
14. *Proposals Relating to the Education of Youth in Pensilvania* (Philadelphia, 1749), *ibid.*, II, 386-396.
15. V. W. Crane, *Benjamin Franklin, Englishman and American*, Colver Lecture (Providence, R.I.: Brown University, 1936).
16. D. H. Lawrence, *Studies in Classic American Literature* (New York: Thomas Seltzer, 1923), p. 21.
17. Letter to Lord Kames. *Writings*, IV, 12-13.
18. *Writings*, III, 408.
19. *Ibid.*, II, 157-170.
20. *Ibid.*, III, 457.
21. P. Russell, *Benjamin Franklin, the First Civilized American* (New York: Brentano, 1926), and B. Fäy, *Franklin, The Apostle of Modern Times* (Boston: Little, Brown and Co., 1929).
22. P. L. Ford, *The Many-Sided Franklin* (New York: Century Co., 1899).
23. J. M. Stifler, *My Dear Girl; The Correspondence of Benjamin Franklin with Polly Stevenson, Georgiana and Catherine Shipley* (New York: George H. Doran Co., 1927).
24. Letter to Josiah Franklin, April 13, 1838. *Writings*, II, 214-216.
25. *Writings*, II, 91-100.
26. M. Farrand, *The Records of the Federal Convention of 1787*, rev. ed., 4 vols. (New Haven: Yale University Press, 1937), I, 450-452.
27. A. de Toqueville, *Democracy in America*, translated by H. Reeve (New York, 1898), II, 1-7.
28. K. Murdock, "The Puritan Tradition," in *The Reinterpretation of American Literature*, edited by Norman Foerster (New York: Harcourt, Brace and Co., 1928), p. 105.
29. R. W. Emerson, *Works* (Boston: Houghton, Mifflin Co., 1903-4), I, 97-98.
30. F. I. Carpenter, *Ralph Waldo Emerson, Representative Selections* (New York: American Book Co., 1934), p. xxxvii.

Franklin on the Art
of Being Human

One of a series of papers commemorating the two hundred and fiftieth anniversary of Franklin's birth, this essay was read at the annual general meeting of the American Philosophical Society, April 19-20, 1956. Other papers in the group emphasized Franklin's importance as statesman, scientist, and journalist. Published in *Proceedings of the American Philosophical Society* C (August 31, 1956): 304-315.

ON THIS MEMORABLE OCCASION I shall attempt to present and defend the thesis that Franklin the humanist and man of letters was as consistent and firm-fibred as Franklin the statesman or Franklin the scientist, and that his humanism, properly understood, can be a tonic for at least some of the distresses of the present. My special equipment for venturing so rash a proposal is that I am a literary historian, a variety of critic that has been extraordinarily rare among the commentators on Franklin. If I remember correctly, Carl Van Doren is the only literary historian who, in all these centuries, has made a thorough study of Franklin from this point of view.[1] James Parton was a professional journalist and even John McMaster, who contributed Franklin's biography to the first American Men of Letters Series, was trained in political and social rather than in literary history. Yet Franklin was, beyond question, America's leading man of letters of the eighteenth century, and the man of letters, perhaps more than anyone else, attempts to understand and to give expression to the whole of experience.

There seems to be little doubt that Franklin, at least in his later years, had come to be recognized pretty generally as a great human being—a philosopher-statesman, a scientist, and a humanist in the pattern of greatness of the Enlightenment. At his death, he was commemorated in France, England, and the United States as a kind of universal man. Even John Adams, who teamed with him on so many exacting political missions but who never achieved much more than an imperfect sympathy for him, testified, somewhat begrudgingly, that "his reputation was more universal than that of Leibnitz or Newton, Frederick or Voltaire, and his character more beloved and esteemed than any or all of them." But then he added significantly, "To develop that complication of causes, which conspired to produce so singular a phenomenon," might require "a complete history of the philosophy and politics of the eighteenth century." [2]

Such a history should probably start in France for it was there that Franklin's fame was so genuinely that of the *philosophe*. When Mirabeau proposed to the Paris Convention of June 11, 1790, that its members should wear mourning for three days in Franklin's honor, he argued that "antiquity would have raised altars to this mighty genius, . . . Europe, enlightened and free, owes at least a token of remembrance and regret to one of the greatest men who have ever been engaged in the service of philosophy and liberty." [3] And the Englishman and fellow philosopher —as he regarded himself—David Hume had, many years before, written to Franklin, "America has sent us many good things, gold, silver, sugar, tobacco, indigo, etc.; but you are the first philosopher, and indeed the first great man of letters, for whom we are beholden to her." [4]

America, France, and Britain thus bore witness to the international fame of this first philosopher of the New World. "Revered for benevolence," as Washington had described him, honored by the academies for his scientific accomplishments, thanked by its people for his achievements in guiding the fate of the infant Republic abroad and improving the comforts of daily life at home, he was also accepted as a great man in the more nearly absolute sense. As long as the ideals of the Enlightenment held sway, Franklin was the acknowledged American spokesman for the wisdom of his age.

I I

To turn from this image of the great and wise humanist to the widespread notion that succeeded it so rapidly in the popular mind is to make the classic descent from the sublime to something not far from the ridiculous. So rapidly did the climate of opinion in the Western European and American world change in the period from 1790 to 1810 that the wise spokesman of his age might well have come to life, like Rip Van Winkle after only twenty years, to find himself greeted as a Yankee tinker and the vendor of a shrewd utilitarian morality that even he did not practice. Although scholars like Jared Sparks, John Bigelow, Paul Leicester Ford, and Albert Henry Smyth faithfully assembled and edited his books, pamphlets, and papers, and more came to be known about him than about almost any other of the founding statesmen of the Republic, the antilegend grew and expanded in the popular mind during the next century. The skepticism of John Adams had early given a hint of what was coming, and perhaps the ubiquitous Parson Weems, who painted one of his inimitable word-portraits of Franklin in 1815, may have had something to do with the growth of the new legend, for the very name of Franklin suggested to him that "clever fellow" of Chaucer:

> Knight of the shire; first justice of th' assize,
> To help the poor, the doubtful to advise.

But it was not so much the actual portrait of Franklin that changed as it was the interpretations that came—usually with the best of intentions—to be put on his familiar words and deeds. Just as the reputations of Chaucer, Spenser, and even Shakespeare were distorted and discounted in the rationalistic eighteenth century, so the reputations of Pope, Voltaire, Swift, Dryden, and the other voices of the Age of Reason went into an eclipse in the unfavorable anti-intellectual climate of the romantic movement and the naturalistic philosophy that followed it. Such revisions and reversals of fashions and reputations are to the literary historian what the rise and fall of empires and parties are to the historian of politics. Values in history are relative to the growth and changes in cyclical human evolution. They should be taken into account in all literary judgment so that one may avoid the mistake of interpreting a great man or a great work of art in the context of a wholly or largely alien climate of opinion.

This is, in effect, what happened to Franklin also. The common image of the philosopher-statesman-scientist dissolved during the century after his death in a climate that belittled the broad assumptions upon which it was based and tended to overvalue the trivial and petty acts of a shrewd and benevolent opportunist. Basically, this change can be attributed, I think, to a shift in systems of value which was already taking place in Western European society by 1790 and which erected a screen of misrepresentation that has only recently shown signs of breaking away. This screen is the view of life adopted early in the nineteenth century by the romantic naturalists and maintained, with variations, throughout the Victorian era and well into our own time. Although many assumptions about life have changed in the interim, there is not too much difference between the romantic egoism of Carlyle, who somewhat scornfully dubbed Franklin "the father of all the Yankees," and that of the modern British novelist, D. H. Lawrence, who attempted to wither him once for all by calling "this cunning little Benjamin" "the first downright American." Both men are emotionally charged themselves and are screaming at a self-controlled rationality that they do not understand.

There are three prongs to this attack, each with its own objective: there is Benjamin Franklin himself as a person and as a thinker; there is American "materialism" in general; and there is positivistic science in all its forms, past and present. Franklin has often been the direct object of the attack, but he has also served as a whipping boy for anti-intellectual and egocentric objections of the romantic naturalist to the ideals of the preceding age.

Carlyle is a good example of the romantic crusader in one of its earlier forms. The first chapter of *Sartor Resartus* contains an attack on that physical science which has made the Creation of the World "little more mysterious than the cooking of a dumpling," and that moral science which, through mercantile greatness and an invaluable Constitution, has impressed a "political or other immediately practical tendency on all English culture and endeavor." In such a climate, the God-given soul languishes and the mystery of life is forgotten.

In another book, *Past and Present,* Carlyle applies the same kind of passion to the solution of society's ills. He can produce, he says, no cure-all, no "Morrison's pill," as can the positivistic reformers, but he can distinguish "eternal Justice from momentary Expediency, and can understand . . . how Justice, radiant, beneficent, as the all-victorious Light-element, is also in essence, if need be, an all-victorious *Fire*-element," which melts down social inequalities and does "in the long-run rule and reign, and allows nothing else to rule and reign."

The assumptions, implicit or stated, in the position of such a romantic naturalist are that God is a remote and mysterious essence that inhabits both Nature and the soul of man; that this essence lies above and beyond the plane of mortal mind and is therefore inaccessible either to logic-chopping reason or to scientific observation and experiment; that man has an innate intuitive faculty by which he can, at least at moments of intensity, perceive the identity of the moral and natural laws—of his own soul in relationship, on the one hand, to God, and, on the other, to Nature—and that therefore the will of the individual man is supreme in the universe. With suitable variations, this is the view of life held by the British romantic poets under the leadership of Coleridge and Shelley, and of the American transcendentalists as expressed by Emerson, Thoreau, Melville, and Whitman. It is the exact antithesis of the views held by Voltaire, Hume, Bentham, and Franklin. The two groups share the conviction of the importance and the centrality of man, but they differ sharply in their views of whether the rational or the emotional faculty of man is paramount. The romantics even went so far as to draft the word "Reason" and to limit its meaning to truth gained through intuition, the higher or spiritual truth, as contrasted to that gained through the "Understanding," or the lower and logical processes of the human mind.

Against this background, the attacks of modern critics like D. H. Lawrence and Max Weber on Franklin take on special meaning. Different as they are in temperament and motive, Weber and Lawrence have many qualities in common. Both take the passages on the art of virtue in the *Autobiography,* sweepingly include Franklin's few prayers and writings on religion, select those aphorisms from Poor Richard which seem to imply a purely utilitarian morality, and set the American sage up as the very image of all that is opportunist in the American character and the capitalistic system. Lawrence's substitute for Franklin's list of virtues itemizes the position of the modern romantic naturalist, point for point: "Resolve to abide by your own deepest promptings. . . . To be sincere is to remember that I am I, and that the other man is not me. . . . Beware of absolutes. . . . Obey the man in whom you recognize the Holy Ghost. . . . 'Venery' is of the great gods, . . . the dark ones." [5] The optimist of the early romantics is gone, but the faith in the inner man and his voice and in the promptings of nature is even stronger. "I am a moral animal. But I am not a moral machine. . . . I'm really not just an automatic piano with a moral Benjamin getting tunes out of me. . . . He tries to take away my wholeness and my dark forest, my freedom." Essentially this is the same egocentric and anti-intellectual romanticism that Carlyle expressed more than a century earlier.

Max Weber presents an interpretation of Franklin which is even harder to combat because, in a limited sense, it is more sympathetic, but which in its underlying premises is not too different from that of Lawrence. Weber argues from the same sources—the Art of Virtue passage in the *Autobiography* and the collateral documents—that Franklin took his basic ethic from Calvinism which encouraged the "self-made parvenus" of the rising strata of the lower industrial middle classes to make a virtue—or even a duty—out of the acquisitive instinct and thereby to create a whole new economic order later to be known as Capitalism. "Capitalism is identical with the pursuit of profit, and forever *renewed* profit, by means of continuous, rational, capitalistic enterprise." [6] The critic does not offer, as does Lawrence, a romantic alternative to Franklin's table of virtues, but his attack on the utilitarian morality of the American is none the less limited and misleading, because it forces a complex individual into conformity with a broad social generalization. One does not have to take sides in order to appreciate the ground of hostility between Franklin and the rational humanists of the eighteenth century on the one hand and Carlyle and the romantic naturalists of the nineteenth and twentieth centuries on the other. With such widely divergent norms for moral evaluation, any meeting of minds between the two groups would be impossible.

But if Franklin's romantic critics misjudged him merely because they proceeded from different value assumptions, what can be said of those hosts of supposed friends who, during the same period, attempted to defend him on the grounds of utilitarian ethics? The nineteenth-century schoolboy was indoctrinated, not only in the Art of Virtue passage and Poor Richard's sayings, but in the supposed morals to be drawn from such trifles as "The Whistle" and "The Ephemera." In the context of pious Victorian moralizing—so foreign to the cool reasoning of Franklin's time—his very whimsies were distorted into parables of opportunistic duty. The self-made man of the Horatio Alger stories was but a step from the portrait of himself which Franklin had so skillfully drawn when he furnished the rationale for the great personal fortunes and the anarchic code of business ethics that guided the era of the so-called Robber Barons. It was obviously all Franklin's fault, and behind him, the fault of his middle-class, mercantile, Puritan, Protestant training. The codifier of American morals could, at the same time, stand for the menacing Puritan who imposed rules of conduct that inhibited the American joy of life, the materialistic opportunist who could turn such rules to his own personal and worldly advantage, and the sly hedonist who could urge self-control on others and at the same time humor his own Dionysian impulses to his heart's content.

If this portrait were not so accurate a drawing of Franklin's image in the popular mind toward the close of the last century, it might well be dismissed for its inconsistencies and obvious distortions. Albert H. Smyth, the most recent of Franklin editors before the present team of Labaree and Bell, concluded his summary account in his school history of American literature with the comment, "Franklin's mind was attentive to trifles, his philosophy never got beyond the homely maxims of worldly prudence," [7] and Charles F. Richardson, the most considerable of the nineteenth-century American literary historians, in speaking of Poor Richard in 1884, remarked, "The inculcation of practices of prudence and economy was always a leading idea in these maxims, and they had a prompt effect in increasing the amount of spare money in Philadelphia." [8] Such was the fame of this first philosopher of the New World a century after his death.

III

If this decline of Franklin's reputation as a philosopher and scientist in the nineteenth century can be identified with an undermining of the rationalism of the Enlightenment by the romantic movement—and I hope that I have made the argument for this view sufficiently persuasive—its rehabilitation should follow a rediscovery of the eighteenth century and its values today. This is exactly what I believe has happened and is continuing to happen. Franklin has more to say to the twentieth century than to any intervening age because the twentieth century, in its emphasis on experimental science as the means of understanding the physical universe and on systematic analysis as the means of exploring the nature of the individual and of society, is more like the Enlightenment than we sometimes are willing to admit. A few modern critics have recognized the validity of this formula and have succeeded in restoring Franklin to his high place in the history of science by reevaluating the basic thinking of his age and thus reconstructing the setting for his experiments with electricity and his other writings on scientific subjects. This is at least a first step toward restoring a just perspective on the whole of his character and achievements.

The classic essay of Carl Becker is perhaps as good a means as any to open our consideration of the modern status of Franklin, for Becker lists Franklin of Philadelphia, "printer and friend of the human race," with Montesquieu and Voltaire and Rousseau, Leibnitz and Herder and the young Goethe, Locke and Hume and Bolingbroke, Adam Smith and Priestley and Jefferson, as *philosophes* in the extended international use of the term. True, Becker was more interested in proving that these radical rationalists were merely dethroning the God of the scholastic philosophers and raising human reason in his stead to the highest authority without otherwise disturbing the Heavenly City or its ramparts; but he succeeds in describing the nature of the new government with convincing clarity. "The laws of nature and nature's God," he concludes, "appeared henceforth to be one and the same thing, and since every part of God's handiwork could all in good time be reasonably demonstrated, the intelligent man could very well do with a minimum of faith—except, of course (the exception was tremendous but scarcely noticed at the time), faith in the uniform behavior of nature and in the capacity of reason to discover its *modus operandi*." [9]

Thus the Enlightenment dethroned the theistic God of its inheritance and substituted a sensible deity who had planned so well ordered a universe and so rational a race of men that he could afford to sit back and watch the consequences with only the occasional qualm of the permissive parent who sees his offspring take his first uncertain steps alone. In Deism, the eighteenth-century man found the basis of both his science and his morality. The application to science comes first, for the physical universe must be proved to be a consistent product of a reasonable God before man could hope to discover reason in human affairs.

Becker himself did not single out Franklin for special study in this book, nor did he explore the progress of experimental science in the eighteenth century in its application to the thought of the American sage. It was Carl Van Doren, in his monumental biography, who, a few years later, became the first among moderns to call for a reevaluation of the experiments with static electricity which Franklin performed and reported.

In the six years between the summer of 1746, when he first saw electrical experiments in Boston, and the summer of 1752, when he flew the electrical kite in Philadelphia, he made all his fundamental contributions to electricity. He made them because he had a fundamental mind, which almost at once mastered the general problem as it then existed and went deeper into it than any observer had yet gone. He found electricity a curiosity and left it a science.[10]

This statement of Franklin's importance as a natural philosopher is unequivocal, but Van Doren did not pursue either the sources of Franklin's scientific thinking or its further influences on his other activities. Where he as biographer left the problem in order to pursue his narrative, a younger scholar, Chester E. Jorgenson, took up the study, calling Franklin a "scientific deist," and following down all the possible influences of earlier scientific and metaphysical thinkers upon him. But however much he overstated his case, Jorgenson reconstructed the Newtonian universe of immutable laws and the Lockean mind of the *tabula rasa*, as well as the belief in man's capacity for self-improvement, which were the stock-in-trade of the Philadelphia printer as well as of the French philosophers.

The way was now open for the modern critic to follow up Van Doren's hint and to make a definitive restudy of Franklin as a scientist. This task was undertaken in 1941 by I. Bernard Cohen with the republication of the *Experiments and Observations on Electricity* (1774). Franklin's specific contribution to science thus became clear. His electrical theory is important in the history of science, says Mr. Cohen, because "it afforded a basis of explanation for all the known phenomena of electricity," and "gave a single unified account of all the data of the subject and thereby for the first time congealed a miscellaneous collection of knowledge into the rigid form of a single unified scientific discipline." [11]

The discovery of such a discipline was exactly what Franklin had hoped for when, in 1748, he had given up his printing business in order, as he wrote at the time to Cadwallader Colden, to gain "leisure to read, study, make experiments, and converse at large with such ingenious and worthy men as are pleased to honor me with their friendship or acquaintance, on such points as may produce something for the common benefit of mankind." [12] His reward came quickly in his discoveries of electrical laws which could be immediately applied to the control of lightening and to other services for mankind. Franklin the inventor of gadgets in the interest of human comfort was an integral part of Franklin the empirical and speculative scientist. Even though they are probably apocryphal, it is not hard to believe the anecdotes which Parson Weems tells of the good Doctor and his parlor tricks, in which he used his electrical jar to shoot off a pop pistol, illustrate a biblical story with miniature dancing figures, or so charged the most beautiful of his younger guests with static electricity that her lips sent off unexpected fire when she was approached by her startled swain.[13] The wisest of scientists may still retain his sense of humor.

He may also apply the principles and methods of empirical science far beyond the limits of physical law. This phase of Franklin's thought Mr. Cohen develops further in his recently annotated volume of selections to illustrate Franklin's contribution to the American tradition. "Franklin firmly believed," he states, "that truth could, by his definition, survive every experimental test which falsehood would necessarily fail. . . . Over and over we see Franklin embodying his conclusions in acts rather than concepts. It is misleading to think of him as the enemy of the abstract and the master of the concrete, however, because this description would rob his empiricism of the role of reason." [14] He further hints rather than demonstrates that it is this same empirical and scientific quality of mind which made Franklin a successful statesman. Because he held firm to the axioms of his science, he could manipulate details without sacrifice of his fundamental principles. Many other of his contributions to the welfare of the infant Republic and of mankind in general are understandable once the scientific nature of his thinking is recognized. As an empiricist, he believed that discovered truth was valuable only after it had been reapplied in the light of reason to the improvement of life on this earth.

I V

This reapplication of discovered truth to the welfare of man was thought of by Franklin and his fellows as an "art" in distinction to the discovery itself, which was "science," a distinction which has survived to the present in the academic phrase, "a college of arts and sciences." Art, as the eighteenth century used the word, was as precise and empirical a pursuit as science. As one should seek to understand the laws of physical science in order to establish basic truth, so one should explore the moral laws which govern human behavior in order to improve man's condition by bringing his conduct more nearly into line with immutable reason. To the rational and pragmatic mind of the American man of the Enlightenment, it would seem only proper that the Deistic God who designed a harmonious universe would not be content with placing in it a creature who was merely whimsical in his thought and haphazard in his actions. One might fairly assume, therefore, that human motivation and human conduct would be as rational as natural law if the proper arts of living were discovered and systematically applied. Thus the eighteenth

century made arts of everything that could not quite be reduced
to sciences: an art of love (learned from Ovid), an art of garden-
ing, of preserving health, of criticism, of coffee-drinking, and of
growing old. At the roots of them all was the art of arts, the Art
of Virtue, which was but another way of describing the art of being human. With this art Franklin was deeply concerned throughout his life.

This is the point at which Franklin the natural philosopher
stops and Franklin the moral philosopher takes over, but modern
criticism and scholarship have done little with the problem of
restudying this phase of Franklin's thought and setting it firmly
in the context of the thought of the Enlightenment. Such a task
is far too great for me to undertake here, but perhaps with the
background that I have attempted to supply, I can now turn to
Franklin's own writings on the art of virtue and partially rescue
them from the charge of meanness, materialism, and pettiness
with which the romantics have shrouded them. Franklin as a
moral philosopher shows the same intellectual detachment, the
same faith in empirical rather than logical procedure, and the
same belief that the purpose of acquiring knowledge is its application to the improvement of man, that he reveals as a natural
philosopher. On this level he is the artist of the good life, as on
the other he was the scientist of nature.

The young Franklin in Boston and the old man in Passy were
equally persistent in tossing this problem back and forth without
reaching a final and satisfactory solution to it. Knowledge and
virtue were always paired in his mind as the twin goals of human endeavor, and in science he found the way toward knowledge.
His projected work on *The Art of Virtue* was never written unless
it be incorporated in the *Autobiography,* but the idea for it was
never far from his mind. It was on May 3, 1760, that he wrote
from London to his friend Henry Home, Lord Kames, in speaking
of the latter's *Maxims for the Conduct of Life:*

I purpose likewise a little work for the benefit of youth, to be called
The Art of Virtue. . . . Most people have naturally *some* virtues, but
none have naturally *all* the virtues. To *acquire* those that are wanting,
and secure what we acquire, as well as those we have naturally, is the
subject of *an art.* It is as properly an art as painting, navigation, or
architecture. If a man would become a painter, navigator, or architect,

it is not enough that he be *advised* to be one, that he is *convinced* by the arguments of his adviser, that it would be for his advantage to be one, and that he resolves to be one, but he must also be taught the principles of the art, be shewn all the methods of working, and how to acquire the habits of using properly all the instruments; and thus regularly and gradually he arrives, by practice, at some perfection in the art. . . . My *Art of Virtue* has also its instruments, and teaches the manner of using them.[15]

Here is an explicit statement of the intention behind the famous passages in the *Autobiography,* which have given so much trouble, but before Franklin could arrive at so firm a position, he had made a long search for the principles of moral excellence and the best ways of applying them. The trail of that search carries us back to his boyhood in Boston, which he recalls in an oft-quoted and friendly letter to his one-time adversary Samuel Mather, dated from Passy, May 12, 1784.

When I was a boy, I met with a book, entitled *Essays to do Good,* which I think was written by your father. It had been so little regarded by a former possessor, that several leaves of it were torn out; but the remainder gave me such a turn of thinking, as to have an influence on my conduct through life; for I have always set a greater value on the character of a *doer of good,* than on any other kind of reputation.[16]

The interest was something more than theoretical because Mather's *Bonifacius,* or *Essays to Do Good* (1710), is described by Perry Miller in its historical context as, "possibly the most important work of the early eighteenth century." [17] It derives its importance from being the central document in the battle between the entrenched Massachusetts clergy and the witty and insolent Franklin brothers, James and Benjamin, for command of the New England soul. The story of the founding of the *New-England Courant* by James Franklin in 1721, of his attacks on the vested interests and subsequent incarceration, and of apprentice Benjamin's taking over the paper in fact when he was only supposed to do so in name, has been so clouded by the younger man's account of the quarrel that its larger significance has been forgotten. But it was in the early phases of this battle that the young Ben learned the rudiments of the Art of Virtue by fighting for it in the market-place before he had had time to consider what the

philosophers designated the four or seven of twelve cardinal virtues actually to be.

Mather's unpretentious little book became the most popular of
all his writings largely because it fell in with a dominant movement of the times which, in England, had taken the form of
"rallyings of the Noncomformist conscience in an effort to recapture, by nonpolitical means, moral territory lost to the Restora-
tion." [18] With the total loss in England and the weakening in
Massachusetts of the political power of the clergy, Protestant
orthodoxy as represented by the Mathers was finding it more and
more difficult to control the popular conscience and, through it,
the conduct of the individual. An obvious answer to the dilemma
was to find new reasons for "doing good." Mather's essay was a
weapon in this campaign, an effort to rally popular opinion to
reform the manners of its own society by supplying it with a
handbook of conduct in which the role of each individual was
defined and his moral obligations to others described in detail.
Not only the clergy, but physicians, lawyers, rich men, men in
political or judicial positions, sea-captains, and military commanders are instructed in these pages as to how they may direct
their normal roles to the benefit of society. Families are urged to
group themselves in order better to do good, and societies of
young men are suggested for the same purpose.[19] The rewards of
future bliss are reserved for the "useful man" who has directed
his life to the improvement of his fellows. Faith and dogma are
either assumed or forgotten; all that remains is proper conduct.

It was obviously not Mather's intention to undermine formal
religion and to substitute secular for theological controls over
conduct, but when his *Essays* are paired, as they were by the
young Franklin, with Defoe's *Essay on Projects,* they become completely secular and defeat the purpose for which they were designed. By removing the practical need for faith, they opened the
door to reason as the primary guide to the good life. The controversy between the Franklin brothers and the Mathers hinged
on this issue and started Benjamin on his career of pragmatic
humanism. No wonder he remembered the book as a turning
point in his development.

His "Dogood Papers," published in the *Courant,* are the first
step in this career. They are obviously the work of a prodigy, for

Franklin was only sixteen when he wrote them. It would hardly be necessary for their author to tell us that he had made a careful study of Addison's *Spectator,* so closely do they follow the form and style of the periodical essay which was so popular in eighteenth-century England and so widely copied in the early American newspapers. In creating an imaginary correspondent through whom to attack the morals and manners of the day in a tone of good-natured innocence, Franklin was far from original, but in selecting for his character a middle-aged widow and in pointing his letters directly at the powerful Mathers, he showed that he was witty and daring in his own right far beyond the capacities of his contemporaries. *Silence* Dogood was a direct hit at the loquacious (at least on paper) author of the Dogood essays, and the "Editorial Preface" to the *Courant* on February 11, 1723, published when Benjamin was taking the editorship, is overingenuous in claiming that the paper now "is designed purely for the diversion and merriment of his readers."

Modern criticism would probably call Franklin's position "ambivalent" and he himself christened the "perpetual dictator" of his journal "good old Janus the Couranteer," two-faced because he really shared with Mather the rational Do-Good philosophy of the ecclesiastical party at the same time that he was protesting the right of any party to attempt to control the public conscience by any means. Franklin's position, as expressed by the genial widow of his invention, was that Vice and Virtue are not learned in church or college but are matters of individual choice, and that the wise man or woman will choose the virtues of sobriety and temperance because "no pleasure can give satisfaction or prove advantageous to a *reasonable mind,* which is not attended with the *restraints of reason.*" [20]

During the next twenty-five years in Philadelphia and London, when he was busy establishing himself financially, politically, and socially, Franklin pretty much took virtue and vice as they came without further attempts to discover or to formulate the rules of the art by any means other than practice. But there were two more-or-less abortive exceptions to this pragmatic procedure. In the *Dissertation on Liberty and Necessity, Pleasure and Pain* (1725), he made his only thoroughly systematic attempt to establish an ethical basis of operations through the use of logic.

In an experimental rebuttal to Wollaston's *Religion of Nature,* he argued that, because God is good, man is good, and therefore, because there is no evil, man may do as he likes, measuring his actions only by their returns in pleasure. This genial determinism, so different from that of the Puritan conscience, may have been what was needed by a young man on his own in London, but it did not satisfy his inner needs and he concluded that Logic had tricked him so basely that he would never use it again. His other attempt at formulating a faith, the *Articles of Belief and Acts of Religion* (1728), was a statement rather than an argument and was therefore somewhat more rewarding because in it he established a working relationship with God which served him for the rest of his life. The two most important planks in this platform were:

> I conceive for many reasons, that he is a *good being;* and as I should be happy to have so wise, good, and powerful a being my friend, let me consider in what manner I shall make myself most acceptable to him.
>
> Next to the praise resulting from and due to his wisdom, I believe he is pleased and delights in the happiness of those he has created; and since without virtue man can have no happiness in this world, I firmly believe he delights to see me virtuous, because he is pleased when he sees me happy.

What use would he have for a complex ethical system when so simple a formula would serve?

This was also the era of *Poor Richard's Almanack,* his most overtly moral production. Again it is necessary to turn to contemporary literary fashion and the climate of ideas of the times to counteract the unhappy anti-Victorian reaction of the modern reader to what usually seems to him but a haphazard grab bag of sententious pontifications. But perhaps it is now well enough known that by 1730 almost every printer either published, or aspired to publish, an almanac, that one of the customary marginal decorations of such productions was the aphorism, and that Franklin's aphorisms are more apt, more shrewd, more witty than those of any of his competitors. For he alone at the same time could preach the Art of Virtue in practical maxims which had the value of a good recipe in that they not only advised but "taught all the methods" of working the art, and while doing so he could laugh at his own pomposity. In the torrent of maxims that are quoted with such apparent reverence in the famous Preface for 1758 known as "Father Abraham's Speech," the reader is likely to forget that Franklin pictures himself in the audience, so overcome by his own quoted arguments for providence that, whereas the people "approved the doctrine and immediately practiced the contrary" by buying extravagantly in the subsequent sale, he, the author, was so moved that he went home with his old coat, fearful of the consequences of buying the cloth for a new one. Wit of this sort is the salt for the most earnest of his preachments. It provided the ironic base for the political satires which brought sanity to the strained nerves of the Revoluntionary era and it made a literary masterwork out of the simple chronicle of his own life.

There are many good reasons for recognizing the *Autobiography* as one of the finest literary products of the eighteenth century, but most of its critics have been somewhat puzzled by the frankness of its admissions and the apparent casualness of its composition. It has suffered too, like other of Franklin's writings, by the refractions of romantic naturalism. By nineteenth century standards, the egocentricity of it is naïve; the ideals it expresses, materialistic and opportunistic; the style bare and utilitarian. Yet it has never once ceased to be accepted as required reading for the literate American even thought it has been laughed at almost as much as it has been praised.

The posthumous edition of Max Farrand (1949), which attempts to solve the complex problem of an accurate text, has done much to encourage a more scholarly approach to this great work, but once again the gem must be reset in its original setting before its full lustre can be appreciated. The *Autobiography* is a characteristic product of the Enlightenment in its humanistic emphasis on reason as a guide and explanation of life; it is characteristic of Franklin and the challenge of the New World that it offers a practical system of measurement of success or failure in the application of reason to daily conduct. Checks and balances are now supplied and *errata* carefully noted, in actually working out the admonishments of Cotton Mather and the sweet reasonableness of Shaftesbury and Hutcheson. The Art of Virtue should be capable of a precision as great as that of the science of electricity if, as reason proposed, the moral law were but a higher reflection of natural law, and man were the sole shaper of his own destiny. What more logical method of developing and testing a pragmatic moral system than the analysis and inventory of conduct in a single human life; and what life more ready for this purpose than one's own?

The point of view, style, and form of the *Autobiography* reflect many of the literary modes of the age. Eighteenth-century British literature placed strong emphasis on personality and self-revelation as guides to conduct. Not only was this trend characteristic of the periodical essay, but it gave rise to the long pseudobiographical novels of Richardson and Fielding, the letters of Lady Montagu and Lord Chesterfield, the biographies and autobiographies of Gibbon, Boswell, and Johnson, and the satires of Pope and Swift. The individual in his society was the obsessive subject matter of all forms of literary effort and the simplest writing became literary in its self-consciousness and its emphasis on the standards and forms of expression. Franklin had given study to the requirements of the essay, the literary letter, the political satire, and even to poetry; it was logical that he should try the the autobiography. Through this form he could best explore the Art of Virtue—in practice as well as in theory—and protect himself from the charge of pride by the cool objectivity and bantering wit of the prevailing literary fashion. Even should these fail, he had his thirteenth virtue, humility, in reserve. Here perhaps was the most effective form for his book on the Art of Virtue, long deferred.

The book was written at four separate sittings, widely spaced. The first and most revealing section deals with his childhood and youth and analyzes the whole process of maturation with a careful list of *errata* committed in the first edition. It bears the dateline of Twyford, the home of his friend Jonathan Shipley, Bishop of St. Asaph, 1771, when Franklin was sixty-five years old. Twelve years later, when he was living in Passy, he received letters from Abel James and Benjamin Vaughan urging him to continue the narrative. Claiming that the first part had been written primarily for his family, he deliberately changed his tone and wrote a supplement for the general reader in which he stated and discussed his famous method of acquiring virtue. Now seventy-eight, Franklin spoke in more impersonal tones and with increased confidence in the principles he had learned by his early experience. When he again took up the writing, he was back in Philadelphia, now eighty-two and failing in health. Quoting his memorandum of 1731 on Cotton Mather's proposal for a society of young men to create a "united party for virtue," based on a Deistic creed and exercising a worldwide influence, he then proceeded to recount the various projects to which he had applied his benevolent and utilitarian philosophy in the years of his maturity. The fourth section, written just before his death, is a brief fragment continuing the narrative of the third and leaving it unfinished.

There are therefore but three parts to the work, organically considered: the education in virture, the principles and methods of the Art of Virtue, and the application of the rules of virtue to public life. Although probably not thus consciously planned, the book has a unity as a tract on the art of being human which it lacks as the mere narrative of a life. Like the autobiographies of Rousseau, Henry Adams, Goethe, and Wordsworth, the subject of the narrative is an alter ego of the author, as much a symbol or projection of his controlling views on the experience of living as it is a portrait of his actual self. The painter's self-portrait usually has the same character: it is as much a product of imagination as of observation. Franklin, like these others, was using his knowledge of the facts of his own life for a purpose which lay beyond the limits of literal reality.

His opening address to "My dear Son" may therefore be taken as but the first of a series of literary devices, common enough at the time but out of fashion now, which Franklin used to establish the factor which T. S. Eliot has called the "objective correlative," a literary counterpart to experience by means of which the author may gain his needed aesthetic detachment without losing the authenticity of the intimate object or event. In the same way, he uses the Vernon money, the defection of Governor Keith, his unsuccessful attempt to seduce the mistress of his friend Ralph, his experiment with typesetting at Palmer's, the dire croaking of Samuel Mickle, and many other incidents, to illustrate and symbolize specific virtues and his success or failure in practicing them. From the mass of detail, there gradually emerges a whimsical but consistent character, a sort of New World Tom Jones who has rejected conventional ethical canons and substituted a pragmatic natural morality which can accept life as it comes but at the same time bend and control it through the exercise of a free will granted by a benevolent deity. Franklin's account of his early years has the naïve delight of Huck Finn's wanderings and confessions; they are impersonally personal, gently ironic, while maintaining a seriousness and sincerity of underlying purpose, and endowed with the narrative gift of a first-rate writer of fiction at work with facts.

The second section, which is the real heart of the book, caused most of the intellectual indigestion which became epidemic among nineteenth-century romantics, and is even somewhat difficult for us to accept today. With unbelievable candor, he sets forth his working scheme for improvement in virtue, complete with tables and score-sheets, and describes how and for how long he experimented with the scheme himself. His belief that the virtues were individually capable of precise description, and that they could be sharpened one by one by merely giving each a day of concentrated attention, has seemed to later readers a gross violation of fine feeling. It is rather an evidence of clear and consistent thinking in the framework of the empirical rationalism of his time, without the emotional coloring of sentimental humanitarianism.

The idea that virtues can be particularized and cultivated goes back to Socrates and Plato, who agreed on four: prudence, courage, temperance, and justice. The twelve moral virtues which Spenser, in his *Faerie Queene,* says he borrowed from Aristotle, are but refinements on this fundamental set. Neither list includes the Christian additions of faith, hope, and charity, which constitute, with Plato's four, the Cardinal seven. Franklin is wholly Greek in his choice of twelve, realizing that the list could be reduced but preferring "for the sake of clearness, to use more names with fewer ideas annexed to each than a few names with more ideas" (p. 101). To the twelve he added a thirteenth, humility, as a safety valve. His list follows closely, with a general modernization of terms, that discussed by Aristotle in the *Nicomachean Ethics,* and his main emphasis is on Plato's four. Faith, hope, and charity are not mentioned because the purpose of the Art of Virtue is self-improvement rather than self-immolation. The plan is based on the theory that, if each human being took thought for his own weaknesses and did his best to eliminate them, the human race might approach perfection. Sharing with the Greek philosophers and with the contemporary rationalists like Shaftesbury, who had recently included in his *Characteristics* (1711) an "Inquiry Concerning Virtue or Merit," the belief that virtues could be isolated and defined by a method of a priori reasoning, and could then be tested empirically, Franklin merely took the next step of spelling out in detail just how all of this might be done by the average man or woman. For it is not enough, he had said to Lord Kames, to advise and to recommend an art; one must supply all the working principles and the instruments. Actually, if one could maintain the benign calm of sweet reason which was so completely at Franklin's command and avoid the self-conscious prudery of his critics, it would be hard to find anywhere a more helpful set of rules and instruments for self-improvement that that which he proposes. But it would also be necessary to share with him that irony and wit which he in turn shared with the other great prose satirists of his day and thereby avoid the subjectivity and emotional coloring which makes the sanest of advice a mockery.

The latter part of the *Autobiography* is the least interesting of the three, partly because it was written when Franklin was really an old man and lacked some of the youthful zest he had exhibited at the age of sixty-five, and partly because it is largely a factual record of his civic, national, and international activities. The same self-confidence and pride in his achievement, tempered by the same modesty about his own worth, are evident in this part of the narrative, but there is less discussion of his motivation, less character analysis of others, fewer interesting events, and less warmth of human effort. The reason for the change is mainly that he now has presented his formula for the Art of Virtue and his struggle to realize it in his own character; all that remains is the account of his largely successful application of its principles and methods to a fruitful and happy life.

The conclusion which many of his biographers and critics have drawn from this record is that versatility of gifts and variety of activity characterize this great man, and the traditional "Many-sided" Franklin emerges. I would rather point out the singleness of his purpose and the magnificent focus and the direct aim of all of his actions. The pursuit of the Art of Virtue had become for him identified with the pursuit of happiness, and the instruction of all mankind in its principles and methods, the one activity to which he could wholeheartedly devote his life. To push back ignorance by exploring and applying the physical laws that govern the universe and to improve man's lot on earth by teaching him the equally precise and effective moral laws that govern conduct seemed but two parts of the same great purpose. Science and art were the twin agents of the new, free, and democratic society that was even then becoming a reality in the New World. Not being a man of theory, Franklin devoted every ounce of his energy to the job of popular education: through civic enterprise, international politics, scientific experiment, and effective writing. In all he was the great teacher of the masses, making complex knowledge simple, confused issues clear, strained relations helpful, and distant goals within reach of sincere effort. All that was needed for peace on earth was the realization on the part of each human being of his right to be completely human in a universe in which he rightfully belonged. There is a magnificent unity in this American man of the Enlightenment. Naïve, yes, and pragmatic, as the spokesman of an emerging new civilization should be, but rational, consistent, of tireless energy and devotion to the welfare of others, and lightheartedly ironic in his contemplation of man's ignorance and follies. To his conquest of static electricity should be added his realization of the dynamic virtues of prudence, courage, temperance, and justice.

V

The time has come for me to bring my remarks to a close by indicating in what ways Franklin's literary life and moral philosophy—his art of being human—may provide us with a "tract for the times." It would be too easy to point out that his pragmatic humanism is a rewarding philosophy at any time or place, and to recommend merely that we should study and imitate his principles and actions. This might be sound advice, but there is more to my assignment than the making of a simple recommendation. I have tried to suggest that Franklin is best understood as an American man of the Enlightenment, and that, because the basic philosophy of the Enlightenment was more akin to that of today than to that of any intervening era, a restudy of the man in the setting of his own climate of opinion should make both man and times more intelligible and useful to us today.

There are two aspects of this comparison of the then with the now that must be disposed of immediately. American civilization in the twentieth century, with its increased and heterogeneous population, its vast territorial expansion, and its urban and industrial economy, is not the simple, experimental, democratic, and agrarian colonial civilization that Franklin knew. Furthermore, modern philosophy has not only dethroned the ruler of the Heavenly City of the Scholastics, as Carl Becker accused the eighteenth century of doing; it has destroyed the City itself, ramparts and all. We live in a much more complex and far less orderly universe of the mind than did Franklin and his contemporaries. The big questions are, therefore, whether or not these changes are fundamental; whether or not there is anything left of the philosophy of the Enlightenment after the removal of its limited and secure mental universe; whether or not, if there is anything left, it can be applied to the complex problems of American life today.

Underlying the eighteenth-century view of life are the principles of empirical science and pragmatic humanism. Neither of these sets of principles requires a guarantee that truth is capable of complete realization or that man will at any certain further date reach perfection. Both function better on a foundation of skepticism that on one of absolute idealism. The general movement of modern American philosophy [21] seems to have been, during the present century, away from dialectic systems of ideas—either idealistic like that of the transcendentalists or materialistic like that of the Marxists—and toward one or another form of rationalistic analysis for its own sake. This movement began in the late nineteenth century with the pragmatism of Peirce and James, and was carried forward by the instrumentalism of Dewey. The influences of G. E. Moore, Bertrand Russell, Albert Einstein and Rudolf Carnap have been further in the direction of a reliance on the power of human reason, with the tools supplied by experimental science and mathematical formula, to resolve if not to solve the mysteries of the universe one at a time by a process of analysis without reference to any single view of the whole of knowledge. At least one secret of the physical universe has recently given way to a blackboard and a piece of chalk when Einstein perfected the formula which released atomic energy for the use and destruction of man. The experience was not unlike that of Newton and the apple; it was a triumph of the human reason, working with mathematical principles which are closely correlated with observed scientific phenomena.

Similarly, twentieth-century America has tended to turn toward pragmatic and experimental systems for the examination and the reform of both society and the individual. Our sociology and our psychology function best when their assumptions can be tested by experience because their methods are based on natural rather than on any form of supernatural law. Our day-by-day management of our group and personal experience is governed by the relative and pragmatic tests of our courts of law, the will of the electorate, the measurable data collected by the social scientist, and a system of mental therapy which closely parallels that of physical therapy. In all aspects of our life, we maintain a skeptical empiricism: we observe, we compare, we test, we measure, we prescribe. We may not have much faith left in universals, but what faith we do have is based on our belief in the immutability of physical law and the validity of human reason. Even our poetry and criticism have turned from insight and emotional uplift to analysis and rational order in the fashion of eighteenth-century neoclassicism. We have survived the romantic movement and are back to something very like the rationalism of the Enlightenment.

It is not my intention to declare this state of mind either good or bad. Sometimes I regret it for purely temperamental reasons and, as a displaced romantic, feel like an alien in my own land. But I would like to propose that any state of mind can be fruitful only when it is understood and accepted by those who profess it. What we can learn from Franklin is that pragmatic humanism, based on the acceptance and application of scientific evidences, can be a workable and rewarding philosophy. Our one grave danger is that of rejecting the world we live in and sinking into a mood of mass despair. It is impossible to think of Benjamin Franklin, were he living today, as in danger of committing this *erratum,* for if he could know how much more we know than he did about the laws that govern the physical universe and the ways of applying them to human comfort, as well as how much more we know about the principles that determine individual and social motivation and the ways of reshaping conduct toward more enlightened self-interest and mutual improvement, he would groan with envy in his grave. Perhaps we should put an end to his torture and reincarnate him as a guide to our pursuits of the science of nature and the Art of Virtue today.

NOTES

1. Since this paper was written, there have appeared studies by Theodore Hornberger, Bruce I. Granger, and others, not to mention the Yale edition of the *Papers*, which might call this statement into question.
2. *The Works of John Adams*, edited by C. F. Adams (Boston: Little, Brown and Co., 1856), I, 660-664.
3. *Gazette Nationale, ou le Moniteur universel* (June 12, 1790). Quoted by Carl Van Doren, *Benjamin Franklin* (New York: Viking Press, 1938), p. 781.
4. *The Writings of Benjamin Franklin*, edited by A. H. Smyth (New York: Macmillan Co., 1905-7), IV, 154. Hereafter cited as *Writings*.
5. D. H. Lawrence, *Studies in Classic American Literature* (New York: Thomas Seltzer, 1923), pp. 24-27.
6. Max Weber, *The Protestant Ethic and the Spirit of Capitalism*, translated by T. Parsons (London, 1930), p. 17.
7. A. H. Smyth, *American Literature* (Philadelphia: Eldredge and Brothers, 1889), p. 20.
8. C. F. Richardson, *A Primer of American Literature* (Boston: Houghton, Mifflin Co., 1884), p. 20.
9. Carl Becker, *The Heavenly City of the Eighteenth Century Philosophers* (New Haven, Conn.: Yale University Press, 1932), pp. 21-22.
10. Van Doren, *Franklin*, p. 171.
11. *Benjamin Franklin's Experiments*, edited by I. B. Cohen (Cambridge, Mass.: Harvard University Press, 1941), p. 73.
12. September 29, 1748. *Writings*, II, 362-363.
13. M. L. Weems, *The Life of Benjamin Franklin* (Philadelphia, 1815), pp. 168-171.
14. I. B. Cohen, *Benjamin Franklin: His Contribution to the American Tradition* (Indianapolis, Ind.: Bobbs-Merrill Co., 1953), p. 63.
15. *Writings*, IV, 11-14.
16. *Ibid.*, IX, 208.
17. P. Miller, *From Colony to Province* (Cambridge, Mass.: Harvard University Press, 1953), p. 410.
18. *Ibid.*, 411.
19. Mather offers only moral reasons for the forming of such societies of young men, but Franklin, in adopting Mather's idea, sees them as means toward the development of international understanding and world peace.
20. *Writings*, II, 42.

21. See Morton White, *The Age of Analysis* (New York: New American Library, 1955). A contrary view is presented by Brand Blanshard, "Speculative Thinkers," in *Literary History of the United States* (New York: Macmillan Co., 1948), II, 1273-1295.

Fenimore Cooper: The Critical American in England

From *The American in England During the First Half-Century of Independence* (New York: Henry Holt and Co., 1926), pp. 318-345. Based on Cooper's then almost forgotten *Notions of the Americans, American Democrat,* and five volumes of travels in Europe, this largely accidental discovery that Cooper was as much an "American Carlyle" as an "American Scott" was subsequently developed into *Fenimore Cooper: Critic of His Times* (New York: Minton Balch and Co., 1931).

THE MOST IMPORTANT FIGURE in the controversy and the harshest critic of England among all these travelers was James Fenimore Cooper. The fact that his criticism was vigorous, founded firmly on seasoned theories of government, and in many essentials justified by subsequent events is often obscured by the more obvious fact that it frequently sounds ill-tempered and, in its expression, not always consistent. Cooper's name belongs with those of Carlyle, Ruskin, Mill, and Emerson as a penetrating critic of nineteenth-century social conditions as well as with that of Scott as a popular writer of romantic fiction. His two-edged commentary on America and Europe occupied the central portion of his life, and not only did it turn his novels from the open avenues of art to the less pleasant ones of propaganda, but it produced his *Notions of the Americans* and his ten volumes on European scenery, society, and government, which may be grouped (although published by him as separate studies) under the single title of *Glean-*

ings in Europe 1826-33. The custom of Cooper's critics has been
to hasten over or to gloss over these years and their literary products as an interlude of blindness in the career of a great artist,
the beginnings of that unfortunate series of controversies with the
press and public which so damaged his reputation that it was
many years before it even began to recover. The reason for this
attitude is that Cooper was already becoming involved in controversy when he wrote these books and their temporal significance has largely clouded the real basis of thought which prompted them.

The penetrating comment that Cooper was "an aristocrat in
feeling, and a democrat by conviction" [1] is a necessary premise to a
discussion of his excessively paradoxical position. He was charged
with having defended America when he was in England, only to
return and defend England at the expense of his own country.
This accusation is superficial, but has in it the elements of truth,
as have the statements that he was temperamentally a Puritan
who could not appreciate the Puritans; that he was the first novelist to depict primitive American life with fidelity and yet misunderstood and spurned his countrymen; and numerous other
contradictory interpretations of his character. The simple fact is
that his temperament was too passionate to keep step with his
thought.

As a young man, Cooper was in England at least twice. When
it was suggested by the authorities that he leave Yale College because of a frolic in which he had been involved, his father put
him on a merchant vessel in preparation for a career in the Navy.
He was seventeen when his ship first put in at the port of London
in 1806. It has been frequently suggested that the picture of English society which Cooper draws in his first novel, *Precaution,* was
second hand, but one chief source of his knowledge has been
rather neglected. In his *Gleanings in Europe: England,* he tells
us that a certain old custom-house officer named Swinburne,
formerly the personal domestic of an English gentleman, regaled
him with the lore of the servants' hall for a week and then es-
corted him to the West End and reverentially pointed out the
scenes of these romantic and mysterious happenings. Among other
adventures, says Cooper, "Mr. Swinburne bristled close up to me

. . . and putting his hand to his mouth, as we passed a quiet old gentleman, he whispered ominously, 'An Earl'!" Later the performance was repeated when its object was Horne Tooke, and the enthusiastic young American ran after this dignified and celebrated personage for some distance in order to get a better look at him.

Later, Cooper took a fellow sailor over the same ground and one of the sights of the trip was an elderly lady, followed by a gentleman in black whom the Americans took to be a minister. What was their surprise when this "minister" stepped aside with all the deference of the footman he was, took off his hat, and opened the door for the lady when she arrived at her residence.

His view of England on this trip was not extensive, but he recalled later that it had moved him to theorize on the English idea of liberty. The two sailors were debating whether to enter Green Park or not when a gentleman came up and said, "Go in, my lads; this is a free country, and you have as much right there as the King." This attitude of considering the entrance to a royal park as a favor, says Cooper, "left ground for reflection on the essential difference in principle that exists between a state of things in which the community receive certain privileges as concessions, and that in which power itself is merely a temporary trust, delegated directly and expressly by the body of the people." Such was the basis of his later criticism of society.

This experience, together with his reading of the novels of English life, then so popular, and perhaps some information gained from his wife's English relatives, furnished the material for the almost accidental writing of *Precaution* in 1820. Hints of the later critic of aristocracy are almost as scant in this novel as are its promises of the author's future fictional power. For the most part, he accepts the dicta of fashionable London in questions of manners and morals, and his one point of adverse criticism, personified in the character of Mrs. Wilson, is his comment on the irreligious tendency of the times, especially manifest in the difficulty of keeping holy the Sabbath in the society of London, "where the influence of fashion has supplanted the laws of God." But the novel as a whole conforms to its English pattern and it was even issued anonymously with the implication that it had

been written by an English author. For this one instance of the
current subserviency to England in literary matters, Cooper amply
atoned by his later writings.

I I

When he next went abroad in 1826 it was as the head of a party
of ten, comprising his wife, children, and servants, and as a writer
of international reputation. He had turned from the English to
the American scene and had enjoyed a decade of sensational success at home and abroad, especially on the Continent. The English
reviews had at last deigned to recognize him as "the American
Scott," an epithet sufficiently condescending but not particularly
welcome to his independence of spirit. Scott himself, as well as
Mary Russell Mitford, Barry Cornwall, Maria Edgeworth, and
others, had declared themselves his unqualified admirers. His
friend, Samuel F. B. Morse, who was on the Continent in 1829,
bears further testimony to his foreign reputation. "In every city of
Europe that I visited," he writes, "the works of Cooper were conspicuously placed in the windows of every bookshop. . . . They
have been seen by American travelers in the languages of Turkey
and Persia, in Constantinople, in Egypt, at Jerusalem, at Ispahan."

"It is my intention," Cooper wrote to his English publisher just
before sailing, "to remain in Europe a year or two. My object is
my own health and the instruction of my children in the French
and Italian languages. Perhaps there is also a little pleasure con-
cealed in the bottom of the cup." His stay in Europe, which at
first he had planned should be short, extended to seven years,
and he even feared, like many another transatlantic traveler, that
he would never return.

"Four years in Europe are an age to the American," he says in
his preface to *Switzerland*, Part II, "as are four years in America
to the Europeans. Jefferson has somewhere said that no American
ought to be more than five years, at a time, out of his own country,
lest he get *behind* it. This may be true, as to its *facts;* but the
author is convinced that there is more danger of his getting *before*
it, as to *opinion*. It is not improbable that this book may furnish
evidence of both of these truths."

During these years he was engaged in writing a series of novels, the first of which, *The Prairie, Red Rover, The Wept of Wish-ton-Wish*, and *The Water Witch*, were on American themes, and the last of which, *The Bravo, The Heidenmauer*, and *The Headsman* were located on the Continent. Although none of these stories deals with England, a study of them, especially with reference to incidental passages, furnishes an excellent introduction to their author's transition from pure fiction to political and social propaganda. In 1828 appeared his anonymous *Notions of the Americans; Picked up by a Travelling Bachelor*, his only direct statement at this time of his criticism of society.

The first four of these novels are significant chiefly for their intense, almost belligerent Americanism. Cooper, looking back on his country from across the water, was proud of her, especially of her history, and set out to vindicate her by a wider range of subject matter than that of his earlier novels. He wrote of the Puritans, of the early shipping in New York and Rhode Island, and of the great middle western prairie, instead of concentrating his attention on his own wilderness of northern New York. But even in these novels, the seeds of his later debates are apparent. In *Red Rover* he takes occasion to make some disparaging implications on the English character, particularly in the matter of deference to presumed hereditary rank in the person of the Captain of the *Dart;* while in the preface to *The Water Witch* he criticizes the "virtuous and infallible voters" of America who have decreed that there shall be no more estates. "The curse of mediocrity weighs upon us," he exclaims, but in the same book he compares the youthful vigor of America in "covering the wilds of the West with the happiest fruits of human industry," to the Queen of the Adriatic "sleeping on her muddy isles," and to Rome itself, living only in its antiquities. The double-edged quality of his criticism is apparent thus early. Even in his intellectual enthusiasm for democracy and progress, the aristocrat in him finds a discordant note in American crudity; and in the despised limitations of Old World society the same aristocrat discovers a congenial warmth of culture.

Again, in *The Wept of Wish-ton-Wish*, he speaks in his preface of the Europeans, who, "accustomed to despotic governments," naturally gave the title of "King" to Indian chiefs; and he, later in his story, goes into a considerable analysis of American civilization. In Europe, he says, "the arts of life have been the fruits of an intelligence that has progressively accumulated with the advancement of civilization; while here improvement is in a degree the consequence of experience elsewhere acquired." It is therefore dangerous to generalize from single phenomena, for "in order to understand the actual condition of these states, it should be remembered that it is equally unjust to believe that all the intermediate points partake of the improvements of particular places, as to infer the want of civilization at more remote establishments, from a few unfavorable facts gleaned near the center."

These identical factors in his criticism are even more apparent in the *Notions of the Americans*. Cooper, like many another ardently patriotic American, resented the charges of the English traveler in America, and to this resentment was added a reading of the reviews and a personal contact with Englishmen, chiefly during his travels on the Continent. On his way to France in July, 1826, he had spent a little over a week in England, and in 1828, he lived in London something over two months. On the knowledge gained during these two brief visits, he based his criticism of England and the English. It was enough, however, to bring his resentment to the point where he felt the necessity of an answer to the English charges. His one fictitious travel book was published immediately upon his return to the Continent.

The primary object of his attack in this book is the English traveler in America. His letters are supposed to have been written by one of these gentlemen who, having met an American, by name Cadwallader, in Europe, and having been struck with the manliness and liberality of his character, decided to visit America for himself and find out the truth of the matter. Cadwallader carefully prepared his intinerary and his mind, furnishing him with such data and opportunities as he thought needful. The result was a trip and thereafter a book which exhibits America at her best, and Cooper does not hesitate to color, yet he never misstates, his facts. His America is dangerously near to Paradise, and yet he is accurate as far as he goes. His study gives exactly what he promised it would, the other side of the picture. The English traveler had already portrayed in full the black side of America and the American traveler; all that was left was white.

Cooper's attitude is not vindictive. He explains rather than reviles the blindness of the visitor from Europe. His natural instinct, says Cooper, is to compare the new country with the old, and he would be more than human if he did not, consciously or unconsciously, blacken the one in favor of the other. The very fact that he considers America sufficiently on a par with England for comparison proves a great truth in favor of the former. "What should we think of the boy whose intellect, and labors, and intelligence were drawn into bold and invidious comparison with those of aged and experienced men!"

His criticism of the American social state is a thoroughgoing idealization, exhibited for English and not American eyes. Its starting point is the advantage gained by an absence of hereditary rank. "Servility," he says, "forms no part of the civilization of New England, though civility be its essence." And he generalizes from this to the conclusion that "the great desideratum of the social compact would then seem to be, to produce such a state of things as shall call the most individual enterprise into action, while it should secure a proper consideration for the interests of the whole." This state of affairs, he finds, in general, to be the true one, but in the same passage in which he proclaims the virtues of wealth and industry in commercial New York he implies a distaste for the sordid money-seekers who may, by the laws of democracy, sit at the same banquet table with the cultivated and urbane scion of one of "the principal and longest established families." The instinctive reaction of the author's temperament to the results of the democracy which he is so enthusiastic about in theory is apparent even in this panegyric on America.

I I I

The other side of the story is also told, although incidentally, in the pages of the *Notions of the Americans*. The faults of the Americans in matters of taste, such as an overemphasis on food and the use of carpets, is attributed to the hereditary or commercial influences of England, and frequently direct comments on English life are brought in by way of contrast with affairs in America. "The tendency of everything in England," he says, "is to aristocracy. I can conceive that the King of England might very well set a fashion in the pronunciation of a word," for his dictum would easily find its way down through her "powerful, wealthy, hereditary, but subsidizing aristocracy." He confesses that this state of affairs somewhat puzzles him. "Beyond a doubt," he says further, "what is called English high society is more repulsive, artificial, and cumbered, and, in short, more absurd and frequently less graceful than that of any other European nation. Still the English are a rational, sound, highly reasoning, manly and enlightened people. It is difficult to account for the inconsistency."

In the *Notions of the Americans,* Cooper's denunciation of the English social order is firm, but not as yet bitter. He discusses many aspects of America's spirit, but he always returns to the principles of honesty, integrity, and industry which he finds at the root of her character. He presents her as a young nation which has still much to learn, but which is acquiring knowledge rapidly. With her democratic form of government he is in complete accord, but he is equally free to recognize her crudity, though here only by implication. He looks forward to the day when America will have an aristocracy of culture rather than of inherited rank. "I am of opinion," he says, "the two nations might benefit a good deal by a critical examination of each other. Indeed, I think the American has, and does, daily profit by his observation, though I scarce know whether his kinsman is yet disposed to admit that he can learn by the study of a people so new, so remote, and so little known, as those of the United States." The book was addressed to the English people, and its tone, on the whole, is conciliatory. His interest is not primarily in the weaknesses of the English state and character, but rather in the ignorance of America prevalent abroad. Nevertheless, his deep-rooted prejudices and principles are already apparent. He shows himself an ardent, and yet, even in this eulogy, a critical believer in democracy in government, and in aristocracy of merit in personal relationships. To the social weaknesses of democracy and the hypocritical intolerance of an aristocratic form of government he allows no quarter.

In his following four novels, Cooper's obsession with the idea of social liberty became more and more dominant until, in *The Monikins,* it reached its height in involved satire. "A history of the progress of political liberty," he says in his preface to *The Bravo,* "written purely in the interests of humanity, is still a desideratum in literature." These four novels, together with his

Gleanings, may be regarded as Cooper's contribution to this end. "Governments are usually called either monarchies or republics," he says again. "The former class embraces equally those institutions in which the sovereign is worshipped as a god, and those in which he performs the humble office of a manikin. In the latter we find aristocracies and democracies blended in the same generic appellation. The consequence of a generalization so wide is an utter confusion on the subject of the polity of states." He then continues with the interesting theory that small republics are more likely to err than large, because in the latter, the popular interests are sufficiently diverse to prevent the dominance of sinister passion.

His story is an analysis of the actual despotic character of the so-called republic of Venice and must be judged chiefly as a tract in illustration of his adverse criticism of such a social order. As narrative it is heavy and dull. His conclusion is that the failure of the Venetian Republic "teaches the necessity of widening the foundations of society until the base shall have a breadth capable of securing the just representation of every interest, without which the social machine is liable to interruption from its own movement, and eventually to destruction from its own excesses."

It will not be necessary to follow the development of this theory through Cooper's next two novels, *The Headsman*, which deals with the republic of Switzerland, and *The Heidenmauer*, which carries the reader back to an analysis of such social liberty as formed the rule of the Benedictine monasteries of the Rhine. The author's entire absorption in his quest is witnessed by the concluding words of the latter novel: "To this tradition—true or false—we attach no importance. Our object has been to show . . . the reluctant manner in which the mind of man abandons old, to receive new, impressions," and the eternal antagonism between selfishness and inherent good throughout the history of the conflict.

The Monikins is Cooper's most extensive excursion into the fields of the political and social sciences. It is in the form of an allegory, after the fashion of the last book of *Gulliver's Travels*, of *Penguin Island*, and of other satires in which the habits and abilities of the human species are transferred, on the terms of a given principle, to animals of some sort, and are thereby exhibited in an extreme and presumably illuminating guise. The animals in this case apparently derive their name from a crossing of the words "manikin" and "monkey"; they have the nature and appearance of monkeys, but they act consistently according to their principles, as we might presume that manikins would. They are divided into the two nations of Leaphigh (England) and Leaplow (America), and the governments and social conditions in the two furnish commentaries on their parallels in the real countries which Cooper wished to satirize.

In this novel, Cooper has resorted again to the device of fictitious authorship. He pretends that a manuscript by an English gentleman, John Goldencalf, Viscount Householder, has fallen into his hands, and that his function has been merely that of an editor. The name itself is part of the allegory. This gentleman has inherited a vast sum of money and determines to attain happiness through philanthropy, and philanthropy through the "social stake" theory. This theory is best given in Goldencalf's own words: "Happiness is the aim of society; and property, or a vested interest in that society, is the best pledge of our disinterestedness and justice, and the best qualification for its proper control. It follows as a legitimate corollary that a multiplication of those interests will increase the stake, and render us more and more worthy of the trust by elevating us as near as may be to the pure and etherial condition of the angels." Acting on this theory, Goldencalf buys first a rotten borough, then a title, and finally lands, slaves, and shares in commercial companies all over the world. The satire on the English reverence for property is apparent.

The second and more intricate phase of the allegory opens when, in the company of an American sea captain, Noah Poke, Goldencalf meets some citizens of the land of Leaphigh and returns with them to their country. Here he finds that the monkeys have a highly organized society, the basis of which is social caste. Each citizen is classified and numbered, and all fit into their respective niches with the servility and accuracy of parts of a well-regulated machine. The very exaggeration of the picture renders the whole system ludicrous, as when the archbishop is much relieved at hearing that England has a national church, and he does not inquire into the question of whether Goldencalf is pagan or Presbyterian in his faith. "We shall meet in heaven some day!" he exclaims, with holy delight; "men or monikins, it can make no great difference, after all."

Neither is Cooper's satire of American social organization notable for its gentleness. When the travelers arrive in that land, they are confronted with election posters in which the same candidate is proclaimed, on the one hand, a known patriot, an approved legislator, a profound philosopher, and an incorruptible statesman, while on the other he is denounced as a bigamist, the father of seven illegitimate children, a bankrupt, and a sheep-stealer. The two parties making these statements are the Horizontal-Systematic-Indoctrinated-Republicans and the Perpendiculars.

In his comparison of the two societies, Cooper carries his satire even further. He derives the conclusion that in America (Leaplow) political and social facts are in advance of opinion because they go blindly ahead without guiding principle, while in England (Leaphigh) opinion is ahead of facts because facts are rooted to their bed of vested interest.

His allegorical picture of the governments of the two countries is ingenious. In England, the machine of state is a pillar resting on the tripod of the King, the nobles, and the people. If any one slip, the whole structure is doomed to fall. The Americans merely inverted this structure so that the tripod was on top with its legs up in the air. In this way they could be changed periodically and if any one made a blunder and fell, he would only break his own neck.

All of this is destructive and bitter criticism without a noticeable amount of leavening humor: but Cooper draws a long list of conclusions in his final chapter, some of which are ineffectual attempts to be clever, but a few of which are exceedingly pertinent:

That of all the 'ocracies (aristocracy and democracy included) hypocrisy is the most flourishing.

That nature has created inequalities in men and things, and, as human institutions are intended to prevent the strong from oppressing the weak, *ergo,* the laws should encourage natural inequalities as a legitimate consequence.

That liberty is a convertible term, which means exclusive privileges in one country, no privileges in another, and *inclusive* privileges in all.

That the whole people is not infallible, neither is a part of the people infallible.

And finally:—

That men have more of the habits, propensities, dispositions, cravings, antics, gratitude, flapjacks, and honesty of monikins, than is generally known.

Whatever may be said of the unreadability of *The Monikins* as a novel, or of its clumsiness as political and social satire, it must be accepted as a unique and vigorous commentary on two similar, yet contrastive, social orders. In addition, like all good social satire, it lays its final charge against human nature rather than against any particular social or political organism.

I V

The Monikins was published in 1835. During the next three years Cooper devoted his attention to editing and publishing the letters which he had written from various countries of Europe to his friends and relatives in America. Most of these were issued simultaneously under different titles in England, France, and America. They may, however, be grouped under the general title of *Gleanings in Europe* as they embrace his observations on France, England, Switzerland, the Rhine and Italy. Although addressed to some fifteen or more different people, and divided into separate works, they form a very well-connected record of his years in Europe and repeat more of comment and sentiment than of narrative of events.

These letters, he says in his preface to *France,* "contain the passing remarks of one who has certainly seen something of the world, whether it has been to his advantage or not, who had reasonably good opportunities to examine what he saw, and who is not conscious of being, in the slightest degree, influenced, 'by fear, favor, or the hope of reward.' "

His contemporaries, in so far as they noticed the volumes at all, accepted them on this basis. They were eager for entertaining comment on the passing show of the Old World, and an early reviewer, who obviously was inoculated against their real meaning, described them as "extremely amusing, light and piquant, and abounding in anecdotes."

The *Quarterly Review,* however, took a different attitude. The publication of *France* was greeted in April, 1837, as an entertaining and instructive criticism of France and, more particularly, America, by a writer of established European reputation. The implied references to English aristocracy contained in the volume are glossed over with supreme complacency. What was the Editor's horror, therefore, when *England* appeared the same year! "As a literary work," he cries in his rage, "it is really below contempt. . . . It has nothing solid but its ignorance. . . . The title should in truth have been *J. Fenimore Cooper, Esquire, in England, with Sketches of his Behavior in the Metropolis.*" The English critic who could patronize Irving, Rush, and Willis, and who could administer a lashing to the unfortunate Paulding, had at last met an antagonist to make him cringe.

As travel literature, apart from their social significance, these books have undoubted value. Cooper's descriptive powers, because of his experience as a novelist and his determination to express only what he saw in terms of his own mood, are equaled by Irving's alone, while in anecdote he is second to none but perhaps Willis. Few Americans enjoyed an opportunity equal to his for meeting the great of the Old World. In France, Lafayette was his close and constant friend, and Scott, who was abroad in quest of materials for the last volumes of his *Napoleon,* met him at the home of the Princess Galitzin. A few days later, as Cooper was leaving his apartment one rainy morning, he saw a carriage drive up and from it step a large, heavy-molded man, somewhat gray, who limped a little and walked with a cane. The visitor was half way up the steps before Cooper realized that he was probably looking for him. Turning back, he hailed him on the landing. *"Est-ce Mons. Cooper, que j'ai l'honneur de voir?"* asked the "Unknown," in French, but with an indifferent accent.

"Monsieur, je m'appele Cooper."

"Eh bien, donc—je suis Walter Scott."

In a few moments the Scotsman was firmly entrenched in the comfortable *bergère* which Lafayette had quitted but a minute before, and the two were discussing like old friends, business, international copyright, experiences in writing and with publishers, and national characteristics. Scott sympathized with Cooper's expression of despondency after seeing his novels in proof, remarking "that he would as soon see his dinner again, after a hearty meal, as to read one of his own tales when he was fairly rid of it."

The next morning the two took breakfast together and met once more thereafter at the hotel of the Princess Galitzin, parting in the ante-chamber to renew their friendship later on the other side of the Channel. "The manner of Sir Walter Scott," concludes Cooper, "is that of a man accustomed to see much of the world without being exactly a man of the world himself. . . . I have seldom known a man of his years, whose manner was so different in a *tête-à-tête*, and in the presence of a third person."

Cooper's books on his continental travels are, however, rather more notable for his description of natural scenery and his lively recounting of the ordinary incident of the journey, than for anecdotes of the great. The first volume of *France* and the two of *England* tell the story of his brief sojourns in the latter country. His description of the transatlantic passage in *France* is among the best written by an American. He sailed on an American packet, the *Hudson,* on June 1, 1826, from New York harbor and landed with his family at Cowes on July 2. The trip was a very usual one, but Cooper, with his nautical knowledge and experience, omits no detail which could make his narrative more vivid, colorful, or accurate. The mate of the vessel recognized him as a fellow seaman immediately, for, in mounting the side of the ship he had used the single technical expression, "send it an end." The result was that as soon as the other passengers were forced below, the sailor gave him a wink and remarked, "A clear quarter-deck! a good time to take a walk, sir." It was three days before the "land-birds" came crawling out one by one.

As the responsibility of his family was almost as heavy as would be the responsibility of a ship, the American kept in close touch with every movement of the boat or manifestation of the elements. The fact that a great number of ships had recently been lost made the captain steer a southerly course to avoid ice and shoals. One curious point which Cooper makes is the superstitious belief in the existence of rocks and shoals which had never been seen because they had always been so carefully avoided, but which nevertheless were charted. The "Three Chimneys," off the west coast of Ireland, is cited as an example.

The south coast of England presented a glorious view as they skirted it in the early morning. "The day was fine, clear, and exhilarating," says Cooper, "and the wind was blowing fresh from the westward. Ninety-seven sail, which had come into the Channel, like ourselves, during the thick weather, were in plain sight. The majority were English, but we recognized the build of half the maritime nations of Christendom in the brilliant fleet. Everybody was busy, and the blue waters were glittering with canvas. A frigate was in the midst of us, walking through the crowd like a giant stepping among pigmies. Our own good vessel left everything behind her, also, with the exception of two or three other bright-sided ships, which happened to be as fast as herself." She was not a particularly good sailer at that, but her speed is attributed by Cooper to a general superiority of American seamen, whose sense of ownership and achievement made them eager to take advantage of every fair wind.

His first impression of the English was that they were less foreign than they had appeared to him on his earlier visits. He accounts for this by the fact that, in 1806, England had been isolated so long by wars that provincialisms of costume and manners were apparent in all walks of life. This had largely died out in twenty years and Englishmen were, in externals, more like the rest of the world, notably Americans.

In the "toy-town" of Cowes, with its tiny, neat houses and narrow, crooked streets, they stayed long enough to see the sights of the island; and he comments on their difficulty in becoming accustomed to the saltless butter, realizing at the same time his own provinciality in the criticism and improving the opportunity of pointing a moral to those travelers who judge everything abroad in the narrow terms of the things at home. "The moral," he notes, "will be complete when I add, that we, who were so fastidious about the butter at Cowes, after an absence of nearly eight years from America, had the salt regularly worked out of all we ate, for months after our return home, protesting there was no such thing as good butter in America." In this casual confession lies the key to Cooper's later attitude toward his countrymen.

One of his first experiences with the English church was, like Irving's, with a country funeral, but in no passage is the contrast between the two men more apparent. Two bodies were brought in, laid out in coarse black coffins denoting the extreme of poverty. "The mourners," continues Cooper, "evidently struggled between natural grief and the bewilderment of their situation. The clergyman was a good looking young man, in a dirty surplice. Most probably he was a curate. He read the service in a strong voice, but without reverence, as if he were doing it by the job. In every way, short measure was dealt out to the poor mourners." Cooper and his companion followed him into the church and there found him accepting the funeral fee, while the graves were still open. It was "such a view," he exclaims, "as I had never before seen, and hope never to witness again. . . . In one ear was the hollow sound of the clod on the coffin; in the other the chinking of silver on the altar."

Carisbrooke Castle and Netley Abbey were the Coopers' first real taste of ruins, and the head of the household was moved to a particularly illuminating and Cooperesque bit of philosophy. "The greater force of the past than of the future on the mind," he says, "can only be the result of questionable causes. Our real concern with the future is incalculably the greatest, and yet we are dreaming over our own graves, on the events and scenes which throw a charm around the graves of those who have gone before us."

When he first saw Westminster Abbey he did not roam about it in either a melancholy or a scoffing mood as had his countrymen, but instead he paused outside with the deepest sensations of reverence, more for the richness of its architecture than for its mere antiquity. "All the architecture of America united," he says, "would not assemble a tithe of the grandeur, the fanciful, or of the beautiful (a few imitations of Grecian temples excepted) that were to be seen in this single edifice." Among all the experiences which aroused "strong and excited feelings," Cooper places this view of Westminster Abbey as the first, for it was his introduction to the Gothic, "an acquaintance pregnant of more pure satisfaction, than any other it has been my good fortune to make since youth."

In London he found many Americans, for his country had "long been giving back its increase to England, in the shape of admirals, generals, judges, artists, writers, and *notion-mongers,*" but he attended to his business and hurried back to his party at Southampton, only to find that they had spent the week in doing little else than admire ruins. "The European who comes to America," he concludes, "plunges into the virgin forest with wonder and delight, while the American who goes to Europe finds his greatest pleasure, at first, in hunting up the memorials of the past. Each is in quest of novelty, and is burning with the desire to gaze at objects of which he has often read."

The trip back to Southampton was enlivened by the other passengers in the coach; an English gentleman who admired nobility, a specimen of nobility itself, and a radical who was somewhat free in the expression of his opinions on both nobility and the Americans. Such a cross-section of English society furnished Cooper material for several pages in his best caustic style.

When the party returned to England in 1828, the background of Cooper's impressions was the mellow though turbulent culture of France rather than the raw vigor of America. The one point upon which his commentary had been favorable to England, the contrast of antiquity with crudity, was no longer fresh and vivid, while the emphasis upon caste in the continental social system made his chief object of adverse criticism seem even more oppressive to him. The result is that his antagonism to the English social order is strong at the start and becomes increasingly bitter as new evidences of its evils are added. His impressions of Dover are, however, favorable. "The place is both naturally and poetically fine," he says, "for, when one reflects that this accidental formation is precisely at the spot where the island is nearest to the Continent, it has the character of a magnificent gate-way to a great nation." But London he considered a "focus of coal-smoke," Windsor disappointing inside and out, and the Tower not at all imposing. To visit such conventional sights was to Cooper, in a sense, a weakness, and to describe them an unpardonable sin, unless the purpose were to correct popular error or probe to more essential meanings. Nevertheless, Westminster had still retained its qualified charm and St. Paul's its impression of grandeur. He gives a full description of the "antics of the House of Commons," which he finds quite as ineffectual as those of the American Congress, and the House of Lords appeared to him gentlemanly, quiet, and unbusinesslike. He did a small share of sightseeing, but he confesses that his purpose is to give a comparative study of manners rather than a description of scenes, and he devotes almost no space to the latter.

His contacts with English society furnished, however, more

fruitful material. It was the Cooper habit to make a temporary home for themselves wherever they were, and it was not long before they were settled in a small house in St. James's Place with a tiny drawing room, quite plainly furnished, a dining room, and three bedrooms, with the use of offices, etc., for a guinea a day. The people of the house did the general work and cooking, while the Coopers' own man and maid did the personal service.

Cooper had consistently scorned the use of letters of introduction, partly because there was too much hypocrisy involved in the practice, and partly because he hesitated to force himself upon others. He had become acquainted, however, in Paris with a certain Mr. Spencer, who mistook the reasons for the American's hesitancy and undertook to write letters to Rogers, Campbell, Sotheby, and others. Had it not been for this enforced kindness, Cooper might have spent his full quota of time in London without his presence becoming known to anyone of importance.

He had hardly been settled a fortnight when "a quiet little old man" appeared in his room and announced himself as William Godwin. He had confused Cooper with another of the same name, but the resultant conversation on American affairs was none the less cordial on both sides, howbeit the visitor's childlike ignorance of America somewhat grated on Cooper's sensitive patriotism. Nevertheless, he was impressed with Godwin's sincerity and freedom from cant, and confessed that several times he wished to pat the old man's bald head in approval.

Samuel Rogers, however, was his first visitor from Mr. Spencer's list, and his call was the beginning of all Cooper's other knowledge of the London *élite*. An invitation to breakfast at the poet's home was speedily accepted. His house was almost as small as Cooper's, but was tastefully lined inside with pictures by the old masters, valuable books, literary curiosities, and rare relics of art. It was the "nucleus of the best literary society of London," and its famous *petits déjeuners* were among the most exclusive of the fashionable festivities of the town—a curious haunt for the uncompromising American! Nevertheless Cooper found the society of his neighbor very enjoyable, if we may trust the testimony of his daughter, and spent many pleasant hours in this "charming *bijou* of a house." It was there that he met Chantrey, the sculptor, the American artist, Leslie, Sir James Mackintosh, Richard "Conversation" Sharp, Lockhart, and Scott himself once more. In one of these gatherings Scott sat silent most of the time, but Mrs. Siddons, who was also of the party "dialogued to him in a very Shakespearean manner." The three—Scott, Rogers, and Cooper— later planned a party to visit Hampton Court, and the intimacy of the neighbors on St. James's Place is witnessed by a letter, dated December 25, 1835, from Rogers, in which he thanks Mrs. Cooper for a sugar cake, her children for Christmas wishes, and her husband for a fragment of a farming journal, adding the remark: "You say you are not reckoned a first-rate writer in America. Pray let us know who your rivals are. We are dying to know."

Sir James Mackintosh lived up to his customary hospitality to Americans by showing the Coopers marked attention, but it was at a dinner at the home of the rather unknown poet, Sotheby, that the American first met Coleridge. After the ladies had retired, a remark on the unity of Homer called forth "not a discourse, but a dissertation" from Coleridge. For more than an hour he held the floor, with only occasional brief comment from his opponent, who was Sotheby. "His utterance was slow," continues Cooper, "every sentence being distinctly given, and his pronunciation accurate. There seemed to be a constant struggling between an affluence of words and an affluence of ideas, without either hesitation or repetition. His voice was strong and clear, but not pitched above the usual key of conversation. The only peculiarity about it was a slightly observable burring of the *r-r-r's*, but scarcely more than what the language properly requires . . . I was less struck by the logic than by the beauty of the language, and the poetry of the images."

The effect of this oration was to hush the company to silence. "Scott sat, immovable as a statue, with his little gray eyes looking inward and outward, and evidently considering the whole as an exhibition, rather than an argument," while Lockhart, catching Cooper's eye, expressed his comment by a hearty, though entirely silent, laugh. A half hour later they rose and Scott led the company "deliberately into a maze of petticoats and . . . let them play with his mane as much as they pleased."

In all this, Cooper was completely in his element, and was therefore scarcely critical at all. A charge has been brought against him that, after accepting English hospitality he returned only hostile criticism for their kindness, once the ocean intervened. If we accept his own testimony, he did nothing so out of keeping with the direct honesty of his character as this. By act as well as by word he made no attempt to court favor. When it was suggested that he might enjoy a presentation at a royal drawing room, his convictions were sufficiently strong to make him refuse such a hollow show, and when invited to the most fashionable balls, he frequently refused to go or left early. At one dinner of this impersonally *élite* sort he was utterly ignored by all present, including the host, and, being a stranger, was unable to help himself. When the gentlemen had all entered the dining room with their respective ladies, the American followed in the company of a guest who later proved to be a member of the family, and found the lowest place at the table reserved for him. He was so infuriated by the slight that he made a cutting remark about British policy, which was whispered about the table amid much shaking of heads, and when the meal was finally concluded, he shook the dust off his feet in quitting the house. Such experiences, clearly the result of his uncompromising lack of sympathy with the English social order, did little to add to the pleasure of his brief stay in the country.

This was not, however, his usual experience. He could distinguish between the gentleman and the haughty fashionable. For Lord Holland and Earl Grey he has little but praise. Of the latter, he says: "I find that the English look upon this statesman with a little social awe, but I have now met him several times, and have dined twice with him at his own table, and so far from seeing, or rather *feeling*, any grounds for such a notion, I have been in the company of no distinguished man in Europe, so much my senior, with whom I have felt myself more at ease, or who has appeared to me better to understand the rights of all in a drawing room."

These personalities and anecdotes may serve to give Cooper's opinion of the English character and social organization rather better than his frequent bitter but penetrating generalizations. He found the Established Church "prostituting the meek doctrines of Christ"; he was disgusted at the obsequious attitude rather than delighted with the respectfulness of English servants; he regarded the snobbery of London society in the matter of pronunciation as an evidence of narrow principles; he considered English propriety

a mere "boarding-school finish"; and in all he ridiculed the substitution of the "seemly" for the "right." The chief fault of the
aristocracy he found to be the "widespread system of studied misrepresentation," and he prophesied its downfall in the none-too-
distant future because influence was narrowing down to fewer
and fewer individuals, because the new commercial elements of
society were already deriving power in terms of money rather than
property, and because the entire existing system was based on a
network of lies. For the same reasons that he prophesied a downfall of her internal social organization he anticipated a dissipation of her colonial power, and he saw in the growing reform
spirit of the age a complete revolution in the political, social, and
all other aspects of the imperial organization. When we realize
that this analysis was first made three years before the great Reform Bill passed the English Parliament, Cooper's insight into
the underlying factors of human organization is brought forcibly
to our attention.

For the English ignorance of American conditions and their
willingness to criticize without knowledge, he has nothing but the
most unqualified scorn, but he is even more bitter against the
American servility of mind which was willing to swallow insults
in silence and return only sentimental reverence. "Heaven bless
the *Quarterly Review!*" he exclaims, for shocking the American
mind into an assertion of its manhood. "God knows what is to be
the final result. We may grow out of this weakness, as children get
the better of the rickets; or we may succumb to the disease, as
children often die." "Here then," he concludes, "we take our leave
of England—England, a country that I could fain like, but whose
prejudices and national antipathies throw a chill over all my
affection, . . . a country that all respect, but few love."

Two more novels, *Homeward Bound* and *Home as Found*, both
published in 1838, carry Cooper's analysis one step further, revealing the disillusionment of a belligerent idealist on his return
to his own country. The comparative crassness and vulgarity of
American culture was even more abhorrent to him than the glossy
hypocrisies of Old World aristocracy. Whichever way he turned
he was faced with materialism, and, like many another prophet, he
flew in the face of his own times and was lashed and battered by
the forces against which he struggled so valiantly and with such

effect. His experiences with the Old World had given him a broader basis for his attacks on the evils and the hollow appearances of his day. His ideals were deep rooted; but his one mistake, from a tactical standpoint, was his tendency to take personally those wrongs which a milder temperament would have viewed with a more objective detachment. Samuel F. B. Morse knew Cooper perhaps better than any one else during his days in Europe. "If he was at times severe or caustic in his remarks on others," he said just after Cooper's death, "it was when excited by the exhibition of the little arts of little minds." [2] The same attitude was at the root of his criticism of society.

NOTES

1. T. R. Lounsbury, *James Fenimore Cooper* (Boston: Houghton, Mifflin, Co., 1882), p. 82.
2. Samuel F. B. Morse, *Letters and Journals* (Boston: Houghton, Mifflin, Co., 1914), II, 314-315.

Second Thoughts on Cooper
as a Social Critic

The Centenary of Cooper's death, held by the New York State Historical Association in Cooperstown, New York, in September, 1951, resulted in a series of critical and biographical studies by various hands, which were published by the Association under the title, *James Fenimore Cooper, A Re-Appraisal* (Cooperstown, N.Y., 1954). This reappraisal of a reappraisal concludes the volume, pp. 170-189.

FIFTEEN YEARS AGO I promised myself that I would never write another word about James Fenimore Cooper. He and I had maintained an uneasy intimacy for a decade or more and we were wearing each other down. Living with the master of Otsego Hall must never have been a very relaxing experience; and I had specialized in reexamining his quarrels. My admiration for him as man and writer had risen constantly with the years, but I wished by then—this was in 1936—to move on to further if no greener fields.

He agreed, as we both felt that my view of his work, however friendly, was somewhat restricted; and he was happy to turn the management of his reputation over to younger scholars. But the centenary of the death of this great romancer stirred my conscience. Here was my chance to satisfy another and quite contradictory promise to myself—the promise that someday I would review my thought on Cooper and try again to solve a problem that I had left unsolved—namely, the relationship of his theory and practice of romance to his intense concern for social criticism. My generation had stated the problem more precisely than had Cooper's contemporaries and his first biographers and critics; but we had not solved it. Perhaps my impatience with Cooper in the middle 1930's was in part caused, not by his recalcitrance, but by my own feeling of inadequacy. The more intensively I explored his criticism of America, of society at large, of life itself, the more hopeless I became of arriving at a formula which would resolve the critical dilemma.

But now I could do what he could not—except in spirit—I could return to the problem after an interval of absorption in other matters. Cooper couldn't escape from himself, but I had succeeded in escaping from him. In those fifteen years I had grown older and American literary scholarship had matured. Further exploratory research on Cooper had been done by others. A restatement and review of the case might bring results now which would have been impossible before even though the corrosive action of time on the memory might rob me of the knowledge of detail that I once had. In fifteen years one could forget a good deal.

I I

When I began to work with Cooper in the early twenties, the two volumes of his correspondence had just been published and there were three biographies in addition to Bryant's "Memoir": an illustrated sketch by Mary E. Phillips, an excellent short one by W. B. Shubrick Clymer, and the classic American Men of Letters life by Thomas R. Lounsbury. To the last we owed, and still owe, most of our fundamental concepts of the author of *The Last of the Mohicans*, as well as of the master of Three Mile Point—not always the same person. It is a sane, scholarly, well-informed, but largely and admittedly unsympathetic view. The closing or destruction of his personal records by the deathbed wish of the author had not only limited the sources available, but had irritated the biographer to the point where he was in no happy mood about his task. At the same time that he gives us a just analysis of all of Cooper's works and speaks of the author as a manly upholder of principle, he so emphasizes Cooper's prejudices and irritability by repeated apologies for these traits that the final impression is one of a writer whose great gift of narrative was sadly damaged by his addiction to ideas. "Nature," says Mr. Lounsbury, "he could depict, and the wild life led in it, so that all men stood ready and eager to gaze on the pictures he drew. He chose too often to inflict on them, instead of it, the most common place of moralizing, the stalest disquisitions upon manners and customs, and the driest discussions of politics and theology." [1] So the biographer's own prejudices and irritability are excited to statements as narrow as Cooper's at the worst.

The injury done by this authoritative biography stems from its perpetuation of the contemporary notion that Cooper's system of political and moral ideas intruded upon his art as a novelist and destroyed an otherwise great talent. This is the genteel perversion of the sound romantic theory that the primary aim of literature is to give pleasure, a view which in the last years of the nineteenth century withheld recognition from Whitman and Melville, distorted our pictures of Poe, Hawthorne, and Emerson, and exalted Longfellow and Irving to absurd heights of adulation. When the time came—in the later 1920's and early 1930's—for a general reversal of our classic literary judgments, Cooper also came in for reconsideration. Perhaps it was his good fortune that his reputation was then at a low ebb. Instead of a debunking of idolatry, the new biographical and critical studies set about systematically to restore a damaged reputation. Henry W. Boynton explored Cooper's personal life from the few remaining family documents which the novelist's grandson now was giving to the public, emphasizing the strength and sweetness of character that Lounsbury so often mentioned without conviction. But the rest of us concentrated on the more difficult task of discovering intellectual and aesthetic values in his system of ideas and in its form of expression. Vernon L. Parrington, Marcel Clavel, Dorothy Waples, Ethel R. Outland, John F. Ross, and I suddenly realized that we were working on essentially the same job: the analysis of Cooper's social criticism, and an attempt to discover an organic connection between his ideas and his romantic narrative.

The problem thus proposed could have been treated either in general terms or with reference to the specific case, for its implications extend far beyond the mere body of Cooper's thirty-two romances. There is the larger question as to whether the romance, as developed by Scott, Dumas, Hugo, Cooper, and others of that day, is by its nature antipathetic to the concept of art as a means of commenting upon life. Is it inevitably and always an escape from life, a mere instrument of entertainment? Certainly throughout its history it has been used, especially by lesser writers, for the creation of thrills and horrors far more than for bridging the meaning of the past to the meaning of the present; but the greater romancers, from Shakespeare to Thomas Mann and William Faulkner, have taken it as perhaps the most versatile and effective form for serious fiction. Hawthorne, Melville, George Eliot, and Tolstoi cry out against the idea that romance and triviality are in any way synonymous. Cooper always claimed, as a writer of romance, the right to "a poetical view of the subject," at the same time that he argued that the only distinctive trait that could be expected of American literature is "that which is connected with the promulgation of their distinctive political opinions." Part of the "poetical view" was the right to be faithful to ideas rather than limited to facts. Cooper's attempt to use romance as it had been developed in his day to contain his whole reading of life challenged critical intelligence on the highest level.

My own work with Cooper never aspired to such heights; instead it attempted a more circumstantial consideration of the problem. I asked, and I now ask again: Were his social and moral ideas, as Lounsbury seemed to believe, merely narrow prejudices which interfered with a richer form of narrative art? Or had they validity both in themselves and as an organic and necessary component of that art?

The first task was obviously to reexamine Cooper's system of ideas without reference to his art of romance. The formula as it presented itself to us in the early 1920's was a simple one. James Fenimore Cooper was recognized as "the American Scott" (however much he might protest the implications), the writer of romance, the literary discoverer of the American wilderness, the first seaman-novelist to keep his ropes and sails as well as his tenses straight, the first American novelist to undertake the task of creating a "usable past" for American literature. But he was also, in his own view, a commentator on the American way of life and the principles of democracy, and his romances were often merely a means of conveying his views on the political and social evils of his day. Should we continue to apologize for him in the second role? By a series of coincidences, or by some more subtle agency in human affairs, a half dozen of us suddenly shouted, "No!" at the same time—after criticism had remained virtually silent on the point for almost half a century.

There are times in the affairs of men when ignorance has its uses. My special qualification for this task of reexamining the neglected side of Cooper's work was the fact that his social criticism was the only part of his work that I knew. I probably had read *The Last of the Mohicans* as a boy, but I had no interest whatsoever in Indians or wilderness scouts or crackling twigs when in 1922 I first discovered Cooper. I came to the study, so to speak, by the back door. I was not concerned with Cooper; I was concerned with social criticism. And I discovered that, whatever his excellences as a writer of romance, he was the leading literary critic of American society prior to Thoreau and Whitman. It was not long before I also discovered that this was the way Cooper had, at least in his own opinion, undertaken his career as a writer. From *Precaution* in 1820 to *The Ways of the Hour* in 1850 he thought of himself as a critic and reformer of the ways of men. His first concern was with the moral duty of parents, and his last preface begins: "The object of this book is to draw the attention of the reader to some of the social evils that beset us."

An author's own judgment of his work may not be the best index to its value, but it is always a factor in determining that value. An author may succeed or fail either because of or in spite of his intention, but without that intention, the work should be something quite different from what it actually turned out to be. Unfashionable as the historical method may be at this time, it seemed to me in 1922—and it still seems to me—important to consider an author's plan and purpose as the starting point for critical analysis. And Cooper's primary conscious purpose was always that of the social critic, an intention but vaguely realized in his early novels but becoming consistently stronger and clearer as he studied his own work and developed his methods.

My first attempt at appraising this side of Cooper's work came in a brief chapter in *The American in England* (1926), a study in the growth of American cultural independence, as seen by American travelers. I had not thought Cooper important to this study when I first made up my list of names to be included. Irving, Willis, and the official envoys were of course the important travelers, but there were, it appeared, some travel books on the Cooper list which Lounsbury had grudgingly called, "the best of their kind." An effort to obtain copies of these works testified to their rarity; a reading of them confirmed Lounsbury's impression of their vigor. Cooper forced himself into the position of climax in my story. The appearance of his five books of travel (1836–38) was simultaneous with and confirmatory of Emerson's plea for the cultural independence of the American Scholar (1837). Here was the American "Man Thinking"; and his struggle to discover a meaningful relationship between literary expression and American life was the epitome of the birth-struggle of a national culture. Because of Cooper, my book suddenly became something more than a review of travel writings of a given time and place. He made me reshape and completely rewrite a nearly finished book-length manuscript.

The rest of my Cooper story is very much like his own. Just as he was drawn further and further into the writing of fiction almost against his will by a series of challenges, so I was drawn to him by the opening up of one problem or question after another. Once the value of the *Sketches* and *Gleanings* was established, it was obvious that their scarcity should be corrected, and new editions were called for. Examination of the circumstances of original publication of these works led to the astounding discovery that no one knew why Cooper's novels were usually issued in England prior to their American appearance. A study of international copyright conditions followed, with the establishment of a formula that goes far toward explaining the practical difficulties in an American writer's career during these formative years of our literature.[2] And the intimate knowledge that I had thus gained of the seven central and formative years, 1827–33, challenged me to broaden my perspective, to study the early and the late novels, and to produce works of overall bibliography and criticism for which biography supplied a convenient pattern. The reprinting of a couple of minor works and the inevitable anthologizing followed as the excitement of the chase led me further and further into territory where I continued to think of myself only as a pioneer and never as a colonizer. But in 1936, with my special job of resurveying done in a half dozen different ways, I felt that it was time to turn Cooper over to others who could bring to him more of the old and primary spirit of romantic adventure that my work with him might have tended to obscure.

In spite of my emphasis on social criticism, I have tried through all of this work never to reduce Cooper to the role of social critic at a sacrifice of appreciation of his gift for romantic narrative. His social criticism is a part—perhaps the most important part—of the material of which his stories are made, but they are still stories. The two elements in his art enhance each other. His moral, religious, economic, and political ideas furnish the equipment of a writer of fiction rather than of a preacher, statesman, journalist, or politician. Literary ideas need not add up to a final and consistent position on any one problem because they are parts of human experience and human experience is always fluent. We sometimes try too hard to pin our writers down to intellectual systems; we should try more earnestly to study their ideas as controlling elements in their art.

Nevertheless I was worried by my own failure to relate him in any significant way to the political wars between Jackson and the Whigs, to the economic theories of Malthus, Ricardo, and Adam Smith, and to the breakdown of Puritanism or the position of the Anglican Church in the colonies. Against such specific correlations I revolted instinctively, even though my conscience was not altogether easy. I see now that my primary concern was that of the literary rather than the social historian. I was interested in discovering the relationship of Cooper's work to the domestic novel of manners and morals, to the novel of political and social purpose, to the Gothic and historical romance, as they flourished in the literature of England and of Europe in his day; and I was even more interested in figuring out just how and just how well he had succeeded in defining and expressing the distinctively American body of facts and opinions which, according to his own theory, alone could make his work original and native. Miss Waples tried to be charitable when she charged me with dismissing very lightly the whole matter of politics and being "as anxious as other critics to ignore that subject as if for Cooper's sake." [3] Her own work did that job much better than mine, for I was always inclined to relate him more to the instincts of the Federalist squire that was his father than to the battles of the Democratic and Whig parties of his own day because he accepted the terms of nonexistent Federalism much more deeply and emotionally than he could the political partisanship of his own times. The correlation was psychological rather than consciously intellectual. Similarly I tried to relate his economic ideas more precisely to general economic theory and history by inviting an economist to collaborate with me on a new edition of *Satanstoe,* only to find that he had studied enough literature to realize that Cooper's economic ideas were not precise and that the fact of their vagueness did not seriously injure their use in his novel. After all, Corny Littlepage was a gentleman of taste and action, not a scholar, and to have pictured him studying Adam Smith rather than the rules of surveying would have been a falsification of fictional truth.

My final case rested, therefore, on such proofs as I could gather that Cooper's general ideas about men and society were important to his own intentions and methods as a novelist; and that his novels were far more important than they otherwise would have been as a result of the serious and critical interest their author had in the life of his own times. I failed—more or less deliberately —to sort out and organize any single body of those general ideas apart from their share in his equipment as an artist; and I failed— even more seriously, but more excusably too because Cooper also failed in this—I failed to show that his general ideas operated within his fictional method to help or hinder his art. It is this second failure rather than the first that makes me willing at this late date to come back to Cooper and raise the old questions about him again. Perhaps I am foolish to hope that some future Cooper scholar may come closer to success than have the scholars of the past.

III

The first two volumes of Parrington's *Main Currents in American Thought* appeared the year after my *American in England* and was the chief incentive to my further work with Cooper. His challenge was sufficiently thrilling to a beginning scholar who had already opened up the trail. "No other major writer, unless it be Whitman, has been so misunderstood," he wrote.[4] "That

America has been so tardy in coming to know him as a man and a democrat, as well as a romancer, is a reflection upon its critical acumen." [5] Here was my laying on of hands by an elder scholar, and I took it in that spirit.

The fine mixture of economic and political theory of which the Jeffersonian Parrington was master gave his brief essay an authority which none of the full-length books on Cooper that soon appeared would command. But his book was not a history of American literature as its author believed it to be, and the weakness in his interpretation of such writers as Poe and Emily Dickinson, where specific social content is almost nonexistent, is also apparent in his interpretations of writers like Cooper and Whitman, where social content is central if not paramount. His essay on Cooper was a vigorous and needed correction of both the genteel critical perversions of Lowell and Lounsbury and the noncritical acceptance by the general reader of the day; but it did not go far enough to help with a new understanding of his art. Rather it prepared his novels for use as social documentation by the social and cultural historians from Dixon Ryan Fox to the present.

Two other books on Cooper as social critic appeared within the following decade. Both made their contribution to the subject by doing what I had hesitated to do. Both developed theses as to what Cooper's position on the political issues of his day might have been and both assumed or stated that his primary importance lay in his defense of a political position. Mr. Ross [6] opens his monograph with the statement, "James Fenimore Cooper, 'one of the great romancers of the world,' [quoting Brownell], was not primarily a romancer, but a purposeful critic of American civilization." For Mr. Ross, Cooper represented "individualism thwarted by conflict with the herd," [7] and served as a useful prophet of the degeneration of twentieth-century society at a time when young followers of H. L. Mencken were imitating his braying tactics. It is a comment on the young Mr. Ross and his times rather than on Cooper and his.

Miss Waples is to be taken more seriously. Building upon the earlier monograph of Ethel Outland,[8] she analyses the political context in which Cooper found himself between 1833 and 1851, and reaches the valid conclusion that because Cooper's legal bat-

tles were prompted by his Whig detractors they were of specific
political significance. She then carries her argument one step further and concludes, I think without evidence, that Cooper was
therefore a partisan Jacksonian Democrat. We must put her statement over against Cooper's to appreciate the positive misuse she
has made of negative evidence. She says, "Comparing Cooper's
publications and his letters with the network of intrigues which
politicians were weaving in the state, we can discern in Cooper's
remarks a pattern of conscious adherence to such Democratic
party as there was." [9] Cooper, on the other hand, declares his non-
partisanship: "Party is the most potent despot of the times. Its
very irresponsibility gives it an energy and a weight that over-
shadows the regular action of government." [10]

None of these critics realized that Cooper was merely doing
what any thoughtful historical novelist must do: he was attempting
to recapture his own past and to establish a critical relationship
between himself as artist and the material, past and present, of his
art. In so far as they supply insight into one half of the equation—
i.e., the facts of Cooper's political thinking and associations—they
contribute to our understanding; but in so far as they warp the
artist out of his orbit and point to his political actions and conclusions as ultimate values in themselves, they befog the issue
more than they clear it.

Only two other books of importance on Fenimore Cooper appeared during the period of my own active work, both of them
by the same man, a French scholar to whom I owe a lasting debt
of gratitude for his generous aid, especially while I was working
on the bibliography of foreign editions. Marcel Clavel's biography
of the young Cooper—up to 1826—and his study of contemporary
foreign criticism of all of his novels are each standard in its field,[11]
but neither is immediately relevant to my present inquiry.

There was a lapse in publication of books about Cooper between this date, 1938, and 1949 when Mr. Grossman's biography
appeared; but this lapse is not reflected in the publication of
articles. Once the Cooper revival might be said to be established
—about 1928—there were each year in learned and popular
journals an average of three articles about Cooper or about some
subject closely related to him. The total of such articles between
1920 and 1945, the period covered by the Leary list,[12] is sixty-

seven, as compared with almost exactly the same number for Irving, a few less for Bryant, 138 for Melville, 177 for Emerson, and 331 for Poe. The period 1946–51 shows a swing from Poe and Emerson to Melville and Henry James, but Cooper's average does not change greatly. This evidence seems to indicate a revival of interest in Cooper—principally in his social ideas—between 1926 and 1936 which had sufficient momentum to continue but not to advance it for another decade or so. Interest in other American authors, notably in Melville, Thoreau, James, and Twain, shot forward in the 1940's, but that in Cooper, Irving, and the earlier group seems so far to have been static or retrogressive.

A dozen of the Cooper articles on the Leary list appeared in the journal *American Literature,* four in *New York History,* and only one in the *Publications of the Modern Language Association* (a deficiency which was somewhat corrected after 1945). Many of these articles are, however, brief bibliographical or biographical notes or single unpublished letters in such journals as *Modern Language Notes, Publishers' Weekly, Notes and Queries,* and *Colophon.* Several of them are French or German; a half dozen are of local interest through Cooper association. Single articles of more general critical interest appeared in *Saturday Review of Literature, Yale Review,* and *American Mercury.*

An assessment of the value of these articles is a somewhat depressing experience. Trivia is the word to describe most of them. Among the subjects discussed are the Bread and Cheese Club, Cooper's Naval career (fit subject for the careful study it is now beginning to get), his visits to Michigan, Long Island, Italy, and France, his association with Scott, Lafayette, and others, the discovery of his one play "*Upside Down,*" and further historical information on upper New York State politics, particularly the Anti-Rent War, and biographical information about his daughter Susan. Articles by the social historians in general carry more weight than do those by the literary historians, but neither group really comes to grips with any of the central critical problems suggested by the novels themselves or by the specifically critical prose.

The classic type of article on literary sources and influences shows slightly more encouraging results. Recently scholars have begun to take up the hint provided by Thomas R. Palfrey in his article on "Cooper and Balzac," [13] and by Dorothy Dondore in her piece on Satanstoe,[14] that Cooper's material was, in appreciable part, supplied by his reading, and that he was an avid reader of travels and treatises as well as of the novels published in his day and of the Bible and Shakespeare. We have long known that such novels as *Lionel Lincoln, The Bravo,* and *The Spy* were the products of genuine research, but the destruction of the personal diaries and many of the letters and books has obscured the facts of his reading and study to an extent that is not true of Poe, Melville, Hawthorne, Thoreau, and Emerson, for whom such sources are extant. Fortunately, Mr. James Beard has already shown by collecting many new letters that at least some of these sources are merely hidden and were not destroyed. H. H. Scudder, W. B. Gates, and others have made special source studies of *Precaution, The Crater, The Sea Lions,* and several other novels and have demonstrated that internal evidence alone is often enough to establish sources and demonstrate reading and study habits. More extensive studies of this nature (for example, the influence of Shakespeare on Cooper's plots, themes, characters, and general ideas) are in process, but much is still to be done.

The existence of such studies is not so surprising as is the long time it took to produce them, even in the hey-day of the source-hunting method in American literary scholarship. Yet it is obvious that such stories as *Mercedes of Castile, The Two Admirals, The Crater, The Monikins,* and *The Ways of the Hour* must have specific sources. The influence of Scott too has been generally recognized but never closely examined, probably because of Cooper's own horror of the idea; but Cooper was troubled by the idea of a confusion of his democratic political ideas with the feudal world of Scott and not necessarily by the possibility of a literary influence. Palfrey's suggestion of a possible direct influence from Balzac has not been followed up, nor until very recently has Cooper's debt to contemporary treatises like that of Henry Carey on economics or to Cook, Wilkes, and other travel narratives been determined. It is apparent that the influence of his reading began with *Precaution* and continued straight down the thirty-two volumes of his romances. The rule works the other way too, for no one would protest the evidence of influence of Cooper on Simms, Kennedy, Bird, and other writers of American backwoods romances as well as on other writers of Germany, France, and throughout the world. There are enough subjects of this kind to keep graduate students busy for a decade.

But after all the returns are in, will the problem with which I began my remarks and began my work on Cooper be solved at last? I think not. We will still be asking questions about his fundamental ideas and about his use of those ideas to create works of romantic art.

IV

It is in this spirit that Mr. Grossman reopened the Cooper case two years ago with his remarkably satisfactory biography, a warmly appreciative study of the man and a thorough and discriminating explication of his work. Doctors and lawyers are often the best literary critics because, to judge literature fairly, one must have a rich knowledge of humanity in its weakness and in its strength. Mr. Grossman is the first critic to realize fully that Cooper's work was a quest for a "wholly adequate symbol in which to concentrate his tragic vision." [15] He found no Dynamo and no Whale, but his intention was none the less noble for its failure.

I would like to conclude these scattered remarks by calling all the younger Cooper scholars to take up the lines of thought that Mr. Grossman has suggested. To come nearer to its solution than we of my generation did, these scholars will have to use some of the newer methods of critical and historical study that have developed since 1925; for example, the methods of Parrington and Lovejoy in the history of ideas and the methods of Richards and of Lowes in the analysis of the psychology of the creative process. Because we know more about society and the ways of humans in group action than we once did, we can now better tackle problems in the history of literary ideas, whether in the sociological method of Parrington or the concept method of Lovejoy. Because we know more about the functioning of the human mind than we once did, we can now better tackle problems related to the work of art itself and its creation, whether in terms of the method of psychological analysis of process of Lowes or of the semantic analysis of the work of art itself of Richards.

I note that in recent lists of topics of work in progress disser-
tations have been announced or completed on "James Fenimore
Cooper: Craftsman of Democratic Fiction" and in "The Moral,
Social, Political, and Economic Ideas Underlying Cooper's Attitude toward America." There are hints in the phrasing of both
of these topics that these scholars are attacking the old problems
in new ways.

The analysis of Cooper's ideas must sort out the chaff from the
wheat by distinguishing the different levels of value in them.
First, there is the level of custom, fashion, manners, and etiquette.
Because of his provincialism and his sensitivity as an American
criticized by British travelers for social deficiencies, Cooper was
overexpressive in these matters and intrudes discussion of them
into his stories. This fault is especially manifest in stories where he
is deliberately attempting the novel of manners, such as *Precaution, Home as Found,* and *Satanstoe.* It is responsible for the
charge of snobbery in his own day, and it has long interfered with
just critical appraisal of his work. It is the costume part of a
costume novel, of interest to the antiquarian and to the social
and cultural historian, often in ways that Cooper himself did not
anticipate. Where implicit in the story, it is an essential part of
the fictional properties; where explicit as part of author's comment on his work, it seems to us today to be tactless and clumsy,
even though the habit of author intrusion was common in Thackeray and other nineteenth-century novelists.

The next level is the body of moral, religious, economic, and
political assumptions which formed the intellectual environment
in which the boy Cooper grew up and which he could alter but
never could totally reject. Here we find the doctrinal body of the
Anglican Church, the Federalist political philosophy of Squire
William and the laissez faire economic doctrines of the philos-
opher-statesmen of the first republic.

Next we have the context of ideas of his own day, the Jacksonian and pre-Civil War period in our history, a confused and
uneven time which we are only now coming to understand more
accurately with the aid of such creative historians as Roy Nichols,
Paul Buck, and Arthur Schlesinger, Jr. This is the territory into
which Miss Waples and Miss Outland ventured, a territory which

has not even yet been sufficiently charted to save the amateur historian from the perils of quicksand.

Finally, we have, in the Lovejoy sense, the intellectual concepts which serve as constants in Cooper's mind, which recur and develop in his work, and which can be correlated with such constants in the American mind and with the human mind in the broader phases of its modern development. This is the ultimate form of Cooper study insofar as the history of ideas is concerned, a form to be regarded respectfully by the unseasoned scholar. Sooner or later, however, such complete Cooper concepts as the Democratic American Gentleman, the Noble Indian, and the Wilderness Garden must be sorted out and defined as constants in his work, by which he may be accurately related to the history of ideas. Some progress has been made in developing this method by Constance Rourke and Henry Nash Smith who seek the fundamental folk and myth-making elements in Cooper's work as contributions to the creation of the American myth.[16] Difficult and tricky as this kind of scholarship is, it holds an exciting promise of enrichment of our understanding as literary historians.

The real Cooper job, however, is only just begun when the myth content of his work is thus more adequately defined. The problem still remains: How, in what stages, and to what extent was this content converted to the purposes of art? The one basic principle of which we can be sure here is that of free experimentation. Cooper was an insatiable experimenter with methods but he was constant in his aim. He knew—and no other American writer of his day approached him in the keenness of his awareness—that American literature had to be different in aim and method from the literature of the Old World because it was dealing with a new human experience. He also knew that original literary forms and modes could not be created on demand, that they would have to develop from the experimental application of the old ways of expression to the new material. His failure to evolve a literary methodology is token of his success as a pioneer, and he still has companions in his failure to solve the technical problem. Sinclair Lewis, Theodore Dreiser, William Faulkner, and John Steinbeck were still experimenting in the 1920's and 1930's with the problem of reducing comment on a contemporary society to the terms of fictional art. May the problem remain forever unsolved, and the creative effort always a vital and experimental process! But in comparing Cooper to modern writers of romantic fiction, we should recognize that his emphasis on social commentary rather than on mere entertainment would put him more in a class with such writers as William Faulkner than with such writers as Kenneth Roberts. His very failure at a synthesis of the narrative elements of his stories with his unflinching critical examination of human social and personal conduct in his times speaks the ambitious scope of his creative mind. *The Crater* is more daring as an experiment in fusing adventure with life than is *The Monikins,* and *The Monikins* is more daring than *The Pioneers. The Pioneers* is by far the most satisfying work of art of the three, and it is bettered by *The Last of the Mohicans,* yet if Cooper's contribution to American fiction had stopped with its nearest approach to success, the Leatherstocking tales, he would have been unfaithful to the terms of the American experiment. His art and thought are vital today because they were germinal in their own. We must stretch our academic minds in this fresh mountain air of Cooperstown if we are to tackle our problem again.[17]

NOTES

1. T. R. Lounsbury, *James Fenimore Cooper* (Boston: Houghton, Mifflin Co., 1882), pp. 169-170.
2. See the Preface to R. E. Spiller and P. C. Blackburn, *A Descriptive Bibliography of James Fenimore Cooper* (New York: R. R. Bowker Co., 1934).
3. Dorothy Waples, *The Whig Myth of James Fenimore Cooper* (New Haven: Yale University Press, 1938), p. 4.
4. V. L. Parrington, *Main Currents in American Thought* (New York: Harcourt, Brace and Co., 1927), II, 222.
5. *Ibid.,* p. 237.
6. John F. Ross, *The Social Criticism of Fenimore Cooper* (Berkeley: University of California Press, 1933), p. 17.
7. *Ibid.,* p. 112.
8. Ethel R. Outland, *The "Effingham" Libels on Cooper,* Studies in Language and Literature No. 28 (Madison: University of Wisconsin, 1929).
9. *Ibid.,* p. 43.
10. James F. Cooper, *New York* (New York: William Farquhar Payson, 1930), p. 39.
11. Marcel Clavel, *Fenimore Cooper and His Critics* (Aix-en-P., 1938).
12. *Articles on American Literature Appearing in Current Periodicals, 1920-1945,* edited by Lewis Leary (Durham, N.C.: Duke University Press, 1947).

13. *Modern Philology*, XXIX (Feb., 1932): 335-341.
14. *American Literature*, XII (March, 1940): 52-58.
15. James Grossman, *James Fenimore Cooper* (New York: William Sloan Associates, 1949), p. 264.
16. See Constance Rourke, *American Humor* (New York: Harcourt, Brace and Co., 1931), and Henry Nash Smith, *Virgin Land* (Cambridge, Mass.: Harvard University Press, 1950).
17. I had not thought that I would attempt this task myself but the opportunity to make a complete restudy of all of Cooper's work and to base a reinterpretation of his fiction on what we had learned about his social and moral commitments came with an invitation to do the pamphlet on Cooper in the Minnesota Series (No. 48, 1965), reprinted in *Six American Novelists of the Nineteenth Century*, edited by R. Foster (Minneapolis: University of Minnesota Press, 1968), pp. 10-44.

A Case for W. E. Channing

In tracing Cooper's reputation in England, I noticed that the name of William Ellery Channing was linked with his and Irving's as the leaders of a challenging new American literature. Knowing Channing only as a clergyman and one of the American founders of Unitarianism, I looked up his writings on literary as well as theological topics. This essay was published in the *New England Quarterly*, III (January 1930): 55-81.

THE REVISION OF A LITERARY REPUTATION is a dangerous, and often futile, enterprise. Especially is this true when the name in question has been almost entirely erased from literary history. "We meet to-day to celebrate a great preacher," said Charles W. Eliot[1] in introducing his lecture on the elder Channing. There is no record of a dissenting voice. No one in that audience remembered that the great preacher had once been greeted as "the finest writer of our age," [2] and had been thought worthy of serious, though not altogether friendly, consideration from the caustic pens of Hazlitt and Brougham. Channing as an author has been dismissed and forgotten.

As long as the element of fashion influences literary judgments it will never be safe to leave such ominous silences undisturbed. No such widespread opinions are ever wholly in error. The eighteenth century greeted the romantic revival with hostility and scorn, and the romantic writers fought bitterly and successfully against these attacks. The present age finds much real justice

in both positions. Similarly, American literary judgments deferred
with too great a solicitude to the English critics of the early nineteenth century, and the wholesome self-assertions of Fenimore
Cooper, Emerson, and others which resulted, established a degree
of mental independence which made a national literature possible. It is time for an objective view of this controversy, also.

Channing was caught in both these conflicts and the subsequent
estimate of him has, as a result, been colored. Philosophically
akin to Wordsworth, Coleridge, and Carlyle, he was also accepted
by the reviewers as one of themselves. Recognized by English
critics as a writer of note, he was also among the first to declare
the need for American intellectual independence.

During the years from 1823 to 1849, when his reputation in
England was being formed and developed, he occupied a position
only below Irving and Cooper in the English estimate of American literary excellences. This opinion aroused criticism in America, not because Channing was included, but because Bryant,
Halleck, and many others were not.[3] There is no doubt that
Channing's historical position in American literary history, with
special reference to its relations with English influences, is usually
underestimated today.

But the explanation that his foreign reputation was merely an
aspect of America's early mental servility, is inadequate. Even a
casual examination of the six volumes of his collected works
shows how superficial and unsound such a judgment would be.
Channing not only was among the first American writers to win
British critical consideration; he anticipated, by almost a generation in his thought and by seven years in his public pronounce-
ment, the independence of mind which was proclaimed by
Emerson in *The American Scholar*. Channing's essay on *The Importance and Means of a National Literature* is inferior in literary
quality to the more famous address on the same topic, but it contains the outlines of the same philosophical position and a statement of an identical demand for American mental self-reliance
which was attained by the Emersonian methods of study and
meditation. There is reason now to regard Emerson's essay as a
declaration of New England's rather than America's self-consciousness. The frontier, agrarian, and industrial movements have
given to American literature ideals and forms which are not

included within the metaphysical limits of that document. But insofar as Emerson's work represents a mile-stone in the progress of our national thought, Channing's assumes, by priority, an importance great enough to compensate for its somewhat lower philosophical and literary value.

Finally, if we pass beyond the table of contents and examine the body of Channing's essays, lectures, and sermons, we find at least a larger proportion of nontheological work than the customary literary estimate of the man would lead us to anticipate. This work shows that Channing not only mastered the critical essay, which was recognized in his day as one of the most worthy means of literary expression, but that his thought, in its range as well as its form, spread far beyond the limits of controversial Unitarian dogma and the rhetorical restrictions of the pulpit. His tendency to moralize, which is usually pointed to as a restriction upon his literary worth, was in reality his means of escape from the more rigid mental limitations of his predecessors in New England prose. Deriving from his forefathers, from the idealists of Germany, and the rationalists of France, his mind followed the path which he himself so urgently recommended, and he applied his principles to the state and being of man in theory and fact, as well as to the idea of God. He thus linked Coleridge and Wordsworth with Carlyle and Ruskin. Emerson substituted a deistic conception of nature for Channing's Unitarian God, following the path of Wordsworth, whereas Channing's thought was more akin to that of Coleridge; Emerson approached a democratic ideal of human relationships in his *Representative Men,* whereas Channing, in his *Milton* and *Napoleon,* stated and illustrated the theory of heroism which Carlyle later elaborated; finally, the conception of the dignity of manual labor, which, in the lectures and experiments of Carlyle, Ruskin, and William Morris, proclaimed the transition to a new social order, finds a full and adequate expression in the writings of this New England clergyman, of one generation, at least, earlier than any of these men.

The fact that Channing's work was recognized as worthy of considered thought by both English and American critics in his own day is, therefore, not so unaccountable as it might at first seem. The comparison of his present-day literary position with that accorded to him by his British contemporaries, and even a casual re-examination of those of his essays and sermons which are least dogmatic in aim and method, should be worth the undertaking, even though a revision of judgment as to his absolute importance must await further and more exhaustive study.

I I

The limits of this discussion will not permit a cross-section view of the recent and contemporary estimate of Channing. From Barrett Wendell, who, in *The Literary History of America* (1901), thinks of Channing only as the founder of Unitarianism, to Vernon L. Parrington, who, in *The Main Currents in American Thought* (1927), enlarges the picture to include his philosophical and social ideas, there is no critic who frankly considers the Boston clergyman as a factor in American literature. Even his biographer, J. W. Chadwick, after admitting the *Milton* "to the account of his literary achievement," dismisses it again because "the preacher in him was a jealous sovereign who could admit no brother near the throne." [4] George S. Hellman, in his *Cambridge History* article on "Later Essayists" points the way to a new approach to the subject when he calls Channing "the earliest in that firmament of lecturer-essayists where Emerson shone as the most benignant star."[5] If his entire chapter had been devoted to Channing, the reconsideration of those lecture-essays might now be superfluous.

This exclusion of Channing's work from literary consideration is, however, a fairly recent development. His contemporaries, especially after certain English critics had pointed the way, made no such restrictions.

There is more than coincidence in the fact that his literary began to supplement his theological reputation soon after his visit to Europe in 1822–23.[6] Up to that time he was not known at home for anything more than his sermons, and even his reputation as a Unitarian leader had not penetrated far in the British Isles. As early as 1811, his sermon on *The Day of the Public Fast* had been reprinted in London from the Boston edition of the year before, and his Baltimore definition of Unitarianism in 1819 ran into many English (as well as American) editions within the first few years of its appearance in pamphlet form. On the other hand, his popular sermon on *The Duties of Children* waited from 1807 until 1825 before it was reprinted in England, and it then saw two Liverpool editions within the year.

From the date of his return to America, his tracts and sermons on doctrine, morality, slavery, and the condition of working men were reprinted with great regularity (and sometimes in several editions) in Liverpool, Manchester, Bristol, Glasgow, and Belfast, and were noticed in religious journals. Sometimes these works appeared first in periodical form, sometimes they were printed immediately as pamphlets after their public delivery.

London, however, seems to have specialized on his more strictly literary discussions. His *Remarks on the Character and Writings of John Milton*[7] appeared there in 1826, but was not much noticed until it ran into a second edition in the year of the pamphlet republication of his *Analysis of the Life and Character of Napoleon Bonaparte*[8] (1828). These essays were followed by his *Remarks on the Character and Writings of Fénelon*,[9] in the next year.

Thus by 1830, when his essay on *The Importance and Means of a National Literature*[10] made its appearance, his literary reputation was ready to keep pace in both countries with his theological, and its immediate reprinting in London was a matter of course. From this time until his death in 1842, his works were issued practically simultaneously on both sides of the water, and their definitive edition of 1840–44 was printed in Glasgow more impatiently than in Boston. The *Memoirs,* edited by his son in 1848, completes the story.

The transition from a theological to a literary reputation was not, however, so abrupt as these facts may seem at first to indicate. The *Quarterly Review,* usually so antagonistic to anything connected with America, was apparently the first nonreligious journal to recognize him favorably.[11] The mention occurs, however, in a theological article on "The Progress of Infidelity." A long quotation from the sermon on *Revealed Religion* (1821) is prefaced by a tribute to its author as "one of those men who are a blessing and an honour to their generation and their country." The writer of this article obviously thought of Channing only as a clergyman, although the *Quarterly* later referred twice to his opinions on slavery.[12]

The same critical yard-rule was applied by the reviewer in *Blackwood's Magazine* who, when discussing the same sermon in 1825, expressed himself as "quite convinced that the author was a man of sound judgment and clear understanding. . . . equally correct in feeling and refined in taste." [13]

So great, however, was the literary reputation of these journals and so broad were the current definitions of literature that the English reviewers were not conscious of any revision in their estimate of this American when his first essay on a nonreligious subject appeared in 1826. At first, the *Milton* was greeted with silence, but when the *Napoleon,* two years later, carried the analysis of the nature of human greatness to a more immediate and controversial topic, the clamor of comment became general and its author's English literary reputation was assured.

The London *Monthly Magazine* was the first to acknowledge the worth of these essays. "We rejoice," it exclaims complacently, "in the renewal of the literary intercourse between us and our *brethren* in America—(for such we still consider them, though we no longer live under the same government)." [14] But, in spite of such good wishes, Channing's unfavorable criticism of the revered Dr. Johnson was somewhat difficult for this reviewer to digest. "When Johnson's Biography of Milton is disparaged by mean writers, we turn from them and their cant about liberty with disgust; but when such writers as Dr. Channing reprehend it, we read with attention, meditate with deference, and differ with respect." The same critic found the *Napoleon* "replete with the most useful lessons of virtue, honour, and public duty." [15]

This latter essay of Channing's fell into both sympathetic and unsympathetic hands. "We echo back the sentiment cheerfully—joyfully," said the *Westminster Review,* with reference to the *Quarterly's* praise, quoted above. "He is indeed a benefactor who is constantly contributing prolific supplies of the greatest mental enjoyment. . . . Dr. Channing was the first man, whose bold and mighty breathings dissipated the delusive mist of fame which hung round the brow of Napoleon." [16]

There was one man, however, who was not so ready to see this mist dispelled. The first two volumes of William Hazlitt's *Life of Napoleon Bonaparte* appeared in this year, and there were still two more volumes to come. Scott's *Life of Napoleon,* of which

Channing's essay was a review, had anticipated Hazlitt's by one year. Further, Channing, in his few pages, unsparingly attacked an heroic myth to the enduring preservation of which Hazlitt was devoting his last few bitter years. The fact that Channing was rebel against the religious creed of which Hazlitt's father had been a leader need not be added to make the chances of a favorable review of this American study of imperialism impossible.

It was not until Channing's first essay on Napoleon had been reprinted at least four times and his second at least twice in London, that a preliminary collection of his writings was noticed by the *Edinburgh Review* and was made the occasion of a general article on American literature.[17] "Of the later American writers, who, besides Dr. Channing, have acquired some reputation in England," says Hazlitt in this article, "we can only recollect Mr. Washington Irving, Mr. Brown, and Mr. Cooper." Starting with almost fulsome praise of Irving, the descent is rapid through the other two authors to Channing, and the *Napoleon* discourse is reserved for this emphatic conclusion:

Dr. Channing is a great tactician in reasoning; and reasoning has nothing to do with tactics. We do not like to see a writer constantly trying to steal a march upon opinion without having his retreat cut off. . . . We like Dr. Channing's sermons best; his criticisms less; his politics least of all. We think several of his discourses do great honour to himself and his profession. . . . His notice of Milton is elaborate and stately, but neither new nor discriminating. . . . This is the general feature of our author's writings; they cannot be called mere common-place, but they may be fairly termed *ambitious* commonplace. . . . It would serve no useful purpose, however, to follow him into the details of his *Analysis of the Character of Bonaparte*. . . . We are here forcibly reminded of Fielding's character of Mr. Abraham Adams, "Indeed, if this good man had an enthusiasm, or what the vulgar call a blind side, it was this: he thought a schoolmaster the greatest character in the world, and himself the greatest of all schoolmasters, neither of which points he would have given up to Alexander the Great at the head of his army." So Dr. Channing very gravely divides greatness into different sorts, and places himself at the top among those who *talk* about things —commanders at the bottom among those who only *do* them.

After this ordeal by fire, Channing's place among the few Americans worthy of recognition in England was undisputed. In the first and scornful article of the *Athenaeum* on this subject, Irving, Channing, and Cooper are the only American authors considered worthy of discussion, and all three are disposed of as imitators of their English betters. But even with a critic so little inclined to praise of America as this, Channing receives a higher tribute than that of mere mention: "No one who has read any of Dr. Channing's writings can fail to entertain the highest admiration for him as a man, and a very considerable respect for him as a writer." [18]

The *Westminster* continued to be Channing's most loyal friend when it returned to him in 1830 and considered the essays on *Fénelon* and on *Associations,* together with the *Sermons and Tracts* which Hazlitt had so scorned. Patronage may be as galling as contempt, but it may also be advanced with good intentions. None of the feeling of superiority which American literature as a whole elicited from this writer is visited on Channing. "It is incumbent upon us gladly to recognize, and heartily to welcome the rising of every 'bright particular star' in their literary horizon," he warns, "and distinguish it at once from the twilight meteors that tomorrow will be forgotten. America has a right to be proud of Channing; and shame would it be for the criticism of England were he to be dismissed with affected contempt." Of the *Napoleon,* he says, "There are none of the littlenesses of political party about this critique." And of the *Milton:* "That a perfectly qualified critic of Milton should be a theologian, was not less requisite before the discovery of his posthumous work [*Christian Doctrine*] than it has been since obviously rendered by that occurrence. . . . Dr. Channing is completely unrivalled in his display of the moral grandeur of Milton." [19]

"You do not tell me what the French say about the American Channing," comments "The Lounger" in Colburn's *New Monthly Magazine.* "I am anxious to know. His works are reviewed in the proper spirit of reviewing in the last *Westminster.* It is high time that we should show that we English are willing to be the first to echo an American's praise. The fact is that when the Americans read our periodicals they suppose us hostile to them—no such thing. The Scotch write our periodicals, and it is the Scotch (the last nation in the world to do justice to a new people) who abuse them." [20]

The appearance of the essay on a *National Literature,* therefore, marks the culmination of Channing's ascending English literary reputation. The *Athenaeum* greeted this discourse in a more chastened spirit than it had previously observed, commenting upon the author as "decidedly a man of high literary attainments, of a refined taste, a discriminating judgment, with an acute, vigorous, and comprehensive mind," but objecting to the style of the work as "frequently diffuse and elaborately redundant." [21]

This was perhaps a necessary step from its earlier hostile attitude to the praise which was to pour on to its pages, doubtless from an American pen, five years later. "Even the great Channing," says this later writer, "though always revered for his piety and eloquence by the immediate circle of his sect, was never generally known and admired in America, as the most powerful writer of his time, until the echo came back from England. Then, indeed, his essays were reprinted, and his works collected into a volume, and all the newspapers mentioned the fact, that they *'had been favourably noticed in England.'* Words could convey no more." And later, this critic continues, "Among those whose names have crossed the Atlantic, and whose works are well known in England, is Dr. Channing of Boston. The *lay* productions, on which the literary reputation of this great divine is founded, are very few: a small volume of essays comprises them all. Yet, in these small limits, the hand of the master are [*sic*] so visible—the thoughts are of such broad sculpture—the language is so severely beautiful—and the truth and loftiness of the author's mind are so stamped upon every line, that, if he were not the leader of a powerful sect, and should he never write more, his fame would have pedestal enough: the essay on Napoleon alone would make a reputation." [22] This article is the first of a series dealing with the contemporary literatures of various nations; the editor planned that the article on America should have been by the Rev. Timothy Flint, but there was a misunderstanding and Flint's article was postponed. Nevertheless, internal evidence would indicate conclusively that the substitute critic hastily procured by the editor was also an American.

When a second collected edition of Channing's work appeared in Glasgow in 1837, it was therefore greeted with praise as a

matter of course. Although a reviewer in *Fraser's Magazine* professed the wish that "he had retained his creed and his politics,
and sent across the Atlantic to our literature all else besides," he
nevertheless proclaimed him "the finest writer of our age," [23] and,
in a later article in the same journal, a writer, presumably the
same, remarked that "Channing's reviews of character, be it intellectual or physical, are models." [24]

Not long after, however, Channing had his second experience
with an able and scornful English critic. By 1839 his influence
had become so great that Brougham saw fit to take a third edition
of the *Milton* as a text by way of example for an essay upon
style.[25] In their stylistic creed these two writers had much in
common; but Channing professed one article of faith which
Brougham could not admit: he preferred fitness to lucidity; he
would not suffer a noble thought or emotion to be reduced to
commonplace for the sole purpose of making it clear to a low
order of intelligence. To this rule of "false taste" Brougham, in
theory, refused assent; how he phrased his complaint will appear:

In every page we trace its evil influence in most careless thinking and
most faulty diction—a constant mistaking of strange things for strong
ones—a perpetual striving after some half brought out notion, of which
the mind had never formed to itself any distinct picture—a substitution
of the glare of words for harmonious ideas. . . . Though he is among the
most distinguished, he is yet but one of a pretty large class of writers,
who, chiefly in affectedly written words of exaggerated sentiment, dictated by a Narcissus-like love of their own fancied charms—in many
departments of the periodical press, and still more recently in the annuals written by ladies and gentlemen amateurs, are filling the republic
of letters with productions all the more hurtful to the public taste, that
these great faults of one class cannot be committed, any more than Dr.
Channing's, without some talents, though of a showy and shining rather
than a sterling kind; while the emptiness of the other is balanced and
set off by the arts of the engraver.

After this model of lucidity and force, there is little more to be
said of Brougham's criticism. Channing, in his eyes, not only failed
in style, but his ideas themselves were, most of them, either too
obvious or too confused to be worthy of expression at all. Once
more the American had found no favor before his English judge,

but the dignity of the occasion was an implicit acknowledgment of his importance.

This was the last remark of the *Edinburgh* upon the subject of Channing. The English periodical press as a whole pronounced its final judgment when the *Memoirs* appeared in 1848, but this journal and the *Quarterly* remained silent. The *Westminster,* for the third time, however, proclaimed his praise in the person of the Reverend James Martineau:

> The action of his thought was wide and immediate, rather than deep and slow; tending more to ripen the best fruits of the present, than to crumble the soil, and prepare the seed for growths invisible and future. . . . The numerous editions of his works, and the competition of popular publishers for their English sale, indicate a scope and direction of influence unexampled among writers of the same class. The keynote to the whole of Dr. Channing's character and convictions is found in his sense of the inherent greatness of man. . . . Though Channing was never much of a philosopher, he knew how to resort to philosophy for the confirmation of the favorite beliefs.[26]

But perhaps the best summary of his literary influence in England is a belated reply in *Bentley's Miscellany* to the second *Edinburgh* attack:

> In the year 1826, Channing first came into the world as an author. . . . These three works [*Milton, Bonaparte,* and *Fénelon*] found their way to England, and were highly admired by the men of judgment and reflection into whose hands they happened to fall, not only for their elegance of style, but for the elevated tone and noble spirit that pervaded them. It was seen that no common man had arisen to adorn literature, and to instruct and benefit mankind. . . . Meanwhile, his reputation was extending in spite of the indifference or passive hostility of the English critics. His published lectures on the "Importance and Means of a National Literature," on "Temperance," on "Self-Culture," on the "Elevation of the Working Classes," on "Self-Denial," and on "War," and his letters to Mr. Clay on the annexation of Texas in 1837 [*sic*], were imported into England, reprinted for a wider circulation, and read with avidity by thousands, not of the higher and middle classes alone, but of the mass of the people.[27]

Those thousands of average humanity who heard Channing remain voiceless today, but they must be remembered if his literary reputation is to be explained. The majority of his critics were, in part at least, hostile; they were protesting against something or somebody. The mounting power of his influence can be charted principally by this reaction of the critics to it.

But he never would have attained even an unwilling acceptance as one of the two or three American writers who were considered worthy of their nation, had he not written in a mode familiar to his English reviewers, and written well according to the standards of the time. The critical school of Jeffrey was not guided by aesthetic canons—either in its limitations upon material or in its choice of forms of expression. From the literary point of view, Channing was a member of this school, with his fellows bridging the interval between the great ages of eighteenth-century and of Victorian prose criticism, both literary and social. The nobility of his thought and character, and his mastery of prose style and of the essay form, rank him with the best of his contemporaries of like aims and methods. A study of the career of his English counterpart, the Reverend Thomas Chalmers, or even of Sydney Smith (likewise a clergyman) will leave few doubts as to the reasons for his British popularity. As a social and literary critic, according to the canons of the day, Channing had the necessary cultural background, the breadth of humanitarian perspective, the mastery of medium, and the originality and vigor of expression to make a position of prominence for himself—and maintain it.

III

His own canons of criticism would give him like rank, even though he was too modest to claim it for himself. He did not think of himself as a literary man, but he thought clearly of the nature of literature, and his own writing conforms accurately and creditably to that definition. His essay on *The Importance and Means of a National Literature* is, like Emerson's *American Scholar,* the statement of a creed which its author believed by living. Channing was prompted by the ideals here set forth when he wrote his own essays and sermons, and his work is, in terms of his means and abilities, his own foundation stone in the structure which he planned for his nation.

This interesting essay, overshadowed by its famous successor, is, like it, a declaration of American intellectual independence and also an acceptance of the conservative literary traditions of England. America had as yet produced no literature, according to both of these prophets, because of her wholesome absorption in practical pursuits. To both of them the answer lay, not in the abandoning of those pursuits, but in the arousing of "the sluggard intellect of this continent" and the courageous self-expression of the "man thinking." Channing thought of the product and called it literature; Emerson thought of the producer and called him a scholar. The philosophical concepts of the two men are, however, identical, and their pleas sprang from the same motives and aimed at the same objectives.

We begin, with stating what we mean by national literature. We mean the expression of a nation's mind in writing. We mean the production among a people of important works in philosophy, and in the departments of imagination and taste. We mean the contributions of new truths to the stock of human knowledge. We mean the thoughts of profound and original minds, elaborated by the toil of composition, and fixed and made immortal in books. We mean the manifestation of a nation's intellect in the only forms by which it can multiply itself at home, and send itself abroad. We mean that a nation shall take a place, by its authors, among the lights of the world. It will be seen, that we include under literature all the writings of superior minds, be the subjects what they may. We are aware that the term is often confined to compositions which relate to human nature, and human life; that it is not generally extended to physical science; that mind, not matter, is regarded as its main subject and sphere. But the worlds of matter and mind are too intimately connected to admit of exact partition. All the objects of human thought flow into one another. Moral and philosophical truths have many bonds and analogies, and, whilst the former are the chosen and noblest themes of literature, we are not anxious to divorce them from the latter, or to shut them up in a separate department. The expression of superior mind in writings, we regard, then, as a nation's literature. We regard its gifted men, whether devoted to the exact sciences, to mental and ethical philosophy, to history and legislation, or to fiction and poetry, as forming a noble intellectual brotherhood, and it is for the purpose of quickening all to join their labors for the public good, that we offer the present plea in behalf of a national literature.[28]

This passage is not wholly original in thought or in expression

—but few such exhortations ever are. An all-inclusive definition of literature was the daily working principle of the reviewers; respect for the practical activities of man was a direct inheritance from Franklin and Jefferson; a belief in the unity of man's thought and activity hints of the paternity of Coleridge and the German idealists. But in gathering these strands into a single cord, Channing furnished to Emerson and others a useful piece of philosophical equipment for climbing higher.

The essay itself is but an elaboration of this clear and broad definition. With the characteristic method of rhetorical exposition, Channing carefully distinguishes the steps in his thought and proceeds with leisure and assurance from his premise to his conclusion. A national literature is important for America because an unprecedented liberty of conscience and action should develop a new and superior race of men, of whom literature should be the widest and most effective avenue of expression. America will be great in so far only as she contributes to the good of mankind. As yet she has produced no national literature, because in her praiseworthy diffusion of instruction, she has neglected the higher levels of moral and intellectual training. The result is a superficiality of mind, a paucity of original and profound thinkers. She is too ready to rely for intellectual excitement and enjoyment upon a Europe schooled in political and social conceptions alien to her own.

The causes which have obstructed the development of a cultural self-respect on the part of America are, according to Channing: a reverence for useful knowledge as it ministers to the needs of animal, and not to intellectual, moral, and religious man; and an acceptance of foreign culture without an effort to rise to the level of the imported stimulus.

The more we receive from other countries the greater the need of an original literature. A people, into whose minds the thoughts of foreigners are poured perpetually, needs an energy within itself to resist, to modify this mighty influence, and, without it, will inevitably sink under the worst bondage, will become intellectually tame and enslaved. We have certainly no desire to complete our restrictive system by adding to it a literary non-intercourse law. We rejoice in the increasing intellectual connexion between this country and the old world. But sooner would we rupture it, than see our country sitting passively at the feet of foreign teachers.[29]

Other arguments for a national literature are: the aid which could be expected from it not only in expressing but also in forming the national mind; the improvement of style through exercise; the stimulus afforded to all kinds of investigations, even to those of a scientific nature; and finally, the diffusion of the American doctrine of liberty throughout the world.

The means of producing this national literature he believed to be: its fostering wherever it appears; the improvement of universities as well as of primary and elementary schools; and the cultivation of a new motivation for literature in the freedom of religion from superstition. Finally, the intellectual men in America should seek stimulus from other European countries as well as from England.

Echoes of the old, blend curiously with prophesies of the new in this epoch-making document. The future, Channing believed, held much promise, although, by 1830, his own major contribution to that future had already been made.

I V

"To recover some of our ancestors' real thoughts and feelings is the hardest, subtlest and most educative function that the historian can perform" said Trevelyan; [30] and he might have added, "The literary historian has perhaps, more than any other, the duty of attempting the task."

Channing, in the eyes of his contemporaries and of himself, seems a very different person from the preacher which his commentators have given to us. The importance of his contribution to American literary history has here been indicated in terms of these old critical canons rather than of any arbitrary modern code; the next step should be the application of these ideas to his own writings, but that task can not be attempted in this essay. The problem cannot, however, be dismissed without at least a cursory view of those discourses and reviews upon which his contemporary literary fame chiefly rested—the four essays dealing with the nature of greatness, those on *Self-Culture* and *The*

Labouring Classes, and the introductory remarks to the collected edition of his works, his *apologia pro vita sua.* The essays on a national literature has already been discussed; literary consideration of his other writings must be here restricted to these others.

The contemporary opinion of these essays was based upon two elements: the thought which they contained and the style in which they were presented. The latter can best be judged by the quotations here incidentally embodied. It was conventional and clear, using the accepted devices of the pulpit and of the quarterly review with a sense of mastery. The belief that style should reflect the quality of thought as well as convey its bare intellectual outlines was always a controlling factor with Channing. It seldom led him, however, to an expression which obscured his meaning. Repetition and over-ornateness were his worst qualities, and these are often justified for their emphatic effect. The criticism that he never left the pulpit is just. His writing takes its form because, in the author's mind, it is heard rather than read from the printed page. But homilies have been considered to be literature before this, and there is no reason why a good sermon may not be as fit an object for the discussions of the literary critic as a good poem or an essay.

His contemporaries, however, did not go this far. They based his literary reputation upon his secular writings only, and laid their chief emphasis upon his social thought. The general pattern of that thought is strikingly typical of the nineteenth-century social and literary critic: a conviction of an attainable perfection for the individual and a descending scale of application from a more-or-less deistic God to the working man or slave. The chief difference between him and those who came later lay in his point of emphasis: he devoted more attention to God and less to labor.

"They have," said Channing, with reference to his collected essays and sermons, "the merit of being earnest expressions of the writer's mind, and of giving the results of quiet, long-continued thought." [31] The remainder of this revealing preface is devoted to refuting the charge that the author is a mere "romancer," that he was more concerned with the affairs of man than of God. But in his very attempt at a refutation of this charge, the preacher becomes the essayist and makes for himself a place in English literature of the nineteenth century. Without social criticism, the product of that century in English prose writing would be a frail ghost of past literary memories. Channing won his place by his "deep attachment to liberty in all its forms, civil, political, religious, to liberty of thought, speech, and the press," [32] and by his analysis of power, restraint, and war.

The conviction that true liberty originates in the respect of the individual for himself was the keynote of his social thought. The essay on "Self-Culture" is a summary of a life-long creed:

Self-Culture, is possible, not only because we can enter into and search ourselves. We have a still nobler power, that of acting on, determining and forming ourselves. This is a fearful as well as a glorious endowment, for it is the ground of human responsibility. We have the power not only of tracing our powers, but of guiding and impelling them; not only of watching our passions, but of controlling them; not only of seeing our faculties grow, but of applying to them means and influences to aid their growth. We can stay or change the current of thought. We can concentrate the intellect upon objects which we wish to comprehend. We can fix our eyes on perfection, and make almost everything speed us towards it. [33]

From this second premise of absolute free-will—his first being the unity of the deity—Channing proceeded to his analysis of leadership and labor among men. If he had come after instead of before Carlyle, his statements on these topics would be justly considered to be mere faint echoes. Divorcing the purely doctrinal sections of the *Milton* from the remainder of that essay, we find in the latter a definition of abstract greatness in terms of intellectual and moral superiority almost perfectly embodied in a "serious" poet. "Milton's fame," he says, "rests on his poetry. . . . Of all God's gifts of intellect, he esteemed poetical genius the most transcendent. He esteemed it in himself as a kind of inspiration, and wrote his great works with something of the conscious dignity of a prophet. We agree with Milton in his estimate of poetry. It seems to us the divinest of all arts." [34]

In the concluding sentences of his essay, Channing gives a positive definition of the ideal "hero," although he does not use the word:

We believe that the sublime intelligence of Milton was imparted, not for his own sake only, but to awaken kindred virtue and greatness in

other souls. Far from regarding him as standing alone and unapproach-
able, we believe that he is an illustration of what all, who are true to
their nature, will become in the progress of their being; and we have
held him forth, not to excite an ineffectual admiration, but to stir up
our own and others' breasts to an exhilarating pursuit of high and ever-
growing attainments in intellect and virtue.[35]

The false or negative aspects of heroism he had analysed in the
essay on Napoleon. He was provoked to a second and fuller
exposition of the theory by the criticism which that essay received.
With his final moral judgment constantly in mind, Channing
carefully studied the means by which Napoleon consolidated and
extended his power, and the qualities of his character which
caused his first success and his ultimate failure. His fall resulted
from a mistaking of self-exaggeration for self-culture. "Such was
Napoleon Bonaparte," he concludes. "But some will say, he was
still a great man. This we mean not to deny. But we would have
it understood, that there are various kinds and orders of greatness, and that the highest did not belong to Bonaparte." [36] There
then follows a classification which echoed through the social
criticism of a century. The first order is moral greatness, or mag-
nanimity; the second, intellectual greatness, or genius; and the
third, the greatness of *action,* or the "sublime power of conceiving
bold and extensive plans." Partaking somewhat of all, Napoleon's
actual greatness appears to increase on this descending scale, and
his highest rank, paradoxically, is in the lowest order.

No judgment more thorough, clear, and logical than this has
ever been pronounced upon this man. The second essay continues the analysis of the "principle of action which governed
him, and of which he was a remarkable manifestation," but elab-
orates rather than adds to the central thought of the first.

Channing's application of his principles of self-culture and
liberty to society was not so thorough as that to the outstanding
individual. It is summarized in his *Introductory Remarks:*

Social order is better preserved by liberty, than by restraint. The latter,
unless most wisely and justly employed, frets, exasperates, and provokes
secret resistance; and still more, it is rendered needful very much by
that unhappy constitution of society, which denies to multitudes the
opportunities of free activity. A community, which should open a great

variety of spheres to its members, so that all might find free scope for their powers, would need little array of force for restraint.[37]

In one of his last lectures, delivered before the Mercantile Library Company of Philadelphia, he took a comprehensive view of his age in terms of its material being:

The privileged, petted individual is becoming less, and the human race is becoming more. The multitude is rising from the dust. Once we heard of the few, now we hear of the many; once of the prerogatives of a part, now of the rights of all. . . . The grand idea of humanity, of the importance of man as man, is spreading silently, but surely. . . . The grand doctrine, that every human being should have the means of self-culture, of progress in knowledge and virtue, of health, comfort, and happiness, of exercising the powers and affections of a man, this is slowly taking its place as the highest social truth.[38]

And like other white-handed speakers before audiences of working-men, he had no hesitancy in proclaiming the dignity of manual labor: "I would not if I could," he said on a similar occasion, "so temper the elements, that they should infuse into us only grateful sensations, that they should make vegetation so exuberant as to anticipate every want, and the minerals so ductile as to offer no resistance to our strength and skill. Such a world would make a contemptible race. Man owes his growth, his energy, chiefly to that striving of the will, that conflict with difficulty, which we call Effort. . . . Manual labor is a school, in which men are placed to get energy of purpose and character, a vastly more important endowment than all the learning of all other schools." [39]

There are no picturesque Plugsons and Bobuses in this essay to add a distinguished literary flavor to sound moral doctrine. "I attribute much importance," said Emerson in summing up the work of the elder prophet, "to the two papers of Dr. Channing, one on Milton and one on Napoleon, which were the first specimens in this country of that large criticism which in England had given power and fame to the *Edinburgh Review*. They were widely read, and of course immediately fruitful in provoking emulation which lifted the style of journalism." [40] Even this, it would seem, was a conservative estimate of Channing's literary importance in his day.

NOTES

1. C. W. Eliot, *Four American Leaders* (Boston, 1907), pp. 57-72.
2. *Fraser's Magazine*, XVIII (May, 1838): 635.
3. *Cf.* A. H. Everett's reply to Hazlitt, *North American Review*, XXXI (July, 1830): 26-66.
4. J. W. Chadwick, *W. E. Channing* (Boston: Houghton, Mifflin Co., 1903), pp. 195-210.
5. *The Cambridge History of American Literature* (New York: G. P. Putnam's Sons, 1917–21), III, 109.
6. R. E. Spiller, *The American in England* (New York: Henry Holt and Co., 1926), pp. 226-229.
7. *Christian Examiner*, III (Jan.-Feb., 1826): 29-77.
8. *Ibid.*, IV (Sept.-Oct., 1827): 383-430, and V (March-April, 1828): 135-153.
9. *Ibid.*, VI (March, 1829): 1-35.
10. *Ibid.*, VII (Jan., 1830): 269-295.
11. *Quarterly Review*, XVIII (Jan., 1823): 535-536.
12. *Ibid.*, LXI (April, 1838): 326-362, and LXIV (Oct., 1839): 328.
13. *Ibid.*, XVIII (Aug., 1825): 160-163.
14. *Monthly Magazine*, n.s., VII (April, 1828): 471-478.
15. *Ibid.*, n.s., VII (March, 1828): 442-448.
16. *Westminster Review*, X (April, 1828): 98-101.
17. *Edinburgh Review*, L (Oct., 1829): 125-144. A review of W. E. Channing, *Sermons and Tracts* (Boston and London, 1829).
18. *Athenaeum*, II (Oct. 14, 1829): 637-639.
19. *Westminster Review*, XII (April, 1830): 472-491.
20. "The Lounger, No. 11," *New Monthly Magazine*, XVIII (May, 1830): 469. The writer was apparently unaware of Hazlitt's authorship of the offending article.
21. *Athenaeum*, III (May 8, 1830): 280-281.
22. *Ibid.*, VIII (Jan., 1835): 9-13ff.
23. *Fraser's Magazine*, XVII (May, 1838): 627-635.
24. *Ibid.*, XVIII (Sept., 1838): 286-297.
25. *Edinburgh Review*, LXIX, (April, 1839): 214-230.
26. *Westminster Review*, L (Jan., 1849): 317-348.
27. *Bentley's Miscellany*, XV (Jan., 1849): 88-90. A signed review by Charles Whitehead.
28. W. E. Channing, *Works* (Boston: J. Munroe and Co., 1841–43), I, 243-244. The essay was first reprinted in full under the title "Remarks on National Literature" in R. E. Spiller, *The Roots of National Culture* (New York: The Macmillan Company, 1933).
29. *Ibid.*, p. 261.
30. G. M. Trevelyan, *Clio, a Muse* (London: Longmans, Green and Co., 1913), p. 17.
31. *Works*, I, v.
32. *Ibid.*, I, xx.
33. *Ibid.*, II, 356.
34. *Ibid.*, I, 6-7.

35. *Ibid.*, I, 68.
36. *Ibid.*, I, 118.
37. *Ibid.*, I, xxv.
38. *Ibid.*, VI, 150-151.
39. *Ibid.*, V, 157-158.
40. R. W. Emerson, *Works* (Boston: Houghton, Mifflin Co., 1903–4), X, 339.

Ralph Waldo Emerson: Man Thinking

This essay on Emerson is Chapter XXV of *Literary History of the United States*, edited by Robert E. Spiller, Willard Thorp, Thomas H. Johnson, and Henry Seidel Canby (New York: Macmillan Co., 1948). As the editors could choose the chapters which they themselves wished to write, I chose those on Ralph Waldo Emerson and Henry Adams as (in the words of Henry Adams) the two "points of relation" from which "to project his lines forward and backward indefinitely, subject to correction from any one who should know better."

A HALF CENTURY AFTER THE UNITED STATES had been baptized in political independence, the time had come for confirmation in freedom of the soul. Ralph Waldo Emerson, of Concord, Massachusetts, declared the ceremony performed and became spokesman for his time and country.

His preeminence has caused our literary historians some embarrassment. America was ready for a Shakespeare, a Dante, or a Dostoevski to give literary voice to her achieved majority. She was given an apologist—an Aristotle, a Paul, a Bacon. In the wise and temperate Emerson, the heat became radiant light. It was he who brought into its first sharp focus the full meaning of two centuries of life on the Atlantic seaboard of this continent; of the economic and spiritual revolutions which had unsettled the Old World and settled the New; of the experiment in democracy which was to make a Holy Commonwealth into a world power.

He did this in two ways: by carrying to its ultimate statement the individual's revolt from authority, which marked the transition from the medieval world to the modern; and by formulating the dichotomy between the vision of a Jonathan Edwards and the common sense of a Benjamin Franklin, a conflict and a balance which has always provided the creative tension in American life. But he translated these discoveries neither into formal philosophy nor into fully formed art. His logic and his metaphysics remained without system; his art, like that of all great American romantics, retained its organic freedom.

As Emerson had no Boswell, he must speak for himself, and he spent his life in doing so. Upon an audience he played with the sure hands of a master organist; but the oft shuffled manuscripts in his study were cold. "We do not go to hear what Emerson says," wrote Lowell, "so much as to hear Emerson." A tall blond figure in black, he leaned forward across the reading desk in shy Yankee awkwardness and searched the hearts of his hearers with sincere blue eyes and controlled voice.

"Where do we find ourselves?" he asks in his essay on "Experience," and he gives his answer: "On its own level, or in view of nature, temperament is final." The inner wholeness of the man is his true self; his life "is a train of moods like a string of beads"; temperament, the iron wire on which the beads are strung. Striving to give expression only and always to this central self, Emerson has left a handful of essays and poems which are to many an essential part of their religious literature; but the man himself evades discovery. "So much of our time is preparation," he explains, "so much is routine, and so much retrospect, that the pith of each man's genius contracts itself to a very few hours."

Preparation—routine—retrospect; these are the entries on the calendar, the frame of life for a reticent New England man who is Emerson the seer. He devoted thirty-three years to what he thought of later as "preparation" before he published his first book in 1836; some two decades provided the "very few hours" when his genius was at high pitch and all of his great work was produced from the essential stability and calm of "routine"; and finally there were almost thirty years of "retrospect" before his death in 1882. The central twenty years have left us our impression of a man who always stood firm on moral ground and ad-

monished his fellows to turn their eyes from evil, to have faith
in themselves and in one another, and to seek God through
Nature. But the Emersonian confidence and calm were not
achieved, nor were they maintained, without struggle, doubt,
and self-examination.

I I

The chronicle of Emerson's preparation may be reconstructed
from letters and journals; it would have been alien to his temperament to leave an autobiography of the soul such as *Sartor
Resartus, Dichtung und Wahrheit,* or the *Confessions* of
Rousseau. But the romantic pattern of introspection, doubt, and
psychological crisis found in a Carlyle or a Goethe was his as
well, marked by the familiar circumstances of poverty, loneliness,
illness, idealized love, and the discovery of death.

Poverty was the lot of his youth. The second of four boys, he
was only eight years old when his father died in 1811 and the
congregation of the "Old Brick" Church in Boston granted the
"pious and amiable" widow home and subsistence for a few
years, while the boys shared one winter overcoat and the house-
work, studied their grammar, and ended the "toils of the day,"
as Ralph reports to his Aunt Mary, with their private devotions.

During Ralph's school and college days this diminutive aunt,
appearing suddenly out of her private wandering for visits at
the Emerson home or writing admonitory letters to her adopted
spiritual orphans, became the substitute for both father and
conscience. Her life, writes her nephew, "marked the precise
time when the power of the old creed yielded to the influence of
modern science and humanity." The zeal and consecration of
Puritan ancestors was mingled in the latter-day sibyl with shrewd
common sense and an insatiable intellectual curiosity. Mary
Moody Emerson lived this life in preparation for the next, but
she lived it with gusto. The correspondence between her and
her nephew charts his course as his mind and spirit grew. There
is solemn thought and wiry humor in the letters of both, even
though the boy's sophistication is sophomoric, that of the little
old lady crisp and intricate. For Aunt Mary was both mystic
and critic, Calvinist and skeptic; Ralph could laugh at her because

he profoundly respected her. To her he took both his doubts and his discoveries. She sharpened his wit and deepened his perceptions. Here is at least one source for that mixture of insight and common sense which characterized his thought, that aphoristic directness which sharpened his style.

During these early years, Emerson learned the habit of introspection. His intimate experience with people seems hardly to have extended beyond the family. "The friends that occupy my thoughts," he wrote at Harvard, "are not men, but certain phantoms clothed in the form and face and apparel of men by whom they were suggested and to whom they bear a resemblance." But his intimacy with his brothers, William, Edward, and Charles, was close. The journals which he, and apparently Charles as well, kept from an early age have not all survived, for the first is now dated 1819 from Harvard; but even in these we can see the somewhat affected litterateur gradually recede and the true man emerge. By 1824, the journals have ceased to be a "motley diary" and have become a "soliloquy," a "savings bank" where he can deposit his earnings. Here is the workshop, with saw, hammer, and plane, where the raw lumber of thought, reading, and experience is stored and worked. There is a vast difference between the early and the late volumes. The first four or five constitute a moving autobiography of the spirit, but the others may be read in almost any order and are most enjoyable when dipped into. Between 1820 and 1836, when his inner life was growing steadily, the record of his progress has dramatic conflict and movement. Thereafter the journals gradually become to the reader what they were to him, a mine to be worked rather than a journey to be taken.

To poverty and introspection was added a struggle with sickness and adversity sufficient to supply a romantic hero with all the sorrows he might need. For the shadow of the white plague lay across the Emerson household, and Ralph barely escaped its doom. It carried off his two younger brothers, the one more eager and self-consuming, the other less robust than he; and, if we accept his own theory, he avoided certain death when a depression and cough racked his chest only because of a "sluggish" passivity of temperament which allowed him to give in to the malady and take the rest and care which brought his recovery. But Edward's sudden mental breakdown in 1828 followed Ralph's trip to Florida in search of health by only a year, and the frailty of Charles, "the friend and companion of many years . . . whose conversation . . . has been my daily bread," kept the minds of both in secret morbid contemplation to be confessed only to private notes. "I read with some surprise the pages of his journal," wrote the elder brother after the death of Charles in 1836. "They show a nocturnal side which his diurnal aspects never suggested,—they are melancholy, penitential, self-accusing; I read them with no pleasure: they are the creepings of an eclipsing temperament over his abiding light of character."

It would be a mistake to overemphasize the similar traits in Ralph's character, but the tone of penitential self-accusation is strong throughout the college and following years, driving him in upon himself when external adversity made the way dark. Like Charles too, but again not to the same degree, this mood cultivated an insistently skeptical habit of mind which fought throughout these years a losing but bitter battle with the native optimism of his character and resulted in a strengthening of his affirmation.

Love likewise came to him in somber garb. Within parentheses he confided in 1827, "I am a bachelor and to the best of my belief have never been in love"; but the next year when he took Edward to Concord, New Hampshire, to hasten his recovery, he confessed to William: "The presumptuous man was overthrown by the eye and ear, and surrendered at discretion. He is now as happy as it is safe in life to be. She is seventeen years old, and very beautiful, by universal consent." Ellen Tucker's illness—the same as his own though more acute—had made her already an invalid and emphasized the ethereal qualities that so appealed to suppressed but dreaming youth. Delicate, deeply religious, and altogether devoted, she awoke his protective manhood, spurred ambition, inspired poetic tribute. The marriage lasted a little over a year, and her death left a "miserable apathy" rather than the morbid depression of adolescent sorrow. As pastor of the Second Church of Boston, he had meanwhile become a man. Yet Ellen remained the one great romance of his life, a dream of purity the easier to maintain because illness had protected it from the rigors of living.

Eager for experience and thwarted by his shyness, Emerson sought in books the reality he craved. His tastes were formed in early childhood. Aunt Mary had seen to it that the fatherless boys should grow up in the family tradition of religious zeal and the love of letters. She herself read beyond orthodox theology, and she encouraged her nephews to follow her devious course. Through her, Ralph discovered Milton and Bacon, Shakespeare and Burke, who were to remain through life close friends on his expanding shelves.

As he grew older and moved away from her influence, the eclectic quality of his reading increased. For the formal Harvard curriculum he had little use, and he was content to remain in the middle of his class rather than seek academic distinction. A good sermon from W. E. Channing, or an oration from Everett or Webster gave him more pleasure than the rhetorical instruction of Edward Channing or the cold rationalism of Locke. The influence of the Scottish rationalist Dugald Stewart can be traced in his later writing; but, at the time, the *Elements of the Philosophy of the Human Mind* seemed all cottages and shops after entering the gate of splendor and promise. Doubt knocked at his door in the form of Pyrrhonism, the current undergraduate fashion. Slowly, as he took over his own education, he added Plato (in the translation of Thomas Taylor), Montaigne, Newton, Swedenborg, and Plutarch (both the *Lives* and the *Morals*), to his list of imperatives. More commonly he turned to histories, anthologies, and translations as short cuts to usable ideas: Gérando, Schlegel, Staël, Cousin, Hammer's translations of Persian poetry into German, and Taylor's translations of the Neo-Platonists. Newton's *Principia* and Lyell's *Geology* opened his mind to both the old and the new science. He could read both French and German slowly, but he would "as soon think of foregoing the railroad and the telegraph" as of avoiding translations when they could save time.

In all of this reading two trends are clearly marked. He hoped to learn from the skeptics, the rationalists, and the scientists a common-sense basis for moral truth; and he hoped to meet in the mystics and romantics a validation immediate, instinctive, and final. The one brought him closer to experience, the other to God. He was feeding his moral imagination rather than disciplining his mind. The two-pronged nature of his quest was a reflection of his two-sided temperament and led to a suspended dualism, the necessary creative tension for literary expression. Always Emerson strove to make one of two; but in his own early thinking he did not clearly distinguish between the logical and the intuitive roads to truth. This distinction he owed largely to Coleridge, but it was not to become clear to him until his spirit had been melted and reforged.

The romantic crisis in his life came with his retirement from the ministry in 1832. The independence of spirit to which he had responded in the books he had read was now focused on an issue which had its roots in his own temperament, his traditions, his times. "Whoso would be a man," he wrote later, "must be a nonconformist. . . . Nothing is at last sacred but the integrity of your own mind." The choice lay before him, raw and urgent. He must renounce his own world in order to find himself.

The earnest young clergyman had chosen his profession deliberately. In one of the most remarkable passages of self-examination in all literature, he stated his prospects to his journal on April 18, 1824:

I am beginning my professional studies. In a month I shall be legally a man. And I deliberately dedicate my time, my talents, and my hopes to the Church. Man is an animal that looks before and after . . . and this page must be witness to the latest year of my life whether I have good grounds to warrant my determination.

In the following inventory a strong imagination is balanced against a proportionally weak reasoning faculty, but theology requires, in its highest form, the moral imagination rather than the "reasoning machine" of a Locke, Clarke, or Hume. Lack of self-confidence in society is a serious handicap in the ministry and entirely precludes the law; he finds in himself no taste for medicine; but "in Divinity I hope to thrive." An inherited "love for the strains of eloquence" makes "entire success" in public preaching a reasonable expectation, even though relative failure in the functions of private influence may dull the triumph. As a teacher —he had assisted in the girls' school which his brother conducted —he had experienced little satisfaction. But his trust is that, by discipline of his weaknesses, his profession may be the "regeneration of mind, manners, inward and outward estate."

Three points emerge from this inventory, which are central to an understanding of the later Emerson: his faith in the moral imagination rather than the intellect, his lack of self-confidence, and his choice of eloquence as his natural medium of expression. At this time, he seems to have had none of the doubts about his ability to conform to the requirements of an organized church that later were to invalidate his choice.

His rebellion, when it finally came, was twofold: against the last vestiges of ecclesiastical authority over the spiritual life of the individual, and against the eighteenth-century rationalism which had killed spirituality, he thought, when it denied revelation. The first pointed to a final schism in which each man becomes his own church; the second sought to provide the rules for a new and personal orthodoxy. In the end, self-reliance was sanctioned by submission to the "Beautiful Necessity." As, long before, Jonathan Edwards had paradoxically sought to bring the straying Arminians back to orthodoxy by a personal appeal to the heart as well as to logic, so Emerson attacked the intellectual liberals of his day.

For the faith of the fathers had by the early 1800's once again cooled in the growing Unitarianism of William Emerson and William Ellery Channing of Boston. The new sect had not yet declared itself, but a small company of New England clergymen, liberal in their theology, were "discarding Calvinism by silently ignoring it" and appealing to the intellect, to sentiment, and to literary taste rather than to dogma or revelation. The next step toward heterodoxy, which Emerson heard preached in the "sublime sermons" of Channing, was the doctrine of truth discoverable by the mind rather than the heart. But the spirit of Calvin stirred once more when the boy wrote to his aunt and mentor, "It would assuredly make us feel safer to have our victorious answer set down in impregnable propositions." A new orthodoxy was implied by direct appeal to the God within. His own version of the new revelation was framed in *Nature*, and elaborated in his lectures and poems. It was an indigenous growth in nineteenth-century soil, but the seed was found on a high shelf of the family cupboard.

The inner drama of this struggle is written between the lines of more than one hundred and sixty sermons preached between 1826 and 1832, a selection of which has been published as *Young Emerson Speaks*. In these sermons, we find most of his later and characteristic doctrines expressed in a voice straining for conviction and leaning upon logic and authority where uncertainties still cling. In his first sermon, "Pray Without Ceasing" (1826), man is declared "the architect of his own fortunes"; conscience, the predecessor of the "moral sentiment" of the later essays, is "God's viceregent"; "the preexistent harmony between thought and things" anticipates the later convictions of correspondence between moral and natural law; and nature "helps the purposes of man."

These central ideas together with others equally characteristic are developed more fully in the sermons which follow, while other ideas, expressed perhaps with less confidence, were later modified or rejected. The painful effort to account for "Miracles" (1831) as a special "means by which God can make a communication to men" was scratched out and rewritten only to have its main argument denied in the confident "Divinity School Address" of seven years later. His wife's death made faith in personal immortality an urgently needed "Consolation for the Mourner" (1831), a doctrine which his later pantheism modified to the point of rejection. And his effort to find his vocation within the frame of the Church made him not only acknowledge the importance of the public functions of prayer and preaching, but the validity of the formal sacraments of marriage, baptism, and the Lord's Supper.

The young preacher struggled with these doubts and contradictions as long as he could; but he sensed his main difficulty from the start. With conformity in spite of conscience, he was determined to have nothing to do. In his first personal talk to his congregation he announced that he would not "be so much afraid of innovation as to scruple about introducing new forms of address, new modes of illustration, and varied allusions from the pulpit." The desire of his hearers for sanctity in style and solemnity in illustration would not deter him from the study of secular as well as scriptural wisdom and its use in his ministry. His revolt from formal sacraments might then have been predicted. Not the administering of the Lord's Supper alone, but the whole structure of formal worship was challenged.

It is perhaps ironic that the man who was to free Unitarianism from the last vestiges of dogma and from reliance upon the authority of logical argument should himself have contrasted so sharply in his discourse with the eloquence of his predecessors, W. E. Channing and Henry Ware. These sermons are cold, and the earlier of them follow careful outlines. They remain on the level of the mind and contain no evangelical buoyancy. Gradually, as personal conviction grew, a new form and a new style asserted themselves. As his personal and theological difficulties became more pressing, his heart seemed to awaken. The need for self-justification in the lonely path which was inevitably opening before him brought an emotional power to his discourse which no evangelical technique could supply. His farewell sermon on the Lord's Supper (1832) was his last effort to rest a case upon the principles of logical analysis. His real farewell came a month later in his final sermon to his congregation on "The Genuine Man," who "parts with his individuality, leaves all thought of private stake, personal feeling, and in compensation he has in some sort the strength of the whole. . . . His heart beats pulse for pulse with the heart of the Universe." With this new strength, a new eloquence was born. Hereafter Emerson would start on the plane of the commonplace and raise his hearers with himself to that of the ideal. In "The Miracle of Our Being" (1834) the form of all his later work is declared. From "the fitness of man to the earth" this sermon rises by swift ascent to "an infinite and perfect life." The seeker has become the leader and guide, with conviction in his message and confidence in his medium.

Many volumes have been written to prove that Emerson's final position was based on Neo-Platonism, German idealism, or Oriental mysticism; but a study of these sermons and of his early reading indicates that he never departed from his loyalty to the faith of his fathers, the Christian tradition as developed by Christ, Paul, Thomas Aquinas, and Calvin. Essentially romantic by disposition, he took his place with the rebels and seekers and, like Coleridge and Goethe, sought both confirmation and refreshment from all ages and quarters.

It was this growing romanticism which made the bondage of formal religion insufferable. For his final searching of the soul, he retired to Ethan Crawford's in the New Hampshire mountains, where "life is reconsidered." There the hours passed on, bearing him to the crisis of his fate. "How hard to command the soul, or to solicit the soul." Struggling with "indignation at this windmill," recognizing that "without accommodation society is impractical," he confronted at last his inevitable choice of path: "I cannot go habitually to an institution which they esteem holiest with indifference and dislike." The issue was not one of doctrine or of form; it was a private matter of his conscience. He would not abolish the institution of the Lord's Supper if it had meaning for others; but he could no longer administer it. When he returned to Boston and once more faced his congregation, he had left all conformity behind, for he had at last grappled with himself and conquered. Fears of his own inadequacy could not block his path, for personal success no longer mattered. The self-reliance which he had preached to others was now to be his.

III

This, as Carlyle was writing at the time, is the "Everlasting Yea," the crisis and resolution of romantic doubts. But before full achievement, it must be preceded by a "Center of Indifference." Divorce from circumstance must be complete, that the inner man may expand to full self-recognition.

The way was not clearly charted when he was on the brig *Jasper* bound for Malta in January, 1833. In spite of his lifelong aversion to travel as a means of escape or refreshment, he spent most of that year in Europe. At thirty, his life lay behind him, apparently a succession of failures with no positive accomplishment to show for his efforts and a state of health and mind which promised little for the future. His mood sank to self-disgust and despair: "What under the sun canst thou do, pale face? . . . I did not put me here; yet God forbid I should therefore decline the responsibility into which I am born." With himself he was relentless: "It is doubtless a vice to turn one's eyes inward too much, but I am my own comedy and tragedy." When he warned later that the traveler "carries ruins to ruins," he was doubtless thinking of his own experience; and on his return, he sighed, "I am very glad my travelling is done. A man not old feels himself too old to be a vagabond."

Such moods were occasional only. He gave various reasons for the trip, among them illness and the desire to see great men: "to learn what man can,—what is the uttermost that social man has

done." But his obvious purpose was to be alone, to confront himself, and if possible to find a new vocation unfettered by the
formalities and expectations of others or by his own shortcomings.
"I am thankful that I am an American as I am thankful that I am
a man." His quest ended with a pledge, "if health and opportunity be granted me, to demonstrate that all necessary truth is its
own evidence; that no doctrine of God need appeal to a book;
that Christianity is wrongly received by all such as take it as a
system of doctrines,—its stress being upon moral truth; it is a rule
of life, not a rule of faith."

But his discoveries were not all moral or religious. Much to his
own surprise, he was startled and ensnared by Old World culture.
His senses and emotions were stirred by the incense and the
music of St. Peter's, by the calm beauty of Raphael's *Transfigura-
tion*, by the Sistine frescoes and the Moses of Michelangelo. He
warmed to the monuments of Catholicism, but found no charm in
Geneva, the home of his inherited faith, other than the surrounding mountains. In Paris, he was astounded by the collection of
birds, beasts, and other specimens in the Jardin des Plantes. "I am
moved by strange sympathies; I say continually 'I will be a
naturalist.'" His confessed lack of human sympathy and ease of
approach to strangers was belied by his friendliness with fellow
Americans, the sculptor Greenough, the traveler Dewey, and innumerable others whom he joined for part of his way. But with
Landor at Fiesole, Coleridge at Highgate, and Wordsworth at
Rydal, his hope to discover greatness in the great was disap-
pointed. Carlyle alone fulfilled his expectations. Emerson had
come upon "the latest and strongest contributor to the critical
journals" in 1827–29 when Carlyle's articles in the *Edinburgh
Review, Fraser's*, and *Blackwood's* were scorching their pages. He
sought him out in his lonely farm at Craigenputtock, listened to
his wry and revealing comments on the ingenuity of a pig and
the immortality of the soul, and entered into a correspondence
which continued through life and ultimately filled two volumes.
These two met and talked through the night because they were
exploring the same caverns, not because they had come out into
the same sunlight. When it appeared finally that Carlyle preferred
to remain a struggler in the darkness, the sympathy waned, and
Emerson emerged alone into the affirmation of his middle years.

That affirmation was most intense during the ten years between his return and the *Essays, Second Series* in 1844. In that short time he delivered from carefully prepared manuscripts over seventy-five lectures, most of them in series of ten or twelve at the Masonic Temple in Boston; a dozen occasional addresses, and many sermons. His letters to Carlyle whom he met only at wide intervals of years, to Sterling whom he never saw, and to nearer friends like Margaret Fuller, Caroline Sturgis, Samuel Gray Ward, and Henry Thoreau, were platonic essays in friendship. The pages of his journal were filled regularly and fully, and poems were wrought with care at frequent intervals. Yet only *Nature* and the *Essays* from this mountain of manuscripts were prepared for the press at the time. This was to be his capital upon which he could draw with interest for the rest of his life. A few poems and essays found print in the *Dial,* the *Western Messenger,* the *Massachusetts Quarterly,* and later the *Atlantic,* and there only to help his friends and the cause of enlightenment which they shared with him, not because he wished to publish. He had found his new profession. His was to be the living message, the spoken voice. The town hall was his new church, the Society for the Diffusion of Useful Knowledge his sect.

With this rededication he discovered a new way of life. Within three years after his return from Europe all his major decisions had been made, his life put in order. In the winter of 1833–34 he began his lectures; that summer he made Concord his home; the next year he married Lydia Jackson of Plymouth, bought the Old Coolidge house on the Cambridge Turnpike—regrettably in a meadow rather than on a hill—and delivered to his townsfolk an "Historical Discourse" on the occasion of their second centennial. In 1836 he published *Nature* and his son Waldo was born. He had home, wife, family, career, friends, and associates. "The lonely wayfaring man," as Carlyle was later to call him, was once more a citizen of this world.

But the spirit of revolt did not die in him so abruptly as these facts might suggest. He had dispersed the morbid clouds of introspection and uncertainty. He had chosen his point of issue with his age. He knew what he must accept as well as what he must reject. He was ready to speak and to act. There are two phases of romanticism, that of doubt and seeking, that of revolt in equilibrium.

Emerson had reached the second phase by 1834, and his productive tension showed no sign of breaking for at least ten years.

The immediate release of that tension was *Nature*; the key to its understanding is what he called "the First Philosophy." "I endeavor to announce the laws of the First Philosophy," he wrote in June, 1835. "It is the mark of these that their enunciation awakens the feeling of the moral sublime, and great men are they who believe in them. Every one of these propositions resembles a a great circle in astronomy. No matter in what direction it be drawn, it contains the whole sphere. So each of these seems to imply all truth."

The source of this cornerstone of his reconstructed philosophy may have been, as he himself implied in *English Traits*, his discovery that "Bacon, capable of ideas, yet devoted to ends, required in his map of the mind, first of all, universality, or *prima philosophia*." But it is likely that his inheritance of Christian mysticism then drew him to sympathy with the Quakers, the Swedenborgians, and the Methodists, tempered and extended by his early absorption of Neo-Platonism and Oriental insight.

In announcing these laws, Emerson, who rejected all established doctrine, formulated a new doctrine composed of assumptions which experience had taught him were vital. With logic he could have nothing to do, declaring that "a foolish consistency is the hobgoblin of little minds." As has been pointed out, his propositions constituted for him, as it were, the persons in a drama of the mind, not the steps in an argument or system; they have also been likened to equations. They are based on the definitions of a few key words used by Cousin, Coleridge, Sampson Reed the Swedenborgian, and Thomas Taylor the Neo-Platonist, which these writers derived in turn from German metaphysics, Scottish rationalism, and the literature of romanticism in general. The similarity of Emerson's thought to that of Kant, Hegel, Schleiermacher, and Schelling is deceptive; such influences usually came to him at one or more removes. His attitude toward his assumptions had the quality if not the rigidity of the dogmatism he had rejected. He had discovered a way of setting down his victorious answers in impregnable propositions, in laws which describe relationships rather than essences. They are the stuff of ethics and faith rather than of methaphysics, theology, or logic.

Nature (1836) is the gospel of the new faith rather than, like Thoreau's *Walden,* a record of an experience of earth. Lifted by the excitement of recognition to the plane of prose-poetry, it is nevertheless a concise statement of the "First Philosophy." The primary assumption of this essay is that man, whether regarded individually or generically, is the starting point of all philosophic speculation. His functions, his relations, and his destiny are its only concerns. The self-reliance which results from this assumption is essential to vital experience. Whatever truth lies beyond or outside man can be reached only through him and by him.

Emerson opens his essay with the current distinction between the Me and the Not Me, the Soul and Nature, thereby establishing the first of his provisional dualities. The Me is conciousness, or that part of man which partakes of divinity, the Not Me is the objective of consciousness, that with which the Me is in relation. But Nature, or the Not Me, also partakes of divinity in that "outward circumstance is a dream and a shade"; its reality lies in its being "a projection of God in the unconscious." A second duality is thus established between Nature and God; and a third, between God and Man. Here is a triangle of relationships, the value of which lies not in the absolute identity of Man, God, or Nature, but in the common relationship between any of the factors. Man may learn to worship God through the contemplation of Nature. The stars, the flowers, the animals, the mountains reflect the wisdom of his best hour, first as that which is outside of his consciousness, then as that which shares with his consciousness a "vision of original and eternal beauty," an awareness of a divine principle.

The ability to view experience in this twofold manner is the essential quality of the First Philosophy. Emerson's position, insofar as it approaches the statement of final verities, is monistic; his method invariably dualistic. He declares in the opening paragraphs of his essay that he will use the word "Nature" in two senses: the common sense in which it refers to essences unchanged by man, and the ideal sense in which it is the phenomenal expression of the soul. The possible ambiguity "is not material; no confusion of thought will occur." It is necessary to set up a provisional dualism in order to explore the ultimate unity. This method, established in the opening paragraphs of his first published book, is implicit or stated again in every word that Emerson ever wrote. As he is wholly concerned with the process of thinking rather than with the objects of thought, his position is often declared to be dualistic; it is so only in its method, but its method is very nearly all there is to it.

From Sampson Reed, and later from Swedenborg himself, Emerson borrowed the doctrine of correspondence between the natural and moral laws to validate this primary assumption. "The spiritual part of man is as really a substance as the material; and is as capable of acting upon spirit, as matter is upon matter." In each sphere there is a law the study of which may be reduced to a science; but the law in the one sphere exactly corresponds at every point with that in the other. Thus natural and moral laws are distinguishable from each other but are actually correspondent at every point. "Matter," concludes Emerson, "is a phenomenon, not a substance." "There is a law for man and a [parallel] law for things." This assumption that the one law may be treated in practice as two allowed him complete and open-minded acceptance of the progress of physical science without fear that its findings would invalidate religion. With one stroke he swept away the major controversy of the age by linking it to the persistent Christian synthesis of faith and works.

Emerson came to describe the faculty whereby man might explore the realm of the spirit as "the moral sentiment," and most of his value judgments on men and experience depend ultimately upon the presence or absence of this faculty. It is the capacity of human nature to discover the moral law by means of intuition. In *Nature* and his early essays he more commonly calls it the "Reason" as distinguished from the "Understanding," another instance of his habit of dividing in order to conquer—this time probably borowing from Coleridge, who had stated in his *Aids to Reflection*: "Reason is the Power of Universal and necessary Convictions, the Source and Substance of Truths above Sense, and having their evidence in themselves. . . . The Judgments of the Understanding are binding only in relation to the objects of our Senses, which we *reflect* under the forms of the Understanding." "Heaven," echoes Emerson from the *Aids to Reflection,* "is the name we give to the True State, the world of Reason, not of the Understanding; of the Real, not the Apparent." He uses these two terms specifically in this sense throughout his writing as he similarly makes distinctions on two planes between Imagination and Fancy, Talent and Genius, in common with English romantic philosophers. He thus again clearly distinguishes between the lower and the higher faculties of the mind: Understanding, Fancy, and Talent are means of dealing with immediate experience, but each has a nobler counterpart in Reason, Imagination, and Genius by which man may climb from the plane of the natural to that of moral law.

From these two assumptions, the centrality of man in his own universe of experience and the exact correspondence between the planes of material and spiritual law, Emerson developed the other principles which constituted his working philosophy. From them he derived his law of compensation or balance of conflicting forces in experience, his theory of good and evil, and his beliefs in the inevitable vocation of each man, in the idea of progress, in unimpassioned love among men, and in the Over-Soul. From the same source he developed his characteristic method for lecture and essay, starting in most cases on the level of common or material experience and rising to that of spiritual realization. From them too he derived his theory of art and poetry as an intricate system of symbols or "language" expressing through human agency an organic moral harmony.

Here was a new covenant of the spirit, built upon the foundation of Puritanism, tested by the rigors of American experience, and shaped by the architecture of romantic theory and the democratic ideal. All materials available were carefully studied and built into the structure if they could prove of use; from the past, the wisdom of Plato and his followers, the inductive method of Bacon and Montaigne, and the mysticism of Oriental religion and poetry; from the future, the naturalism of science and the rampant materialism of a growing industrial nation. The result was a tentative organization of opposing forces into a dynamic harmony rather than a static unity, a philosophy of growth and change rather than one of certainty and system. In a single essay Emerson made himself the apologist of a people because he had discovered a formula in which temperamental contradictions were reconciled if not logically resolved. The theological mystic Jonathan Edwards could speak through him across the centuries to the political idealist Woodrow Wilson; Benjamin Franklin could send through him to William James the message that pragmatism was merely "a new name for some old ways of thinking"; and the American habit of testing truth simultaneously by intuition and by action could seem to be merely a rounding out of experience, not a division of personality.

Even though *Nature* was Emerson's first formulation of his position, it was only a beginning. In spite of its organization into topics proceeding on an ascending scale from Commodity through Beauty, Language, and Discipline, to Idealism and Spirit, it asks rather than answers questions, it is a cry of astonishment at the possibilities of life rather than a record of achievement. There was much work to be done, and its author immediately set about the doing.

When Emerson stood before the Phi Beta Kappa Society at Harvard on August 31, 1837, to define the American Scholar, he was delivering an annual address on the conventional topic. Men far more prominent than he had spoken on the same subject from the same platform many times before. Current journals had for a quarter of a century been sprinkled with pleas for a national literature. There was nothing in the announced subject, the mood of the audience, or the appearance of the speaker to suggest an unusual occasion. Yet when the address was concluded Lowell declared it "an event without any former parallel in our literary annals," and Holmes pronounced it "our Intellectual Declaration of Independence." His hearers realized, as we today cannot, the depth and force of his revolt against his times.

In a series of occasional addresses between 1837 and 1844 he announced to his old associates—writers, scholars, clergymen, and men of thought in general—the revolution that had taken place in his conception of his own function and of theirs. The occasions were seized as offered, the Commencement of his old divinity school, convocations of the Dartmouth and Waterville college literary societies, meetings of library associations, or merely sponsored evening lectures at a public hall. In all of these he is eager, excited, defiant, but firm, clear, and relentless. He knew that he was issuing a challenge: "Amidst a planet peopled with conservatives, one Reformer may yet be born."

He anticipated, especially from the clergy, the violence of the inevitable response. He was speaking with deliberate intention to shock, but in carefully considered language. Each of his thrusts was strong and sure, aimed at the heart. To the scholar he said: "Translate, collate, distil all the systems, it steads you nothing; for truth will not be compelled in any mechanical manner." And again, "Man Thinking must not be subdued by his instruments. Books are for the scholar's idle times. When he can read God directly, the hour is too precious to be wasted in other men's transcripts of their readings." To the writer: "All literature is yet to be written. Poetry has scarce chanted its first song." To the student of divinity: "All men go in flocks to this saint or that poet, avoiding the God who seeth in secret. . . . Let me admonish you, first of all to go alone; to refuse the good models, even those which are sacred in the imagination of men, and dare to love God without mediator or veil," even Christ himself. And in discussing "The Times": "Our forefathers walked in the world and went to their graves tormented with the fear of Sin and the terror of the Day of Judgment. These terrors have lost their force, and our torment is Unbelief, the Uncertainty as to what we ought to do; the distrust of the value of what we do, and the distrust that the Necessity (which we all at last believe in) is fair and beneficent." The intention of all these overstatements was the same. They were designed to shock complacency into recognition that each dawn opens a new day. They did not deny the past; tradition must serve the present as one kind of experience rather than as authority. Emerson was challenging his audiences; not announcing measured and final truth.

For the present and the future he had high hope, granted that self-reliance could be restored and assured. "I speak of the politics, education, business, and religion around us without ceremony or false deference." The new literature must be neither Classic nor Romantic: "I embrace the common, I explore and sit at the feet of the familiar, the low. Give me insight into to-day, and you may have the antique and future worlds." This, he announced, is a Reflective or Philosophic age; its concern is with itself. He did not shrink from the abounding energy and the inexhaustible resources of his time and place. "Railroad iron is a magician's rod, in its power to evoke the sleeping energies of land and water." "It seems so easy for America to inspire and express the most expansive and humane spirit; new-born, free, healthful, strong, the

land of the laborer, of the democrat, of the philanthropist, of the
believer, of the saint, she should speak for the human race."

Emerson was not blind to the dangers in all his rampant energy.
He accepted an economy of abundance based, like that of Adam
Smith, on a moral law which allows self-interest full play. He believed in a natural aristocracy, in property, in immigration, in
trade, and competitive industry. A laissez-faire Yankee materialist
on the level of the senses, he relied on the moral sentiment to
transcend and resolve all conflicts. "The materialist takes his departure from the external world, . . . the idealist . . . from his
consciousness." The transcendentalist accepts both views; because
his dualism is a provisional state only, he can "take his departure" from the level of the senses in full confidence that, at the
same time, he is also operating from the level of the spirit. "He
believes in miracle, in the perpetual openness of the human mind
to new influx of light and power; he believes in inspiration, and
in ecstasy."

Ecstasy is not always apparent in Emerson's own life during
these ten years, nor in the many lectures which he delivered. A
substantial number of them still exist, however, in manuscript,
and most of them are listed or abstracted in the appendix to J. E.
Cabot's *Memoir*. Their uniform emphasis upon the moral law is
evident from the titles of the series: "Biography," "English Literature," "The Philosophy of History," "Human Culture," "Human Life," the "Present Age," "The Times," "New England."
With the journals, these lectures bear the relationship to the
Essays that an artist's sketch does to his finished painting. They
were written out with care, but their style has the rhythm of
speech, the loose phrase, the colloquial and often humorous turn.

The energy and eagerness, the security and peace which Emerson conveyed to his audiences had roots at home. His marriage
and family life were steady, rich, and rewarding. Lidian, as he
asked permission to call her because the *n* smoothed transition to
the new name, had the qualities of a Madonna rather than of a
St. Cecilia. In 1836, Waldo was born,

> Boy who made dear his father's home,
> In whose deep eyes
> Men read the welfare of the times to come—

bringing completion during his five years of life and a sorrow when he died more calm than at the deaths of Ellen Tucker and Charles. Emerson gave to his two daughters the names Edith and Ellen; to his second son, Edward. "In the dwelling-house," wrote the father, "must the true character and hope of the time be consulted," for there a man may "stand on his feet."

The town of Concord was a larger home and the circle of friends that gathered in the Emerson drawing room was but an extended family. Near-by towns had succumbed to industry, but the Musketaquid was still navigable only to canoes, and:

> Bulkeley, Hunt, Willard, Hosmer, Meriam, Flint,
> Possessed the land which rendered to their toil
> Hay, corn, roots, hemp, flax, apples, wool and wood.

The Thoreaus, Hoars, and Ripleys were native citizens, but Alcott, Ellery Channing, and Hawthorne were later comers; Margaret Fuller, Elizabeth Peabody, the mystic Jones Very, and many others of the transcendental set were never more than visitors. The Social Circle which met frequently at the Emerson home on Tuesday evenings consisted of "twenty-five of our citizens: doctor, lawyer, farmer, trader, miller, mechanic; solidest men, who yield the solidest gossip."

A very different group had formed the habit of gathering at one another's houses for an afternoon of serious conversation, whether in Boston or Concord, and so the "Transcendental Club" came into being without deliberate intention or constitution. It was, as one facetious member remarked, "like going to heaven in a swing," and Emerson himself at times mocked their earnest aspirations. "Perhaps they only agreed in having fallen upon Coleridge and Wordsworth and Goethe, then on Carlyle, with pleasure and sympathy. Otherwise, their education and reading were not marked, but had the American superficialness, and their studies were solitary," like his own. Bronson Alcott, the Orphic philosopher, existed in an ethereal sphere which he shared with Plato; Thoreau came fresh from the woods and fields; Emerson from his study; Parker, "our Savonarola," and Brownson from their churches, the one a Unitarian, the other inclining toward Rome. Margaret Fuller and occasionally Hawthorne's sister-in-law Elizabeth Peabody shot bolts of aggressive femininity into the company with their radical notion that women are people, seeking friendship on a plane transcending sex.

One such friendship, violent on Margaret's part, acquiescent but at times disturbing on Emerson's, produced "the modest quarterly journal called *The Dial*," organ of the movement for four years. George Ripley, inspired by Owen and Fourier, attempted the most famous of all communistic experiments at Brook Farm, even though the stars of the movement took only a casual part, preferring to shine each in his own sphere. A third practical—if we may stretch the word—result was the Concord School of Philosophy, founded in 1879 by Alcott in his own back yard, a highly successful pioneer of the American summer session. For at least a quarter of a century, the idyllic town was the intellectual seed pod of the nation.

In so stimulating an atmosphere, largely of his own making, Emerson expanded and matured, producing the *Essays, First and Second Series* in 1841 and 1844. These in a very real sense were new works, dependent no more on the lectures he had delivered than on the pages of the *Journals,* for he drew from both sources, running a pencil line across the chosen passage, lifting it from the page, and remolding it to its new purpose. Lectures in form and spirit still, they are written for a larger audience than any that ever could be assembled in one place. Though they retain their quality of voice, they are not meant to be spoken. In every line and every paragraph they bear the evidence of loving workmanship.

The new form which Emerson developed is neither wholly essay nor wholly lecture. Its unit is the carefully wrought sentence, "pure, genuine Saxon"; as Carlyle immediately recognized, "strong and simple; of a clearness, of a beauty." Each contains in crystalline suspension the whole meaning of the essay, of the book, an art learned perhaps in part from the gnomic sentence of Bacon or the *pensées* of Pascal, as simple and direct as the familiar style of Montaigne. "Nature will not have us fret and fume." "All things are double, one against another." "Life only avails, not the having lived." Sometimes they are but a single image: "Life is a train of moods like a string of beads, and as we pass through them they prove to be many-colored lenses which paint the world their own hue, and each shows only what lies in its focus." Longer sentences are broken and rugged, retaining their staccato quality: "The death of a friend, wife, brother, lover, which seems nothing but privation, somewhat later assumes the aspect of a guide or genius; for it commonly operates revolutions in our way of life, terminates an epoch of infancy or of youth which was waiting to be closed, breaks up a wonted occupation, or a household, or style of living, and allows the formation of new ones more friendly to the growth of character."

Carlyle sought coherence in the paragraph and found rather "a beautiful square *bag of duck-shot* held together by canvas." Even less closely are the paragraphs knit to their foregoers and followers, the essays to one another to make a book. But it would be a mistake to conclude that form is lacking. Each paragraph, each essay, has the structure of the circle containing smaller circles within it and itself contained in larger circles. "The eye is the first circle," wrote Emerson in the shortest of his essays; "the horizon which it forms is the second; and throughout nature this primary figure is repeated without end." His method is organic, a reflection of the structure of the universe as he sees it.

But if the movement of logical sequence is lacking, that of direct communication to faculties beyond the reason is not. The units of his style are built upon one another into a rising structure of thought and feeling. Always there is the sense of a man speaking to his audience, catching their attention, focusing it on a central meaning, expanding it to furthest limits of experience, raising it to highest levels of recognition, bringing it back to the center. Each essay opens with a challenge, either by quiet reference to ordinary experience or by sudden shock of overstatement. With text thus supplied, homiletic rather than logical principles elaborate, illustrate, and slowly unfold the theme as writer and reader are borne onward together. In most of the essays, there is a sense of rising intensity in both meaning and form, which suggests Emerson's own images of the spiral, the ladder, the swift flight upward. The conclusion brings a quiet sense of completion, of exhausted possibilities, of whole vision which has the dramatic finality of the curtain of a play.

A similar sense of structure is not discernible in the arrangement of the essays in the two companion volumes, although the first series has more coherence than the second. The wholeness of

Emerson's thought is such that, touched at any point, it immediately embraces experience. The differences between the essays lie in their varying points of emphasis; each includes all. Their unity lies in the "First Philosophy" expressed, not in its expression.

The points of departure are roughly of three kinds: description of the universe and its laws (Self-Reliance, Compensation, Spiritual Laws, the Over-Soul, Circles, Experience, Nature, and Nominalist and Realist); analysis of the moral faculties in human relationships in general (Love, Friendship, Prudence, Heroism, Character, and Manners); and studies of more nearly particular problems of experience (History, Art, The Poet, Politics, and New England Reformers). But even such broad categories soon break down as the elaboration of the primary point of any one essay includes those of all others.

The resulting unity of approach to living is the key to Emerson's hold on his own and later generations. Henry Adams called it "naïf," and others have put it away with childish things. His disregard rather than denial of evil, his lack of logical system, his staccato crispness of style, his didacticism, his appearance of being above torment and suffering, have provided blockages for many. But his morning quality of recognition and confidence, his power of distilling essences that all know to be true, his gift of innumerable texts for the problems of living and thinking, his accurate reflection of the American mind and heart in its moments of aspiration, have made these essays a book in our modern bible. "It is not yet art," wrote the sophisticated Comtesse d'Agoult when she discovered them for her people, but "the mingling heretofore unknown, of the protestant spirit of individualism, or self-reliance, with the pantheistic spirit which inspires this book, the combination and harmonizing of these two antagonisms in a superior intellect forms, incontestably, a new element from whence may be born an original art." For a moment the tensions and contradictions of American experience were held in vital suspension and, in Emerson, found their first clear and authoritative voice.

I V

The "new art" of Emerson is contained in five volumes—all, except some of the poems, written within the decade 1844–54, none published immediately. They are *Poems* (1847), *Representative Men* (1850), *English Traits* (1856), *The Conduct of Life* (1860), and *May-Day* (1867). That in this period he passed from a state of romantic tension to one of "classic" or organic restraint more suitable to the New England disposition is attested by his own statement in a lecture on "Art and Criticism" delivered in 1859:

"The art of writing is the highest of those permitted to man as drawing directly from the Soul, and the means or material it uses are also of the Soul. . . . Classic art is the art of necessity; organic; modern or romantic bears the stamp of caprice or chance." Even though he retained the doctrinal foundations of his thought in historical romanticism, Emerson developed his arts of poem and lecture-essay in this, his own, definition of the classic, by admitting the need for moral restraint in art.

His poetry was written in his own study, the product of walks in the Concord fields or to his "garden," the wood lot on Walden Pond which he allowed Thoreau to use for his cabin. The prose was a reworking of lectures delivered in England (1847–48) and in the "West" from Pittsburgh to Cincinnati, to St. Louis and Chicago (1850–53). During these years he was away almost as much as he was at home, and Lidian made out as best she could, caring for the children and the big white house, aided by the townsfolk and by Henry Thoreau, the master's delegate in residence to tend the fires and the garden.

Had he never written a word of prose, Emerson's achievement as an experimental and epigrammatic poet would give him a primary place in our literature. In his youth he was the admitted poet of the family, but even he refrained from taking his nonsense and imitative verses too seriously. When the time came to woo Lydia Jackson, not only to himself but to Concord, he had attained to better perspective. "I am a born poet," he wrote, "of a low class without doubt yet a poet . . . in the sense of a perceiver and dear lover of the harmonies that are in the soul and in matter, and specially of the correspondence between these and those"; but he was "uncertain always whether I have one true spark of that fire which burns in verse."

A born poet he most assuredly was, in theory as well as fact. Before the publication of his *Poems* in 1847, the United States had

had but one true student and experimenter in the art, Edgar Allan Poe. Bryant, Halleck, and Freneau either had shown no deep interest in the theory and technique of poetry or had conformed to the romantic modes of Wordsworth and Byron, and to the traditions of the English lyric. The early verse of Whittier, Simms, Longfellow, Lowell, and Holmes had accepted similar models without fresh exploration of anything but the American scene. Poe alone had sought to rediscover the nature and function of poetry in itself. Emerson's originality is as profound as that of Poe, and the theories of the two supplement each other. Poe sought an aesthetic base for the art; Emerson, a moral. Poe explored mainly the possibilities of rhythm; Emerson, of symbol. Together they directed the course of American poetry since their time by turning from borrowed conventions and by seeking once more the springs of poetry. Walt Whitman and Emily Dickinson were further to exploit these breaks with the past; others would follow.

Part of Emerson's sense of inadequacy was caused by his high ideals for the poet. He is the seer, but he is more. He is also "the sayer, the namer, and represents beauty. He is sovereign and stands on the center. . . . He is a beholder of ideas and an utterer of the necessary and causal." His office is that "of announcement and affirming." He does not make his poem, "for poetry was all written before time was. . . . The men of more delicate ear write down these cadences." By characteristic overstatement, Emerson would thus make the role of the poet seem almost passive. He is an Aeolian harp that "trembles to the cosmic breath" (a favorite image). But he is also Merlin, the traditional bard, the wise man, the magician, whose "blows are strokes of fate." In the distribution of functions among men, he is the man speaking, the scholar who has an assigned course of action—to express the message he receives. By this test Plato at times seems almost to qualify as poet, and Sir Thomas Browne, Zoroaster, Michelangelo, and the authors of the Vedas, the Eddas, the Koran. George Herbert stands the test and Milton, next to Shakespeare the prince of poets because of his genius "to ascend by the aids of his learning and his religion— by an equal perception, that is, of the past and the future—to a higher insight and more lively delineation of the heroic life of man." And the Persian Saadi becomes for Emerson the prototype of the poet because

He felt the flame, the fanning wings,
Nor offered words till they were things.

Herein lies the insight which caused his spontaneous acceptance of *Leaves of Grass* in 1855. Whitman's words were things.

If the recording of celestial music had been to Emerson the only function of the poet, his verse might have been more melodic than it is. Rather in his prose, especially when it was prepared to be spoken, he came closest to achieving rhythmic freedom, as did Melville, whose philosopher in *Mardi* chants only when he is seized with the frenzy of prophetic vision. Before it was pruned and sharpened by gnomic insight, Emerson's style might flow with the current of his eloquence and climb by the measured but open periods of the Song of Solomon, the Sermon on the Mount, or Whitman's sweeping rhythms. In an unpublished passage from the introductory lecture to the early course on "Human Culture," he used the techniques which Whitman was later to exploit. Freed from the paragraph of prose as well as the meter of verse, his periodic lines are held to a frame by parallel phrasing, assonance, alliteration, and return:

The philosopher laments the inaction of the higher faculties.
He laments to see men poor who are able to labor.
He laments to see men blind to a beauty that is beaming on every side of them.
He laments to see men offending against laws and paying the penalty, and calling it a visitation of Providence. . . .
He laments the foreign holdings of every man, his dependence for his faith, for his political and religious estimates and opinions, on other men, and on former times.
And from all these oppressions is a wise Culture to redeem the Soul.

But Emerson asked more than this of the poet. The active function of poetry, as he saw it, was to make manifest and specific the correspondence between the real and the ideal, a task which rhythm alone could not accomplish. From the English metaphysical poets in prose and verse, Herbert, Donne, Milton, Browne, he learned the connotative value of the individual word, the possibilities for luster and surprise in the image. He turned to them rather than to the contemporary romantics who had acquiesced too easily in a passive pantheism. Milton and Herbert rather than

Wordsworth and Coleridge felt God intensely and struggled to restore him to this world. These elder poets had striven, as did Emerson, to reconcile an intense religious faith with an equally intense
challenge of science, and his method was theirs. In this, he stood
alone in his times among British and American poets, for not even
Matthew Arnold appreciated the full worth of the symbol, however much he struggled with the "two worlds" between which he
stood. The mystic and the scientist must become one, and the
symbol is the only means for the accomplishment of the union.
This Emerson fully appreciated, and it is his gift to modern
poetry. From Bacon he took the Aristotelian view that "poetry,
not finding the actual world exactly conformed to its idea of good
and fair, seeks to accommodate the show of things to the desires
of the mind, and to create an ideal world better than the world of
experience." To this he added the Swedenborgian view that nature must serve man for symbols, that by seeing through the phe-
monenon to the essence, the poet might transform the evidence of
his senses to a higher use and reestablish the correspondence between the natural and the moral laws. "The act of imagination is
ever attended by pure light. It infuses a certain volatility and in-
toxication into all Nature." The poet is "an exact reporter of the
essential law," but he is active rather than passive because he re-
stores the harmonies of the Over-Soul through the counterpoint
of experience; he supplies from his intuition the true, rather than
the apparent, natural image. "The mind, penetrated with its sentiment or its thought, projects it outward on whatever it beholds."
The result is a beauty not of the senses but of the moral
sentiment.

The critic should not be misled by Emerson's frequent references to poetry as music, for his own verse rarely sings. "That
which others hear," he confessed, "I see." Even in his poem on
"Music," the images are almost all visual, and "Merlin's Song" is
"of keenest eye" before it is of "truest tongue." His dissonant
rhymes and limping rhythms are parts of a deliberate effort to
achieve freedom of movement, and they receive at least some authority from their models. Butler used "slanted" or imperfect
rhymes, Milton incomplete lines, and Shakespeare, in his later
plays, a roving accent. Emerson asked for all these freedoms together. He made excessive use of rhyme, because to him it was the

favorite instrument of rhythm in Nature (although again his examples are visual: reflections in a pond or the repeating forms of shadows). He also adopted the eight-syllable line because he was convinced by the theory of O. W. Holmes that periodicity in poetry is determined by human respiration. He never broke loose in his poetry as did Whitman, into the more natural freedom of colloquial speech. But within his limits, all of which he believed are imposed by Nature rather than tradition, he trusted the song as he heard it, even though his hearing was not always true. His rhymes are often little more than assonances; his meter, counted syllables that sometimes miss the count, letting the accent fall where it may.

With the visual image, Emerson's muse can safely be trusted. In his "Mottoes"—verses distilled to provide texts for his essays—he committed Wordsworth's fault of trying to deal too directly with thought. But where the image is given full play, as in "The Sphinx" (his own favorite), "Days" (perhaps his most successful), "Hamatreya" (his most direct), "Uriel," "Brahma," "The Snow-Storm" and the first part of "Merlin," it achieves an intricate pattern of conceit worthy of Herbert or Donne, but fresh from his own experience. Here the poet exerted his full prerogatives with volatile nature, using the evidences of the pines, the sea, the stars to its own purposes and revealing the correspondence of the law of things to the law of God. In other poems like "Woodnotes," "Threnody," and his odes, he achieves sureness and freedom in some passages, but falls into rhymed prose in others; and sometimes, as in "The Rhodora," the message is too explicit, the effect didactic.

At his best, Emerson's keen sensitivity to the larger aspects of nature, his mastery and daring with the visual image, his deep appreciation of the connotative value of single words (a gift not shared even by Poe and not approached by any other contemporary except Emily Dickinson who followed his course in both theory and technique), place him among the most original and provocative if not the most even poets in the language. Add to these qualities the intrinsic value of what he has to say, and his poetry becomes one of the treasures of our literature, greater in some respects than his essays because, when he allows himself full scope, he speaks from and for himself a universal language, without reference to a particular audience even by inference. His art is organic in that it reproduces the organism of moral law as reflected in nature; it is classic, as he would have it, only when his daring experiments achieve unity and, as in "Days," his intricate and climbing images merge into a single symbol of revelation.

The same quality is achieved in the prose of his maturity, *Representative Men, English Traits,* and *The Conduct of Life.* Derived from specific lecture courses, each has a distinguishable central theme upon which the parts play variations: the uses of great men; the values in modern civilization; the principles of individual action. The wise Emerson now speaks in his own church, of his own people, and to his own people. He is on sure ground, no longer defiant; the fight has been won, and he knows that he is heard.

His themes are not new. Back in 1835, in his first lecture series, he had spoken on "Biography" and examined the tests of a great man: Has he an aim to which he gives his whole soul? Is it broad and unselfish? Is it based solidly on fact? Does it set in motion the minds of others? Has it divine sanction? Two of these lectures, "Michael Angelo" and "Milton," were published in the *North American Review* and have come down to us virtually intact. The other three, "Luther," "George Fox," and "Burke," together with the introductory lecture, are unpublished or absorbed into other writings. The design for the series was his own, perhaps suggested in part by Plutarch's *Lives,* where a man's actions and distinctions are judged for their moral values; strengthened by Carlyle's *Heroes and Hero Worship,* which he welcomed in 1841—"a good book, and goes to make men brave and happy," because, from these cases, it describes and evaluates a whole system of conduct. But Carlyle's confusion of worldly with moral power was beginning to show through his transcendental intensity. On this point Emerson was clear. He did not test men for their control of others. "He is great who is what he is from nature, and who never reminds us of others." "Men are also representative; first, of things, and secondly of ideas." In contrast to Carlyle's, his criteria were the measures of democracy: self-reliance, the moral sentiment, experience, intuition.

For *Representative Men,* Emerson chose his cases carefully, each to represent a way of thinking and acting: Plato, the philosopher;

Swedenborg, the mystic; Montaigne, the skeptic; Shakespeare, the poet; Napoleon, the man of the world; Goethe, the writer. All of these ways he had to some degree tried. They were tests for himself and for his hearers rather than essays in criticism. He was asking: By what measures may a man judge his own ambition? He was answering: By these I have judged my own. Only as they guide you and me in our private and single lives by their examples are great men of use.

The first four, "Plato," "Swedenborg," "Montaigne," and "Shakespeare," were written from the heart. These men had given Emerson personal aid as he emerged from the doubts and uncertainties of youth into the calm confidence of his later years. Each he had finally found lacking, incomplete for his purposes, because there is no such thing as a wholly great man. No man but one has succeeded in resolving the dualities of the law of things into the unity of the moral law, has finally identified faith and works. And Emerson did not choose to write directly of Christ, who had succeeded in fact; or of himself, who had striven in theory. But the book begins and ends, by implication, with these two. For Napoleon and Goethe he has less perfect sympathies. They were added to complete the list, for he must include at least one man who did not write, and one whose greatness depended almost wholly on the fact that he did. Carlyle had used Napoleon as the symbol of worldly power, the hero in action; Emerson through him analyzed the values in "experience" and, by revealing the dangers inherent in democracy, made one of his finest statements of the democratic faith.

In each lecture the same series of questions is asked: What is this man? What did he make of his life, and why? Are his values sound? The final test in each case is the moral sentiment, the ability to rise from the many to the one. Unlike essays on more abstract topics, these do not themselves rise except in the questions asked. Each finally records a partial failure which brings the special case back to the central thesis. Except that the weaker essays are at the end, the book thus achieves a greater unity than did the earlier *Essays;* but the individual judgment is warped to the pattern. For true perspective on the misleading final paragraphs on Shakespeare, for example, one must turn to the fragmentary tercentenary address of 1864, where, without reservation,

Emerson declares that he is "the one resource of our life on which
no gloom gathers . . . the most robust and potent thinker that ever
was." In *Representative Men,* Shakespeare serves as a means for
discussion of values beyond his own; in the later address he is
confronted for himself. There is no confusion of moral with aesthetic values as some critics have affirmed.

This lecture series was delivered in Boston in 1845–46, but it
served Emerson as the chief item of his repertory while in England. On his return he prepared no single series on his impressions, but many of his lectures between 1849 and 1856 drew upon
his experience to illuminate his social views. *English Traits,* in the
latter year, was a book freshly written, but it drew ideas and paragraphs from both journals and lectures. At the same time he was
offering his series on the "Conduct of Life" particularly to audiences in the West, the first draft of the book on the same subject.

Emerson did not enjoy himself on these travels, but they were
enriching experiences both to him and his audiences. He was now
carrying wisdom to wisdom, not "ruins to ruins." He was known
for what he was and what he would say. In England he was guest
of honor at the Grand Soirée of the Manchester Athenaeum,
where he addressed several thousand people, among them such
notables as Cobden, Bright, Cruikshank, and Blackwood. A few
years later he faced in Cincinnati a "vast assembly, which sat for
two mortal hours . . . lecture hungry," in anticipation. He met
the great now on their own level: among them Dickens, Ten-
nyson, and Carlyle again. He heard Chopin play: "Could the
denying heaven have also given me ears for the occasion!" Between lectures, he traveled in the new steam trains or in ruder
conveyances, was entertained in unfamiliar homes, or sat in lonely
hotel rooms. He found Paris "a place of the largest liberty that I
suppose in the civilized world," and "the great sweeps of the
Mississippi . . . the loneliest river." In Europe, he studied people
and society; in the West, he bought maps and learned geography.
The demand for him was so great that he was forced to write new
lectures on the road. Seldom were his audiences large—nor was he
uniformly successful with them—but there were many, sometimes
two within twenty-four hours, and the returns from any one were
small. In one course in Chicago the "gate" for Bayard Taylor was
$252; for Emerson only $37—an extreme instance. In spite of the

industry and enthusiasm of Alexander Ireland who made the arrangements, the English trip apparently did not cover expenses; the American did somewhat better. But the real and enduring profit of these journeys lay in his two ripest and roundest books, *English Traits* and *The Conduct of Life*. If he had written nothing else, by these two he would deserve to be called our most representative man.

His report on British civilization was, like all the work of this later period, the fruit of years of study and speculation. For one of his early lecture series, he had chosen the topic "English Literature" and in preparation had read Warton's *History of English Poetry*. The English classics had always been favorites, but his first visit to England was a disappointment. Only when he returned in 1847 did the past become a living part of the present and the meaning of the British character become clear. "England is the best of actual nations," he wrote, "London is the epitome of our times." *English Traits* was the first record of an American's return to "Our Old Home" to achieve critical detachment without loss of sympathy; but it was also an analysis and judgment of the civilization of which America was as much a part as England. This book takes its place of fulfillment in our travel literature with ease and grace; but it marks in Emerson's own work the turn from a personal to a social perspective. In studying the English, he was concerned for the first time with the problem of man functioning en masse.

Set in the frame of his own journey, it opens with accounts of his first visit and of his voyage, and concludes with his trip to Stonehenge, his personal reception, and his speech at Manchester. The intervening chapters constitute an analysis of contemporary British civilization against a background of history. "If there be one test of national genius universally accepted," he writes, "it is success; and if there be one successful country in the universe for the last millennium, that country is England." His curiosity is piqued, and he seeks the answer in geography, ethnology, moral philosophy, economics, politics, education, religion, and literature. He finds it in a never-failing "reserve of power in the English temperament," a Saxon inheritance strong enough to absorb and use other racial strains, to profit by a favorable location, to rise above mistakes without denying them, and to exploit material resources without losing moral integrity. The mother of human liberty, England in her age is perennially young "with strength still equal to the time." She may pay absolute homage to material wealth, she may retain and develop her aristocracy, she may have her established church and her revered universities, she may cling to her traditions and rituals without great harm because she can laugh at her own mistakes and forever hold on to her "original predilection for private independence." As long as she can produce both steam engines and poets, she is sound and safe in spite of her faults.

Like Cooper and many another American traveler, Emerson returned to his own country with renewed respect for her potentialities, but sharp criticism of her crudities. The glamorous faith of his Boston lecture on "The Young American" (1844) was dulled by a keener critical sense when he began working on *The Conduct of Life* soon after his return. Not, like *English Traits,* an overt analysis of a specific civilization, this book was nevertheless his counsel to his own people in contrast to his earlier advices to men in general. He felt himself swept into the current of analysis of "the times." "By an odd coincidence," he began, "four or five noted men were each reading a discourse to the citizens of Boston or New York, on the Spirit of the Times," during the same winter. Carlyle had published *Past and Present* in 1843, and reform was in the air. "To me, however," he warned, "the question of the times resolved itself into a practical question of the conduct of life." The conflicts in prevailing ideas could only be resolved by reference to larger contexts than those of the here and now. Once more he must write a summary statement of the First Philosophy, but this time its generalizations were to be tempered by experience with the actual forces at work in contemporary society, the conduct of men at court and in the wilderness.

Now for the first time he planted his feet solidly on the ground and looked critically about him. His new task was to evaluate civilization in his day with the tools and criteria he had spent a lifetime in perfecting. No part of his earlier position, as defined in *Nature,* was denied, but no longer did he confuse what he saw of men and things with the perfection of which he believed life to be capable. The critical realism of this third period followed the balanced tensions of his earlier work with a more sharply defined duality of view: keener observation of the world as it is, on the one hand; firmer convictions of the unity of the ultimate moral principle, on the other. His conclusions and inconsistencies are now intellectual more than emotional. His equations have almost the certainty of the formula; his art is firm rather than fluid. To those who enjoy his work for its romantic fervor, this is a loss; to those who look for restraint and form, there is positive gain in firmness of texture.

The Conduct of Life marks the culmination of Emerson's work. He has become social critic as well as moral philosopher. He is willing to explore the pragmatic as well as the ideal test of conduct, and to evaluate men as well as man. Inconsistencies between the material and the ideal are the more glaring, and the ascent from the one plane to the other can no longer be made with the careless abandon of *Nature* and the *Essays;* but made it must be. A wiser and firmer spirit wrote these chapters on "Fate," "Power," "Worship," and "Beauty," because temptation, conflict, and suffering are recognized. The old optimism is not dimmed—we must still build our altars to the "Beautiful Unity" and the "Beautiful Necessity"; but the difficulties of the way are sympathetically explored before they are waved aside. "The young mortal enters the hall of the firmament. . . . On the instant, and incessantly, fall snow-storms of illusions. . . . And when, by and by, for an instant, the air clears and the cloud lifts a little, there are the gods still sitting around him on their thrones,—they alone with him alone."

V

The clouds of the Civil War were already gathering when the lectures on the conduct of life were being written; the War broke in the year the book appeared. It marked a fourth and last phase in Emerson's development, a time for retrospection. His literary powers had reached their meridian; during the last thirty years of life, they were slowly undermined by the distractions of the times, which led him into reluctant participation in public and national affairs, and later by increasing demands and weakening powers, which made for less care in composition.

Never up to the moment of his death in 1882 did he equal the achievement of *The Conduct of Life*. He gathered together one more collection of his essays, *Society and Solitude* (1870), but a second, *Letters and Social Aims* (1875), was too much for him after the shock of the burning of his home in 1872. His friend James Elliot Cabot took over the task and completed it under Emerson's wandering supervision. Cabot culled two more volumes from the stock pile of shuffled manuscripts, and Edward Emerson a third after their author's death. In bulk, these five volumes represent almost half of his published prose; but at best they are fragmentary, however studded they may be with brilliant passages.

Part of the difficulty lies in a new habit of workmanship rather than in declining power. In his early years, Emerson borrowed freely from his own previous writing; but he always copied and revised the borrowed passage, leaving the original manuscript intact. Later, when the demands upon him grew too heavy for this practice, he took to lifting pages bodily, with the result that few of his later manuscripts were whole when the editors set to work on them. No canon of his work during these years can therefore be established, except as Cabot has done it in the listing by title of his lecture series. The lectures themselves as he delivered them are lost.[1] The one collection that he himself prepared, *Society and Solitude,* is on a more familiar level than are his earlier essays, but it has much of the old charm and eloquence. Emerson had settled, after the war, more contentedly into the enjoyment of domestic life, farming, books, clubs, art, and old age, and he gathered together what he had said on these topics, as early as 1841, as late as 1862, to make a single book. "The central wisdom, which was old in infancy, is young in fourscore years, and, dropping off obstructions, leaves in happy subjects the mind purified and wise." This is what his mind would be; and this is what it had become.

In 1870, his lifelong wish to develop "a new method in metaphysics, proceeding by observation of the mental facts, without attempting an analysis and coordination of them" seemed gratified by an invitation to deliver a course of sixteen lectures to the students in philosophy at Harvard. But his mind was too tired to undertake so great a work as the reformation of his theory of the law for man and the law for things, and he drew upon old lecture courses for most of his material.

His *novum organum* remained unwritten at his death. The fragments of the course which survive were published under the title he had chosen for the whole, *The Natural History of the Intellect*. In them he attempts once more to harmonize the powers and laws of thought, instinct, inspiration, and memory with the findings of natural science. The ideas are not new, but the tone is cold and clear like the atmosphere of a late autumn afternoon. Three years before, he had written:

> As the bird trims her to the gale,
> I trim myself to the storm of time,
> I man the rudder, reef the sail,
> Obey the voice at eve obeyed at prime.

The distinction in experience between the moral and natural laws, and their ideal identity, remained the primary message of that voice. It had been a long struggle from youthful doubt to wise serenity, but faith in the "each and all" had not wavered. He had defined and revealed the eternal human verities in the conflicting demands of the new man in the new world.

NOTE

1. There is more order in the later lecture manuscripts than this statement would imply, and at least some of the series are nearly intact as they were written.

II

The Shapers

The Mind and Art of Nathaniel Hawthorne

In his note on the reprinting of this essay in his Norton "Critical Edition" of *The Scarlet Letter*, Sculley Bradley calls attention to the link between Hawthorne's "allegorical romance" and the "condensed psychological fiction of the present," which was here emphasized. The essay was published in *Outlook*, (CXLIX): 650-52, 676, 678, with the editor's note that it was "one of a series of re-valuations of great figures in America's literary past."

A SENSE OF UNFULFILLMENT, almost of failure, seems unavoidably associated with the name and work of Nathaniel Hawthorne. "I thought him a greater man than any of his works betray," wrote Emerson soon after his death, "that he might some day show a surer power. . . . Now it appears that I waited too long." And critics since Emerson have not hesitated to repeat this impression. Yet Hawthorne's position in that small company of pioneers who first brought distinction to the literature of America remains unquestioned. It might almost be said that, if originality of matter and form be one of the more important attributes of genius, his place is preeminent even in this limited circle.

There are a number of factors in Hawthorne's background, in his personality, and in his writings which give reason for this feeling that he failed in his destiny. He lived at a time when his nation was on the eve of its cultural majority. . . . A fringe of wilderness had been converted into a modest imitation of the European scene; the newly cleared ground was ready for cultivation. Men like Irving, Cooper, Longfellow, and Hawthorne cheerfully undertook the task. Lacking tradition, they imported it or they manufactured it from the limited past of their own memories. Lacking original forms, they experimented or imitated. Materials they had in abundance, but even here they sometimes borrowed.

I I

Hawthorne was an integral part of one of the oldest existing traditions in America, the Puritan; and at the same time he was the prophet of its decline. Whatever that tradition may signify in its entirety—and Kenneth B. Murdock's recent plea for an inclusive definition of the term is a timely admonition—Puritanism at its height was a religious conviction which resulted in stability of government, of economic conditions, and of individual conduct. Hawthorne lived at a time when the foundations of that stability were being undermined, when its dogmas and its practices were being questioned; and he pulled away some of the underpinning himself. He felt that his generation had built its house over an unquiet grave—that the very qualities of iron will and certain faith which his ancestors had believed to be virtues, were in reality vices, now living ghosts to torment their children's children. The sense of inherited sin, either that of commission or that attendant upon intolerance, is the keynote of the best of Hawthorne's writings.

But he was not content to view this decay of the New England past with an esthetic objectivity. Neither was he willing to accept the terms which the future laid before him. He viewed the coming age of industry with suspicion and alarm. The Celestial Railroad carries him to the very gates of Paradise, but he hears only the glad angelic welcome of the two poor pilgrims who had climbed by the way of Bunyan. The dream ends before we are told whether or not the last step, the crossing of the river by ferry, was as easy as the others on Mr. Smooth-it-away's improved railroad to Heaven. "The wheels, as they began their revolutions, threw a dash of spray over me so cold . . . that with a shiver and a heartquake I awoke." The chill of the future was as ominous as was that of the past.

A review of the facts of his life leaves a similar sense of unfulfillment. His early hermit-life in Salem, his unsuccessful efforts to take his part in the business and social spheres, and his final inability to enter into the spirit of the European scene, all reveal him as a solitary and a provincial. Such happiness as he found in human associations was concentrated upon his home life both before, but more particularly after, his marriage, and upon his small but intimate circle of friends. Lloyd Morris, in his recent biography of Hawthorne, has felt perhaps too keenly the pathos of a life so spent, and he has painted his portrait of the "Rebellious Puritan" in pastel shades, to the great indignation of Julian Hawthorne, who remembers vividly the wholesome comradeship which he enjoyed with his father. But there is nothing irreconcilable in these pictures. Hawthorne's lonely habits of thought were not the results of a shrinking or morbid temperament. "This claims to be called a haunted chamber," he wrote upon a late visit to his former hermitage (1840), "for thousands upon thousands of visions have appeared to me in it; and some few of them have become visible to the world."

The solitude of Hawthorne was the isolation of self-sufficiency. He is at his best when writing of the scenes of his own life dimmed and merged by long hours of meditation. His romance is of the introvert type. It seeks for strange places and strange times within the mind rather than in the far away. With Sophia and the children, or with Bridge, Ticknor, or even Melville, Hawthorne was friendly and at his ease. But his own descriptions of his experiences at Brook Farm and in the Salem Custom House show how limited was his horizon in these matters. "What, in the name of common sense, had I to do with any better society than I had always lived in?" exclaims Miles Coverdale in *The Blithedale Romance*. "It had satisfied me well enough. My pleasant bachelor-parlor, sunny and shadowy, curtained and carpeted, with the bed-chamber adjoining. . . . Was it better to hoe, to mow, to toil and moil amidst the accumulations of a barnyard; to be the chamber-maid of two yoke of oxen and a dozen cows?"

In the introduction to *The Scarlet Letter* this same bachelor-parlor is again described with fond affection as the proper place for the brewing of romantic concoctions, but, exclaims Hawthorne, "during the whole of my Custom House experience, moonlight and sunshine, and the glow of firelight, were just alike in my regard; and neither of them was of one whit more avail than the twinkle of a tallow candle."

In thus recognizing his need for the proper time and the congenial place for his work, Hawthorne admitted both its strength and its weakness. It was this very quality of dreamy introspection that gave to *The Scarlet Letter, The House of the Seven Gables,* and the best of his seventy-eight short stories their originality and their chief significance. The theme of *The Blithedale Romance* was almost too full-bodied to thrive in such white and moonlit regions; and *The Marble Faun* suffered from being planted in a foreign soil, however native its roots. Much as he professes to have acquired at Rome a home-feeling as nowhere else in the world, and to have retained, from reading the old English wisdom, his feeling for "our old home," Hawthorne was never successfully transplanted from his own study, with its center table and its windows looking out upon the grave New England scene.

I I I

When Hawthorne is considered, therefore, in terms of his background or of his personality, he is apparently hedged about by restrictions and inhibitions enough to make him theoretically incapable of vital and enduring literary work. His success must have been the direct result of concentration upon that small territory which was enclosed by these high barriers. A fair judgment of the work of any author must depend first upon an analysis of that author's aims and methods as he himself conceived them. Secondly, it must question both the validity of those professions and the author's degree of success in their application.

Few writers have so clearly and frequently defined their esthetic creed as has Hawthorne. He was a writer of romance and he strove, by means of romance, to illustrate moral beliefs. Nowhere does he profess an impartial interest in the complexity of a single human soul in all its aspects; nowhere does he attempt the accuracy of the historian, or even of the realist. . . .

"When a writer calls his work a Romance," he says in his preface to *The House of the Seven Gables,* "it need hardly be observed that he wishes to claim a certain latitude, both as to its fashion and material, which he would not have felt himself entitled to assume, had he professed to be writing a Novel." A romance owes fidelity only to "the truth of the human heart"; with particularized facts it need have nothing to do. The author may, with reasonable moderation, "so manage his atmospherical medium as to bring out or mellow the lights, and deepen and enrich the shadows of the picture." The "legendary mist," which the tale brings with it out of the past, aids in this process of blending details for the sake of a generalized truth or belief which Hawthorne finds hidden in its folds.

Similarly, *The Scarlet Letter,* with its scene laid in the familiar streets of its author's own village, requires dim light before it becomes romance. The finest scenes in the book occur in the shadowed depths of the forest or on the village street when the white moonlight reveals the minister standing in his lonely penitence upon the scaffold. Whether it be in his hermit cell, in the Old Manse, or in the Wayside, Hawthorne sees life truly, by his own definition, only when he has withdrawn from it. "From these quiet windows the figures of passing travelers looked too remote and dim to disturb the sense of privacy." The muddy Concord assumed in the sunset glow an ideal beauty which was more true than its own sluggish self. "We will not, then, malign our river as gross and impure while it can glorify itself with so adequate a picture of the heaven that broods above it." And, in *Our Old Home,* he affirms the same theory in no uncertain terms: "Sublime and beautiful facts are best understood when etherealized by distance"—or, he might have added, by any agency which generalizes and falsifies their immediate and confusing complexities.

Right or wrong, this is the creed of the romanticist as Hawthorne believed and strove to follow it. He never intentionally departs from it when he is writing fiction. Even the modern Arcadia of Blithedale failed to reveal a higher truth: "The clods of earth, which we so constantly belabored were definition within the limits of his self-restricted province; when he becomes never etherealized into thought. . . . Our labor symbolized nothing, and left us mentally sluggish in the dusk of the evening." The minister's black veil was in itself a greater truth than the features which it covered. Donatello's ears were better unrevealed; he was a fawn at heart and his ears might have proved after all to be

merely mortal. From the mind of the middle ages comes the belief
that above the truth of facts is a higher and purer truth, compre-
hensible only to the visionary and demonstrable only through
symbols. This Hawthorne believed and upon this belief he built
his art.

I V

Hawthorne was no mere moralist. "A high truth," he continues, "fairly, finely, and skillfully wrought out, brightening at
every step, and crowning the final development of a work of fiction, may add an artistic glory, but is never any truer, and seldom
any more evident, at the last page than at the first." In the distilled
atmosphere of such a truth the story has a life apart from the complexities of this world; yet at the same time it becomes a mere
illustration, a symbol. The ancestral footstep, the scarlet letter,
Alice's posies, Donatello's fountain, and many other symbols oc-
curring and recurring in Hawthorne's fiction point an accusing
finger at a sin, sometimes in itself entirely undefined, but a sin
never to be forgotten. Such thought is but an echo of old Michael
Wigglesworth's insistence upon the eternity of all of that human
action which involves moral good or moral evil.

"But allegory," says W. C. Brownell, "is art only when its
representation is as imaginatively real as its meaning. The mass of
allegory—allegory strictly devoted to exposition and dependent
upon exegesis, allegory explicitly so called—is only incidentally art
at all." Coleridge, on the other hand, attempted to make place
for such an aim within the limits of art by calling it fancy. "The
fancy," he says, "is indeed no other than a mode of memory
emancipated from the order of time and space; while it is blended
with, and modified by the word Choice." This is what Hawthorne
wished to accomplish by his work, and it is significant that Coleridge made his statement at about the time when the American
was writing his romances. Fashions have at least something to do
with our definitions of art.

"In the humblest event," wrote Hawthorne when he had settled
in his first real home after his marriage, "I resolved at least to
achieve a novel that should evolve some deep lesson and should
possess physical substance enough to stand alone." During those

three years in which, to Sophia, dreams became realities, to Hawthorne the reverse was the case. Realities—his life in Salem, the Custom House experience, his brooding upon his own ancestors and upon New England's past—formed themselves into dreams. His mind chose what it wished from the tangled web of his memory to spin a new and patterned fabric as fragile as memory itself. The novel which was to "possess physical substance enough to stand alone" was *The Scarlet Letter,* by the consensus of critical opinion his masterpiece.

The problem of whether the greatness of this book was accidental should furnish the key to Hawthorne's significance as a writer of romance. Did Hawthorne, in spite of his professions to the contrary, write, as Brownell believes, a story "so exclusively a drama of the soul as to be measurably independent of an elaborate setting in a social picture," or do we find in it the expression of its author's obsessing moral vision translated into an allegorical painting of the long-past New England landscape? Herbert Gorman, in his recent study of Hawthorne, calls this book "the completest epitome of Hawthorne's genius," in spite of Hawthorne's own insistence that *The House of the Seven Gables* "is more characteristic of the author, and a more natural book for me to write, than *The Scarlet Letter*—and not only more characteristic, but better as well." Gorman's further statement that the latter novel "is a moving series of symbols within a larger symbol from beginning to end" brings his criticism back to Hawthorne's own terms. But in *The Scarlet Letter* the moral truth is distilled from the particularized lives of the three individuals, whereas in *The House of the Seven Gables* it derives from a generalized sense of the past. Old Hepzibah and young Phoebe alike maintain their own lives, as did Feathertop, by deep breaths of mystic influence, in the one case of past deeds and thoughts, in the other of smoke from Mother Rigby's pipe. A review of Hawthorne's tales and sketches, the forms in which he did by far the greater part of his better work, will demonstrate that the method of *The Scarlet Letter* was the exception, that of *The House of the Seven Gables* the rule. The unity of the latter work depends neither upon plot consistency nor upon character revelation. The sin motif is introduced in the bass strings, and is sustained and tossed about by various voices, forming, over all, a tone poem of rich harmony and graceful dignity. The story is the best of Hawthorne in his most characteristic phase. It is not surprising that he felt it to a more natural book for him to write than that in which he pointed the way to the condensed psychological fiction of the present.

Little has been said except incidentally of the many other volumes of Hawthorne's work. His four great romances, *The Scarlet Letter, The House of the Seven Gables, The Blithedale Romance,* and *The Marble Faun,* were framed by experiments in the same allegorical method: *Fanshawe* in his youth and those four abortive efforts to blend the themes of the ancestral footstep and the elixir of life with which his literary career was brought to a close. Upon his four major romances, however, supported by the many tales and sketches, which are often more apt and more perfect than the longer stories, Hawthorne's ultimate literary fame must rest. His tales for children, excellent in themselves, require no extensive comment, and his endless notebooks, as well as *Our Old Home,* although lighted by occasional glowing passages, are useful chiefly as comprehensive sources for the study of the man and his work.

"Amid the seeming confusion of our mysterious world," he once wrote, "individuals are so nicely adjusted to a system, and systems to one another and to a whole, that, by stepping aside for a moment, a man exposes himself to a fearful risk of losing his place forever." Hawthorne took that risk and suffered that result. In a worldly sense his career was thwarted by his obstinate detachment, and his work began to decline at the moment when it seemed to be taking its first steps toward higher levels. If he became realist occasionally, the attainment was incidental. The truth of *The Scarlet Letter,* for its author at least, lay not so much in Hester's suffering as in the mystic significance of a letter suddenly wrought in fire against dark clouds.

What, then, is the ultimate significance of Hawthorne's work and what is its relative importance to American literature? His own answer to these questions was that, in *The House of the Seven Gables,* he gave form and voice to the spirit of moral truth which dominated his life. Without preaching, he expressed in art what he believed to be the truth of life. In this book he was most faithful to his own esthetic creed, and a generous measure of success in these terms was his. In none of his other works is his purpose as clear and sure, although he never ceased to strive for the same objective.

The validity of this purpose depends upon the inclusion of allegory within the borders of art. The medieval mind thought almost exclusively in these terms and the medieval inheritance was strong in the Puritan Hawthorne.[1] The modern mind tends to exclude allegory or to reduce it to a position of relative unimportance, and in so doing would lessen the value of that part of Hawthorne which he himself strove most ardently to develop and to express. Opinion as to the ultimate importance of much of his work depends upon the answer to this problem.

On the other hand, a survey of his work from the vantage point of the present discloses two values of which Hawthorne was at best only partially and subconsciously aware. The modern short story form evolved from those concentrated studies in motivation which he and Poe developed in America. Further, the interest which he felt in the processes of the human mind has proceeded from his beginnings, even though it has followed scientific rather than moral or theological channels. In many of his short stories and in the longer *Scarlet Letter*, Hawthorne pushed on by a trail which was later to become a highway. On the road of psychological fiction, which has since his time grown firmer and broader, he was a lonely traveler proceeding for a time by a sense of direction of which he was little aware, in the firm belief that it led through his moonlit woodland of allegory and "high" truth. Hester and not Hepzibah speaks for him to the future; yet Hepzibah is more truly his own.

NOTE

1. More recent studies of Randall Stewart, Susan Archer, and others have provided evidence not available when this essay was written of Hawthorne's direct and profound debt to Spenser, especially *The Faerie Queene*, for an understanding of allegory and romance in the medieval sense.

The Private Novel of
Henry Adams

The grandson and great-grandson of Presidents in 1884 wrote a novel (his second) and immediately suppressed it. How I came upon one of the few extant copies of *Esther* in the British Museum I do not recall, but the accident led to its republication in facsimile by the Scholars Facsimiles and Reprints (New York, 1938, now Gainesville, Florida), with the following introduction.

In March, 1884, the novel *Esther,* by "Frances Snow Compton," was published by Henry Holt and Company of New York as the third title in a popular series of higher-class fiction. At the same time there was in Washington a retired Professor of History from Harvard, still young in years and energy, who had, a month before, received from the press the first volume of his *History of the United States*, privately printed for the criticism of his friends. No one, it would seem, found any connection between the two events.[1]

Mr. and Mrs. Henry Adams were, at the time, living at 1607 H Street, although they were already studying plans for their new home, which was being designed for them by their architect friend Henry H. Richardson. Adams was spending most of his days with the archives collecting material, or writing. Mrs. Adams was making her home a center for the cosmopolitan society of the democratic capital. "We generally have the latch up from five o'clock till bed time," she writes, "and we learn more out of books than in." [2]

The comment probably applied to herself rather than to her husband, for Henry was faithful to his books and dogs, Marian to her horses and her comfortable tea or dinner table, frequented by the neighboring Beales, Senator Don Cameron and his young wife, and lone bachelors like Henry James, Aristarchi Bey, and occasionally Clarence King. Others in their social group were Bostonians on their way to Florida, members of the official and diplomatic families who read the *Nation,* and visiting relatives. On Sundays Mrs. Adams took time to write her weekly chronicle to her father, Dr. Hooper, in Boston. Perhaps at the same time her husband retired to his study to write to John Hay in Cleveland or Charles Gaskell in London, or even to turn off a few pages of the *History* or other original work.

There is no evidence that Mrs. Adams knew that he was writing a second novel, although she had shared the secret of *Democracy* and even contributed some details herself. Yet fiction was very much on his mind. The authorship and the identity of the characters in his political satire were still debated in circles where its sting had been felt; and his letters to Hay contain playful comment on the new novel of social criticism, *The Breadwinners,* which the latter was then publishing anonymously. "It has also one curious and surprising quality," he remarks, "least to be expected from an unknown western writer. Howells cannot deal with gentlemen or ladies; he always slips up. James knows almost nothing of women but the mere outside; he never had a wife. This new writer not only knows women, but knows *ladies;* the rarest of literary gifts." [3] Both Hay and Adams had wives; and no other American novelist of the day portrayed a lady with the insight and sympathy of "Frances Snow Compton."

I I

The two novels of Henry Adams deal with two of the most vital problems in human experience, the one with political, the other with religious faith. In each case the seeker for truth is a woman and the self-assumed embodiment of the ideal is a man. Both novels become, therefore, in their closing phases, studies of the inability of woman to accept faith as man formulates it. Both American democracy and traditional Christianity are cast aside; the intuitive wisdom of woman triumphs. But at the same time it fails because it is forced to reject a great personal love which has become inextricably twined with the issue of man-made faith. The problem is stated in a political context in *Democracy;* it becomes far more vital and moving in *Esther* because, in a religious context, it probes to deeper levels of experience.

The scene of *Democracy* is laid in Washington, whither Mrs. Lightfoot Lee, a widow of wealth at thirty, has gone "to see with her own eyes the action of primary forces; to touch with her own hand the massive machinery of society; to measure with her own mind the capacity of the motive power. She was bent upon getting to the heart of the great American mystery of democracy and government." [4]

The picture which Madeleine Lee presents is Adams' portrait of a lady. Like Henry James' Isabel Archer,[5] she feels a vague restlessness and she has sufficient means to attempt an ambitious campaign for the satisfaction of her curiosity about life and the fulfillment of her own strong emotional and intellectual nature. Her mind is completely untrained in the ordinary sense, but she is well read, well informed, and alert, although somewhat hardened by her courageous dealing with her own losses and sorrows. Finding philosophy, social work, and religion equally unable to quench her thirst, she turns, as did Adams himself, to those forces which alone seemed vital enough to motivate the great mass of the American people, the principles of democracy.

In the Honorable Silas P. Ratcliffe, Senator from Illinois and presidential aspirant, she thinks she has discovered the embodiment of these forces. "To her eyes he was the high-priest of American politics; he was charged with the meanings of the mysteries, the clue to political hieroglyphics. Through him she hoped to sound the depths of statesmanship and to bring up from its oozy bed that pearl of which she was in search; the mysterious gem which must lie hidden somewhere in politics. She wanted to understand this man; to turn him inside out; to experiment on him and use him as young physiologists use frogs and kittens. If there was good or bad in him, she meant to find its meaning." [6]

Two other characters are major accessories to this theme:

Sybil Ross, Madeleine's younger sister and temperamental antithesis, and John Carrington, an elder relative who is Mrs. Lee's
guide and friend. Sybil is significant to the theme in that she relies
upon her own charm alone in assuming mastery over the present,
and worries not at all about the past and future or the forces
underlying human experience. John Carrington's meaning lies in
his sophistical scepticism which exempts him likewise from the
agonies of soul to which Madeleine and Ratcliffe are submitted,
the one for her moral imagination, the other for his egotism. Carrington, a Virginian by birth, has attained his detachment
through the loss of his spiritual heritage in the defeat of the
South. "Twenty years of constant responsibility and deferred hope
had added a touch of care that bordered closely on sadness. His
great attraction was that he never talked or seemed to think of
himself." [7]

These four characters present Adams' first literary statement of
the problem which was to occupy his central attention for the remainder of his life. In them he explored, superficially and in-
adequately, the forces which motivate the animate world in their
nineteenth-century setting. Madeleine rejects every hint of conventional and formulated morality in so far as she can. She is completely instinctive woman, and yet, after her exploration of
Ratcliffe has focused upon his proposal of marriage, she rejects
him, even though "she could not reply what was on her lips, that
to marry a murderer or a thief was not a sure way of diminishing
crime." [8] Her final judgment of her own case is in terms of her
intuitive understanding of moral forces, even though the agency
in this case is somewhat artificial, a letter from Carrington which
reveals to her the corruption of Ratcliffe's past. A flight to Europe
with Sybil is not an answer to her problem. The issue which she
had proposed to herself remains unresolved, but she has learned
that only in her own nature can she ever hope to find promise of
resolution. The theme has moved from a consideration of the
nature and principles of American democracy as a force and a
faith, to an examination of the moral force resident in the
feminine soul. The second, but far more significant problem is
carried no further in this novel than a statement that it exists.

Between 1879 and 1884 Adams evidently did some intensive
thinking, for *Esther* is clearer in its statement of his problem, more

subtle and more probing in its quest for a solution. From Madeleine he had asked for a feminine verdict, but he had failed to make her wholly feminine; in Esther he more nearly succeeds in creating a woman who is wholly woman, and the conflict of religion and science provides a richer context than does the corruption of American politics. Yet the central theme of the second novel is that of the first.

Again the plot is concerned with the fortunes of a few main characters, this time three men and two women. Esther's role is similar to that of Madeleine, except that her quest for the meaning of life is implied rather than stated. Wharton describes her: "She gives one the impression of a lightly-sparred yacht in mid-ocean; unexpected; you ask yourself what the devil she is doing there. She sails gayly along, though there is no land in sight and plenty of rough weather coming." [9] She is more subtle than her predecessor and less self-conscious; more really and less obviously gifted. She is less deliberate and purposive, and therefore more feminine, about her inquiry. Madeleine confronts her problem as a man might; Esther feels her way into hers. By giving her this quality, Adams reveals his growth in understanding, and in every step of her progress through the story she is faithful to it. Recognizing almost from the start the tragic conflict between her growing love for the Rev. Stephen Hazard and her inability to accept him and remain true to herself, she does nothing to bring the issue to a head. Instead, she relies upon her own sensibilities and the forces working upon her from without, both to raise and to solve the riddle. It is a further tribute to the author's profound understanding of her that, by so doing, she appears strong rather than weak. Such characters are sometimes found in novels by women, seldom in novels by men.

The other characters do not strike as deeply to the springs of motivation. Hazard must be as he is in order to provide Esther with the dilemma in which she finds herself, but Adams has less genuine dramatic sympathy with him than with her. His esthetic sensibility, moral earnestness, and egotistic dogmatism suggest Channing, Buckminster, even Emerson, and many another clergyman of the days when religion was becoming a matter of personal feeling rather than of divine law. He is a type, but his place in Esther's life is so acutely realized that he becomes human and individual. Even his blindness to what has happened to him in the masterly final interview is in conformity with his essential nature as Adams has conceived it.

The geologist, George Strong, provides a foil for Esther's personal and philosophic doubts, without himself becoming too deeply involved in her emotional life. His function is similar to that of Carrington in *Democracy*, but his detachment is attained by more significant means. Having surrendered faith to the challenge of science, he has nevertheless retained his humanity, and he accepts Esther's doubts without question, her need of him without demanding her love. A lighter story might have paired him off with Esther's friend, Catherine Brooke, the Sybil of this novel, but Adams saw more truly that he could exist in the plot only for Esther and Hazard. It is Strong who realizes intellectually what Esther grasps intuitively: that the conflict in her nature is incapable of resolution by conscious plan and action. Without respect for the Church or any wish to save it trouble, he recognizes that Hazard is moving blindly under Esther's influence toward the ultimate sacrifice of his old forms of belief and his deepest emotional needs. Similarly he sees that Hazard's influence on Esther will inevitably become dominance, not only of her actions, but of her personality. Yet, like Esther, although for different reasons, he takes no deliberate action. His fatalism is of a masculine kind, and it leaves him as helpless as Esther's leaves her. Next to the heroine herself, he is the best drawn character in the story, and the most successful.

Catherine, the charming and vivacious orphaned niece from Colorado, is the prototype of all Henry Adams' nieces. She provides sunlight and humanity for the story without taking any significant part in it except as a foil and a contrast to Esther. And Wharton, the artist, although constantly involved in the main action through his direction of the murals and his interest in Catherine, is provided with his own somewhat melodramatic subplot and is therefore not as necessary as the others to the main thematic structure of the novel. Adams succeeds also in giving William Dudley, Aunt Sarah Murray, and others of his secondary characters a three-dimensional quality.

In plot, action and setting, there is no great originality or technical skill in *Esther*. It is a thoroughly good novel, realistic at its time of writing, but like the stories of Howells and James, acquiring something of a "costume" quality with the passing of time. One is tempted to compare it to James' *The American,* Frederic's *The Damnation of the Theron Ware,* and similar problem novels of the eighties and nineties, without finding that Adams' work suffers by the comparison. It is certainly among the better American novels of its kind and its time. The action is almost entirely mental, as it is in Henry James, and the characters move through scenes without being shaped by the dramatic inevitability of environment as they are in Hardy or George Eliot. Adams' psychology, at this stage of his development, is nonevolutionary; he in no sense anticipates the naturalists. But in Associationist and instinctive terms he analyzes motives and their causes as carefully, if not quite as exhaustively, as does James.

In style *Esther* is superior to most of the novels of its day. The characters talk about important matters in convincing fashion. There is much of the subtle interplay of the mind, delicate innuendo, and irony which make the *Education* one of the wisest and wittiest of books. There is enough of the silvery laughter of the comic spirit playing over its pages to compensate for most, if not for all, of its technical shortcomings. In short, it is the work of an inspired amateur, significant chiefly for its author's profound understanding of the emotional life of a vital and charming young woman, and for its suggestion of the later symbolism of the Virgin of Chartres.

I I I

The source of this understanding and its meaning for the later work of Henry Adams present problems which cannot readily be solved. Even though we have his autobiography and volumes of the letters of both himself and his wife, as well as many records of his actions and thoughts in the writings of his friends, Adams has succeeded thus far in preserving that aura of mystery with which his reticence surrounded his personality. "The general reader of the 'Education'," says Mabel La Farge, "may admire and criticize what the book contains. The 'nieces' are especially interested in what has been omitted." [10] As *Esther* was written at the mid-point of the omitted twenty years, the general reader may perhaps share the nieces' interest and look to it for forgotten clues.

Obviously there is an autobiographical significance in the story for anyone daring enough to read between its lines, but the pitfalls in such an undertaking are many. Of this we can be sure: No man could attain to so sensitive an appreciation of a really noble feminine soul without drawing upon his own experience and reading into her character many of the traits which he found in the women he knew best. The obvious source for the character of Esther is, by the sheer logic of circumstance, Marian Hooper, of Boston and Beverly Farms, Mass. "Clover" Hooper, as she was known to her friends, was twenty-three when she and her father were present at a large dinner party given by Minister Adams and his son on May 16, 1866, in London. That she was intelligent and socially well-schooled, although far from intellectual, we may infer from her future husband's description of her to his English friend, Charles Gaskell: "In fact it *is* rather droll to examine women's minds. They are a queer mixture of odds and ends, poorly mastered and utterly unconnected. But to a man they are perhaps all the more attractive on that account. My young female has a very active and quick mind and has run over many things, but she really knows nothing well, and laughs at the idea of being thought a blue. She commissions me to tell you that she would add a few lines to this letter, but unfortunately she is unable to spell. I think you will like her, not for beauty, for she is certainly not beautiful, and her features are much too prominent; but for intelligence and sympathy, which are what hold me. She is quite ready to like you indefinitely, and as she is fond of society and amusement, I do not fear her separating me from my friends." [11]

They were married on June 27, 1872, and Adams' happy prediction was fulfilled. Instead of separating him from his friends, she made of their Washington home an island of Boston culture in a sea of national political life. By abetting his social prejudices as well as his graces, she increased the numbers of his warmer friends, and made them welcome. The thirteen years of his marriage were marked by more sociability than any other period of his life.

It is somewhat unfair to accept as a faithful portrait the sketch of Marian Hooper which is drawn in Adams' few cavalier remarks, however much affection may be discoverable under the irony. It was the first glimpse of her that emerged from the silence

of the forgotten twenty years. Her own letters and the testimony
of her friends and family draw a more human, if a somewhat
less mysterious, picture. She was not unusually beautiful, witty,
and vivacious, nor was she serious, thoughtful, and moody. Her
letters reveal much liveliness of spirit, with few quick turns of
speech or penetrating comments. Apparently she was a quite
average young woman of her class: intelligent, sympathetic, vivacious, cultured, mentally undisciplined, charming, a lover of animals, and eager for life within the limits which her breeding imposed upon her. Her regular Sunday chronicle to her father (all of
her letters that we have) is probably less colorful than her conversation of her letters to friends, but it gives a fair picture of her
interests and her responses to them. If, therefore, she served as a
model for Esther (as she undoubtedly did, for Esther is average
in the same sense), she did so because she was the woman whom
Adams knew best and through whom he learned to appreciate
more deeply the distinguishing qualities of the feminine character.
A more exact and literal parallel between the personalities of the
real and the fictional characters cannot be drawn without a
danger of doing an injustice to both.[12]

The central conflict of the two novels, the clash between a
woman's desire for self-fulfillment and her love for an egocentric
man of conviction, is not in any sense a statement of the relationship between Marian and Henry Adams. We may not know either
of them well even yet, but we do know that Henry was not distinguished for his convictions, nor did he attempt to bend people
to his will. If his own problems are reflected in his heroes, it is
only by contraries, and perhaps by way of unconcious vindication
of his "failure." He was not a man of unbending will and determined action. We can be sure that he did not confront Marian
with the threat of dominance presented by Ratcliffe and Hazard.
His novels deal with the way-not-taken in his own life. In a sense,
therefore, they ask, not how a woman would deal with life as
Marian experienced it, but rather how a woman would read and
interpret his own record. "Adams owed more to the American
woman than to all the American men he ever heard of," [13] is his
testimony. The masculine way had led him to a conviction of
failure because it was the way of action and achievement; in 1884
he was asking how a woman would judge him, and he was learning

something of the verdict, quite by an accident of circumstance, from one Marian Hooper of Boston. Perhaps there were goals of wisdom which could be discovered from nature through woman, who for generations had been schooled by biology and society to accept rather than to construct life. Woman is a born determinist, whereas only the discipline of scientific inquiry, the discovery of the law of natural selection, and other logical inevitabilities could convince man of the truths that she intuitively knew. Esther was called upon to judge, and Marian was asked to serve as her model.

But Marian failed to provide an easy and acceptable answer, for by her own hand she escaped the issue and died on December 6, 1885.[14] The causes of her action have never been determined. The philosophic fatalism of Adams may well have been shared by his wife, even though providing an emotional rather than an intellectual context for her living. A lack or a confusion of emotional conviction is perhaps more serious to the sensitive nature than is its intellectual counterpart. Marian Adams was not moody, but she had been all her life emotionally sheltered. The fact that she was childless might mean much to those capable of interpreting it. At least it left her without the focal interests which children often bring to the home. Her social life, however gay and interesting, was complete in itself from day to day, without definite objective either for herself or for her husband. There seems, therefore, to have been nothing in her life to provide it with the needed emotional center and sense of direction, other than her affection for her husband and her father. It would be easy to make too much of her choice of a Sunday, the usual day of her letter to her father, as the time for her suicide. He had died a little more than a year before. Loneliness, a sense of old associations, a confusion of emotional impulses and the lack of a conviction of purpose apparently came to an unpremeditated climax. Adams had read Esther aright. Woman is vested with a greater power of understanding of life than is man, but she has no answer to its riddle: what to do? The novel ends, as does Johnson's *Rasselas,* with a conclusion in which nothing is concluded. In this sense only is Marian the original of Esther. And when the final chapters of the real story were being written, its fictional counterpart was dying a death of inertia. There are more reasons than those usually given why Adams wished the novel to be forgotten by all except himself, and why he wrote to Hay concerning its authorship: "Perhaps I made a mistake even to tell King about it; but having told him, I could not leave you out. Now, let it die! To admit the public to it would be almost unendurable to me. I will not pretend that the book is not precious to me, but its value has nothing to do with the public who could never understand that such a book might be written in one's heart's blood." [15] And to Elizabeth Cameron: "I care more for one chapter, or any dozen pages of *Esther* than for the whole history, including maps and indexes; so much more, indeed, that I would not let anyone read the story for fear the reader would profane it." [16]

If this interpretation of Adams' fictional use of the material of his experience be accepted, the problem as it concerns the other characters and the setting is much simplified. It is not necessary in any case to fix upon a specific original and to demand a literal representation, but when the emotional values to Adams of certain people and places are estimated they may safely be related to the material of the novel. In this idiom, we may derive Wharton from John La Farge, George Strong from Clarence King, and St. John's Church, New York, from Trinity Church, Boston. Beyond this point it becomes increasingly difficult to proceed. Catherine Brooke's vivacity suggests that of Elizabeth Cameron, whom Adams knew as the niece of Senator John Sherman, and with whom Mrs. Adams was intimate at the time, but there were other young women who might almost equally well have sat for the portrait; Hazard's task in taking over a fashionable parish as a young man may have been suggested by the coming of Phillips Brooks to Trinity Church, even though the characters and physiques of the real and the fictional clergyman were different in many respects; and there may be some connection between the decoration of St. John's Church by Wharton and the work on St. Thomas Church, Fifth Avenue, New York, which La Farge had recently completed and which he considered to best represent what he thought he could do in the art of painting. Certainly the location of St. Thomas Church is more like that of St. John's, although its Rector at the time of the writing of *Esther* was the Rev. Dr. William F. Morgan, who had been in charge of the parish since 1857.

Whatever of his Boston, New York, and Washington associa-

tions Henry Adams may have drawn upon for the setting, characters, and action of *Esther*, it is at least safe to infer that the
novel was first suggested to him by his recollection of his residence
at 91 Marlborough Street, Boston, when La Farge was doing the
Trinity murals. There is, of course, no St. Cecelia at Trinity, but
there is a window in the North Transept representing St. John's
vision of the Holy City.[17] Adams in his story has moved it from
the western to the eastern wall so that the October morning sunlight may shine through it, and he has consecrated his church to
it, unless we may say that he took the name from St. John's
Church near his home in Washington. There may also be a connection between Wharton's "four great figures of the evange-
lists." [18] and La Farge's Angelesque figures of St. Peter, St. Paul,
David, Moses, Isaiah, and Jeremiah on the upper walls of the
tower of Trinity. The circumstances of the painting of these
figures, as recounted by La Farge himself, are not unlike those
described in the novel, although Adams allowed his Church a roof
before the work was undertaken: "The early part of September,
1876, was the time at which the architect gave me first notice of
the work to be done and the first of January was to be the final
end. That was to include the entire building, from the first talk
to the finished work. The building, as you know, was not finished
then, there being no roof on part of it, nor windows, nor possible
scaffolding, nor designs that were accurate. There were also no
people. I managed to get an extension of several weeks so that
February saw the work through. The designs that were to
be painted in the day had often to be made on the previous night.
We had to enlist any one." [19] The unconventional terms under
which Esther did her painting and the haste and casual character
of the work are clearly suggested in this account.

Perhaps sufficient evidence has been assembled to give an idea
of the degree to which Adams colored fact by imagination and of
the ways in which he used his material. The novel is not literal
autobiography, but on a deeper plane of emotion, it deserves a
major place in any study of its author's development. For *Esther*
provides the lost connection between Adams' discovery of the
feminine soul in his experience and the symbolism of his pagan
worship of the Virgin of Chartres.

I V

The trail from Esther to the Virgin of Chartres is a long and intricate one, but it is straight. Adams took twenty years to travel it, but on Sunday, June 5, 1904, we find him at Coutances, in Normandy, the home of his ancestors. It was merely a matter of days since he had left the St. Louis Exposition, with its exhibitions of mechanical force, and here he found that "the people of Normandy had built, towards the year 1250, an Exposition which architects still admired and tourists visited, for it was thought singularly expressive of force as well as of grace in the Virgin. . . . He never doubted her force, since he felt it to the last fibre of his being, and could no more dispute its mastery than he could dispute the force of gravitation of which he knew nothing but the formula. He was only too glad to yield himself entirely, not to her charm or to any sentimentality of religion, but to her mental and physical energy of creation which had built up these World's Fairs of thirteenth-century force that turned Chicago and St. Louis pale." [20] Twenty years of disillusioning experience and acute thinking had brought Adams to a point at which he could grasp by reason a central truth about life which every woman knows by intuition, but which no woman could express to him in terms of thought. What he had suspected of Esther, he at last found to be true of the Virgin, or at least of man's worship of her. As the creative life force which alone of all the determinants of human experience can bring the soul into focus, Esther was now enshrined at Chartres, the greatest and most impressive of her "Fairs," and Adams wrote another book about her, this time without mentioning her name. That book was *Mont-Saint-Michel and Chartres, a Study of Thirteenth Century Unity*. He dedicated it to his "nieces in wishes," and published it for his friends in 1905.

This is not the place to develop and to defend an elaborate exposition of the symbolism of the Virgin and its place in Adams' matured thought. Her superficial meaning is simple enough; it is the same as the meaning of *Esther*. Adams seems to be saying merely that, at one point in history, mankind succeeded in reducing the multiplicity of life to a unity in the unqualified adoration of Our Lady of Chartres, and that the intense period of this worship lasted less than half a century. This statement may or may not be in violation of historical evidence. It makes little difference whether the facts suggested the theory to his imagination, or he created such a period to suit his concept. The historian is inclined to base his judgment on the former hypothesis and to find Adams at fault. This is unfortunate, for if a poet like Milton or Dante be allowed to create a cosmos or a hell, why should not Adams be granted the right to set up a goddess and put at her feet such adoring worshippers as the case may require, especially when, by doing so, he tells all mankind the truth about a matter of primary importance to the welfare of his soul? Only a poet is qualified to deal in such matters as woman's superior knowledge of nature.

But there is more to Adams' imaginative vision of the progress of man than his creation of a single period of unity for animate force in the thirteenth century. Once having established this polarity he sets out to explain the history of mankind by following the lines of force which he has defined. The undertaking requires a second pole for the inanimate force which seems to be determining the multiplicity of the twentieth century. In his search for the terms in which to complete his dualism, he turns to philosophy, physics, and mathematics, and calls upon such abstruse theories as the law of phase, the second law of thermodynamics, and the law of squares. But debate upon such matters may well be left to the physicist and the mathematician. Art is a safer guide, for art is timeless. Even though the whole vast and intricate structure of Adams' rationalization be thrown to the ground by the simple discovery of some other laws, like that of relativity for example, the two great symbols, the Dynamo and the Virgin, inanimate and animate force, will stand as unshakable images of truth. In the Dynamo, Adams discovered the force which acts from the outside on the soul of man; in the Virgin, he found that force which acts from within. Both are equally submissive at times to reason and control; but both are ultimately beyond man-made law. In his eternal struggle for unity in multiciplity, man is alternately the master and the plaything of these forces. He may attain his peace by either discipline or submission. Without casting his lot with either force, Adams learned from woman the art of submission. The search for a way of life had been long; it had started with his Norman ancestors:

> Simple as when I asked your aid before;
> Humble as when I prayed for grace in vain
> Seven hundred years ago; weak, weary, sore
> In heart and hope, I ask your help again.[21]

This poem, too, was written in his heart's blood. It was found after his death in a wallet containing personal papers, and was probably written by 1902. "True it was, although one should not say it jestingly, that the Virgin embarrassed the Trinity. . . . She was above law; she took feminine pleasure in turning hell into an ornament: . . . To her, every suppliant was a universe in itself, to be judged apart, on his own merits, by his love for her." [22] As she whimsically rejected the scholastic formulation of the Trinity and the whole medieval system of moral law, so Esther had rejected Hazard.

NOTES

1. William Roscoe Thayer, in the *Boston Evening Transcript*, August 10, 1918, seems to have been the first to have called public attention to Adams' authorship, and to have done so with a keen critical appreciation. If there was any doubt as to the identity of the author, it was set at rest by Henry Holt in 1923, and by Adams' own admission in his letters, first published in 1930. See Notes 15 and 16 below.
2. *The Letters of Mrs. Henry Adams*, edited by Ward Thoron (Boston: Little, Brown and Co., 1936), p. 410.
3. *Letters of Henry Adams, 1858-1891*, edited by Worthington C. Ford (Boston: Houghton, Mifflin Co., 1930), p. 354.
4. *Democracy* (New York: Henry Holt and Co., 1879), p. 10. Gossip and conjecture have pretty well settled, for the originals of the main characters, upon Mrs. Bigelow Lawrence and her sister, Miss Fanny Chapman, James Lowndes, James G. Blaine, and Emily Beale. See *Letters of Mrs. H. A.*, pp. 240, 247 n., and 339.
5. *The Portrait of a Lady*, 1881.
6. *Democracy*, pp. 36-37.
7. *Ibid.*, p. 22.
8. *Ibid.*, p. 362.
9. *Esther*, p. 27.
10. *Letters to a Niece and Prayer to the Virgin of Chartres, with a Niece's Memories*, by Mabel LaFarge (Boston: Houghton, Mifflin Co., 1920), p. 6.
11. *Letters of Henry Adams*, I, 227.

12. "The Tragedy of Mrs. Henry Adams," by Katherine Simonds, in *New England Quarterly*, IX (December, 1936): 564-582, cites parallel traits rather than a convincing result.

13. *The Education of Henry Adams*, p. 442.

14. Katherine Simonds (*New England Quarterly*, IX [December, 1936]: 577-578 and note) quotes the death certificate filled out by Dr. Charles E. Haynes and Coroner D. C. Patterson in Washington. According to this record, Mrs. Adams died of heart paralysis induced by an overdose of cyanide of potassium which was self-administered. The author hazards the guess that she was suffering from "a nervous breakdown brought on by the strain and grief of the last illness and death of her father."

15. *Letters of Henry Adams*, I, 377.

16. *Ibid.*, p. 468.

17. *Guide to Trinity Church in the City of Boston* (Boston, 1924), pp. 26-27.

18. *Esther*, p. 74.

19. *John LaFarge, A Memoir and a Study*, by Royal Cortissoz (Boston, 1911), p. 156.

20. *Education*, pp. 468-469.

21. *Letters to a Niece*, p. 125.

22. *Mont-Saint-Michel and Chartres* (Boston: Houghton, Mifflin Co., 1905), p. 276.

Henry Adams:
Man of Letters

This is Chapter LXV of *Literary History of the United States*. It was a radical decision of the editors at that time to give Henry Adams a full-length chapter as a man of letters when R. P. Blackmur alone was struggling to write a biography of him in these terms and the historians were struggling to reconcile his scientific theories of history with his documentary-sound history of the United States between the Presidencies of his forebears. Subsequent scholarship, particularly that of Ernest Samuels, has vindicated the decision.

EVEN AN AGE OF DISILLUSIONMENT must have, if not its prophet, at least its interpreter. Whitman and Emerson gave full expression to the regenerative hope of democratic man in a new world. Mark Twain recorded the first shock of discovery that human nature could not be so suddenly changed, and the confusion and despair of his latter years was reflected in all our serious writers as the nineteenth century came to a close. No one of them confronted the problem as a whole, however clearly an Emily Dickinson, a Henry James, a Stephen Crane, or a James G. Huneker might see a part of it. Henry Adams asked the central question of the age, and explored it with inexhaustible energy. Why had man once more failed? What new conditions made the hope for perfection again seem vain?

Just as the First World War was drawing to a close, a little old man died quietly in Washington, leaving a privately printed book which he had called *The Education of Henry Adams*. For it he wrote a preface which his friend and former student Henry Cabot Lodge obligingly signed, when the book was given to the public a few months later.

Here was the story of an eighty-year search for the meaning of life in a modern world of machines, a story which professed to be a mere record of failure ending with a prophecy of universal dissolution. The tone was almost bantering, the mood dark. The public was slightly shocked, not immediately impressed, not at all amused.

In using the third person for his revelation, Adams had covered his inherent shyness but, whether deliberately or not, he had also created an impersonal voice. In the years that followed, a generation, younger but no less disillusioned than his, gradually discovered that voice to be its own. Like the age in which he lived, this man offered a new paradox at every turn. He spoke its contradictions and its dilemmas, its thoughts, and its feelings; he arranged neat and balanced equations to expound its insoluble riddles; he set up contrary images that could nod to each other across the chaos. With its companion, *Mont-Saint-Michel and Chartres*, the *Education* became a testament of faith urgently needed rather than of faith achieved.

But was the strange power that these books came to exert tragic or merely morbid? Would they survive, would they grow in stature, as the particular problems with which they dealt became history, the dilemmas which they so clearly formulated resolved or forgotten? Had they, like *Paradise Lost*, the *Divine Comedy*, or *Faust*, bored to the subterranean rivers? At least once before this had happened in American literature when the flying turn of the harpooner's line caught Ahab about the throat and snatched him after Moby Dick into the sea. Had it happened again? If so, the little old man, sitting in his low chair alone among the exotic trophies in his big Washington home, would be the most surprised of them all.

I I

As autobiography the *Education* is not altogether satisfactory. Like Walt Whitman, Adams sought to explore himself in order to discover the cosmos. He did not spare himself when he thought confession relevant to his theme, but when it suited his purposes to do so he completely suppressed important facts except by inference. Much must be read between the lines and between the chapters. Even with the aid of his many letters, subsequently published, the life story of Henry Adams is not easily told.

Like Whitman's also is the romantic pose assumed for dramatic intensification—here a pose of reticence and failure rather than one of vigor and success. Unlike the *Autobiography* of his brother Charles, this book is more than a memoir; it is a portrait thrown on a screen for analysis and study. Here, in effect Adams says, is a life—my life. What does it mean?

The reticence was real enough if not the failure. It was a trait common to all members of the Adams clan. Late in life, when rejecting the Buddhist retreat for the more active code of Brahma, he wrote:

> But we, who cannot fly the world, must seek
> To live two separate lives; one, in the world
> Which we must ever seem to treat as real;
> The other in ourselves, behind a veil
> Not to be raised without disturbing both.[1]

This inwardness was Adams' chief source of strength as an imaginative writer, and it made the *Education* "a book deep enough and strong enough to be a bible to some natures"; but it also makes it, as a more recent critic has noted, "a grand-scale study of maladjustment, of the failure of an exceptional individual to mesh with a prodigious civilization." The biographical critic could find no nicer problem. Strength repressed must burst forth somewhere and somehow. In the repression, the maladjustment, must lie the clue to the power of the resultant expression. As Adams himself apparently hoped, the failure of the individual must stand for the failure of man. In recounting the impact of events, facts, and people he reveals the growth of an imaginative mind, an artistic consciousness searching through a long life for an adequate form of expression, and not recognizing it himself when at last he had found it. The account of the search is itself the end of the long trail, the achievement of his destiny.

To be an Adams was by definition to make history rather than to record it. The hand of the fathers lay heavily upon the young boy growing up in the old Adams homestead at Quincy, studying at Harvard and in Germany, accompanying his father to London to help guide the policy of a distraught country through a civil war. Doubtless the progenitors of many a man have shaped his course as much, but the shadow of two Presidents and almost a third in their line made the children of Charles Francis Adams more than usually conscious of their blood. With the Adams and Brooks, admixtures of Boylston, Bass, Quincy, and even Alden had assured a firm planting in Massachusetts soil. The White House was a family homestead like that at Quincy, and the Presidency a family habit. The pattern for Henry Adams was already set when he was born, February 16, 1838, on Boston's Beacon Hill, the third son of Charles Francis, third son of John Quincy, eldest son of John Adams—of the eighth generation of the name in Massachusetts. The Adamses were born to rule.

With so imposing an inheritance, life in Quincy and Boston could be upright and rewarding, but not joyous. Sprung from farmers rather than divines, the Puritan strain nonetheless ran strong in the blood. The father, coming home from fishing on Mr. Greenleaf's wharf on a summer day, records in his dairy: "Perhaps this consumption of time is scarcely justifiable; but why not take some of life for simple enjoyments, provided that they interfere with no known duty?" Such comment was the product of "the only perfectly balanced mind that ever existed in the name," as the boy later records. The mother was a silent partner in this somber household, making no deep impression on his memory. Like Ruskin's, such parents provided much to admire, but little to love. Natural affection, with the exception of family loyalty, was turned inward. There it dwelt for the time with the souls of grandparents, living and dead.

Adams liked to think that he was a variant from the family norm and attributed this divergence to scarlet fever which left him even shorter and lighter in frame than was usual in the family, reticent, and sensitive in nerves although sound in health and vigor. But the "habit of doubt" was common to his brothers, if not "love of line, form, quality." Charles, in his *Auto-biography,* confirms most of Henry's early memories, but he recalls most accurately from these days the gloom of the Boston house; Henry, the sunlight on the yellow kitchen floor at Quincy,

the taste of a baked apple when he turned from sickness to con-
valescence, the smell of rotting peaches and pears on his grand-
father's closet shelf, selected carefully for seed. More than any
other Adams, Henry developed acute senses.

His habit of miscellaneous reading for enjoyment was also formed in these years when he lay on his stomach on a pile of Con-
gressional documents and read Dickens, Thackeray, and Scott.
Later he laid the novels aside and helped in the proofreading of
his great-grandfather's *Works* or did his Latin in an alcove in his
father's library. Such experiences, rather than his schooling, educated him both as the formal writer of history and as the informal
seeker for truth, beauty, and goodness which he was to become.

Perhaps most important discovery of all, the contrast of the
seasons, the severe and sharp winters of Boston Common against
the warm indolence of the Quincy summer, suggested the habit of
balancing idea against idea, impression against impression. In
thought and emotion, this pattern was to provide Adams with his
substitute for singleness of drive, for logic leading to the in-
escapable conclusion. In its balance, life remained for him open
to the end.

This trait was at once responsible for his lifelong sense of failure and for the distinguishing quality of his achievement. He
became more aware of it during his Harvard years, acutely so during his years in Europe. Unable to reconcile his natural inclin-
ation to literature with the family directive toward action, he
developed many of the characteristics of the dilettante unable to
plan his path. The choice of a career was difficult. Even at college
he had known that he must write. The essays which he contributed to the *Harvard Magazine* were carefully clipped and bound.
They show a feeling for form suggestive of the classroom; their
models are Macaulay and Irving. As index to his reading, they
tell much. The interest in novels persisted, but to them he added
the "literary" historians: Carlyle, Gibbon, Niebuhr, Grote. There
is no evidence of concern for politics or contemporary problems;
this was to come later when he went to Germany to study law
and language. Gradually a single objective seemed to form: law
would provide a living and at the same time a core for his study
and his writing. "But how of greater literary works?" he wrote his
brother in 1859. "Could I write a history, do you think, or a novel,

or anything that would be likely to make it worth while for me to try? And he adds later: "If I write at all in my life out of the professional line, it will probably be when I have something to say, and when I feel that my subject has got me as well as I the subject."

His brother replied by urging journalism as a more immediate occupation, and when he returned in 1860 he went willingly with his father to Washington, then to London. Although he had thus early formulated exactly what he was to make of his life, the path was not clear. He could not bring himself to enlistment in the actual fighting as could Charles—besides, his father needed him—yet in the thick of events, even he responded as an Adams and put his pen in the service of family and country. "Our Washington Correspondent" of the Boston *Daily Advertiser* became "Our London Correspondent" of the Boston *Courier* and the New York *Times*. The letters are lively and well written, with flashes of description interspersed with sharply reasoned argument. Irony plays lightly over them. The boy was earnest, and his moods of gaiety and despair alternate with the course of events. Primarily he hoped to support his father's effort to keep England out of the war by giving out accurate information for consumption at home. In this task, he showed energy, fearlessness and skill, but little diplomacy. He did not always succeed in doing "good by sustaining papa at home."

I I I

But the role of "Special Correspondent" was too limited and too shallow to satisfy him for long. He was soon back on his main track with an article in the *Atlantic* and others in the *North American Review*. He wrote to his brother in 1862:

The more I see, the more I am convinced that a man whose mind is balanced like mine [the second of the name!] . . . cannot be steadily successful in action, which requires quietness and perseverance. . . . What we want is a *school*. We want a national set of young men like ourselves or better, to start new influences not only in politics, but in literature, in law, in society, and throughout the whole social organism of the country—a national school of our own generation.

In short, the Adams brothers and their friends henceforth would guide the country through the press rather than from the White House.

Chance and the audacity of a young college president, Charles W. Eliot, further opened the way for the writer in public life by offering respectively the editorship of the *North American Review* and an assistant professorship of history at Harvard. With hesitation as to his fitness and grave fear that he might be wasting his time, Adams accepted both in 1870. That these were steps along his chosen way was not as clear at the time as it appears from the vantage point of the finished career.

One of his students describes him at this time as "a small man, blue eyes, brown hair, pointed beard auburn verging to red, perfectly but inconspicuously dressed in brownish gray tweeds (as I remember), of easy and quiet movement and distinct but quiet speech." Another thought of him as "a man of pure intellect." Laughlin recalled that "his nature was positive, not negative. His smile had in it fellowship, welcome, and heartiness; but his laugh was infectious, preceded by a sibilant intake of the breath, with a gay twinkle of humor in his eyes and in the wrinkles at their corners."

To prepare for his courses, he read assiduously, but his scholarship in the Middle Ages was not yet profound. The syllabus of his course is a mere digest of facts. From medieval, he moved into general European history, and then into American; and his better students followed him. The climax of these seven years was his seminar at his home, 91 Marlboro Street, the product of which was *Essays in Anglo-Saxon Law*, four Ph.D. degrees for his students, and the real beginning of his original historical work.

The same independence of spirit marked his conduct of the *North American Review*, first alone, then with the help of Lodge. He wrote to David A. Wells upon accepting the post that he planned to make it "a regular organ of our opinions . . . which should serve as a declaration of principles for our party." This party was composed of the independents who were discontented with the conduct of both the regular parties and who were called together by Carl Schurz in 1875, shortly after Grant's reelection, when it became apparent that civil service reform was not in the offing. Here was Adams' "national school of our own generation."

The best of the essays from this period are closely reasoned and highly technical arguments in the economics of politics. Confronted by the anarchy of the Reconstruction period, with its rapid economic expansion, its wildcat finance, its government by deals and dickering, Adams made a valiant effort to apply to the situation the traditional family principles of conservative fiscal policy, stable currency, centralization of authority, civil service reform, and planned economic development. The task was hopeless, but he put acid and dynamite in his pen. Two of his essays, "Civil Service Reform" and his second essay on "The Session," were reprinted in pamphlet form from the *North American* as campaign documents even though, like his progenitors, he stood on principles rather than platforms and changed his party affiliations as leaders changed their policies. Other essays in the same and other journals studied the course of nineteenth-century British finance by the way of analogy and warning or exposed and attacked the breakdown of the American political and fiscal structures. Of them all, the most readable today is his account of the Erie Railroad grab, "The New York Gold Conspiracy," where ideas become actions and exposition becomes dramatic narrative.

During all of this discussion of contemporary problems, Adams was gradually forming his working philosophy of history. His reviews in the *North American* reflect his impatience with the narrative method of the English and American schools, his growing admiration for the pioneer research of the German legal and institutional historians. History, he decided, should be both a science and an art. As science, it must examine the laws and institutions of the Middle Ages for in them rather than in the overworked theme of the "Discovery" are to be found the germs of modern American society. His medievalism was a fresh discovery rather than an inheritance from that of Keats or that of Longfellow. History must also be exact. "The Germans have these qualities beyond all other races," he wrote to Lodge. "Learn to appreciate and to use the German historical method, and your style can be elaborated at leisure." He would lead the younger historians away from the easy but unsound narrative method of a Bancroft.

From De Tocqueville and Michelet he learned the art of constructing his story about dominant ideas. Once, Thwing recalls, he boasted to his class that he never tried to remember dates; rather he remembered events, not in relation to time, but in relation to each other, as cause and effect. Laughlin reports that "his disposition to try out all possible points of view led him to say extravagant and fantastic things." This was a tendency which grew upon him and provided the framework for his more imaginative writing of later years.

Following his own precept, he moved from the study of Anglo-Saxon law to the documents of New England Federalism, a volume of evidence in the cases of Pickering, Otis, and others who had tried to separate Massachusetts from the Union in 1814–15. From the Pickering manuscripts in the Massachusetts Historical Society, he was led to the papers of Albert Gallatin, Secretary of the Treasury under both Jefferson and Madison. Gallatin, though of Swiss origin and a Republican, had hewn close to the Adams line in his fiscal policy and had demonstrated that one could be a scholar as well as a man of affairs.

Here was man, theme, and exhaustive documentation for the kind of history which Adams had been preparing himself to write. The result, four heavy volumes, is the most thorough and Germanic work he ever did. He never again wrote with such sureness, such calm, such repression of personal bias. But only about one third of one volume is original work; the rest is a printing of the letters and essays of Gallatin.

As Adams himself might have put it, lines of force were bearing upon a single point—his *History of the United States of America During the Administrations of Thomas Jefferson and James Madison*, a task which required nine volumes and more than as many years. The work on Gallatin led directly to Washington and into the Jefferson and Madison papers, then in the State Department. From there, the trail took the historian to the archives of London and Paris where he spent the summer of 1879 attacking these new sources. Gradually the massive work took form. For the first time, Adams adopted a procedure which became habitual with him of printing his more important work privately in six copies only, interleaved for the corrections and comments of his friends.

To adapt the scientific method of the Germans to the problem of American democracy required first the definition of the problem, then the fixing of a segment of material to be examined.

> The scientific interest in American history [writes Adams in his final volume] centered in national character, and in the workings of a society destined to become vast, in which individuals were important chiefly as types. . . . Should history ever become a science, it must expect to establish its laws, not from the complicated story of rival European nationalities, but from the economic evolution of a great democracy.

The point of focus alone remained to be chosen, not in terms of an individual like Gallatin, or even like John or John Quincy Adams, but rather as a segment of social and economic evolution. About such a trend, the art of history could construct a unified whole.

For this purpose, what period could be more suitable than that which lay between the Presidencies of the two Adamses when the new-formed democracy was undergoing its first major test? Here he could use all the material on which he had cut his eyeteeth as well as the vast store of manuscript which had recently come to hand. If one wished to understand the complex of the present, as well as the principles of relationship between the individual and society in the modern world, these sixteen years of Old World convulsion and New World expansion offered the best possible laboratory material.

Economic determinism had not yet been invented in the sense in which more recent historians have defined and applied the term, but the philosophical base of Adams' theory rests as firmly on its premises as does that of F. J. Turner. The central theme of his history is the incapacity of the individual to control his own destiny or to shape the course of events outside himself. The focus of the opening and closing chapters is upon the American character and the American environment. Individuals and events, whether in Congress, court, or battlefield, are given the fullest treatment in detail of fact and analysis. Leaders, silhouetted against this background, are followed with painstaking care through every step of their progress. But everything happens because it must. Jefferson, the dynamic and determined, left the country in near ruin; Madison, lacking in the gift of leadership, restored it by drifting with the current of events. The point of view is as naturalistic as is Dreiser's in *An American Tragedy,* and the two central figures of the story are as helpless in directing the world over which they preside as is Clyde Griffiths in controlling his minor destiny.

Intellectual exhausion would be the natural result of so great an effort, and the other three historical works which followed were mere by-products. The *History* as a whole had been a study in the capacity of man to survive in spite of the stupidity and helplessness of individuals. The careers of the tempestuous John Randolph and the unprincipled Aaron Burr stood out as extreme cases of the whimsy of fate. Some perverse force within Adams urged him on to separate studies of these two men whom he thought despicable. The *Randolph* (1882) appeared during the course of writing of the *History;* the *Burr,* if ever completed, was never published and the manuscript is either lost, hidden, or destroyed. Basically unsympathetic, the former is nevertheless a vivid portrait and a unified miniature of the method used in the larger work; of the latter we have no real knowledge.

The final volumes of the *History* were yet to appear when Adams fled with his artist friend, John La Farge, to the South Seas in 1890. But he was not to escape so easily. Adopted into the family of Tati Salmon, a Tahitian chief of mixed Polynesian and English stock, his curiosity was aroused by the history of the island as recounted by its last Queen, Tati's sister Marau, and by her mother, "the Old Chiefess." Here was a third and an unexpected by-product of his investigations, for the competition of England, France, and Spain, which formed the backdrop for his drama of American struggle, had served the same function in this remote island. Here was the great theme of modern history in capsule form. The Queen herself became interested in the problem and long hours were spent in helping her mother to recall the family history. The written record Adams took him with him and fitted into the accounts of explorers and missionaries. From these sources he was able to reconstruct the story in outline from 1690 to 1846, when the memories of the Old Chiefess are edited from her own words. With this, Adams' work as an historian came to an end. His work as artist and philosopher had scarcely begun.

I V

"The other in ourselves, behind a veil"—Adams was so eager to suppress the story of his inner life that he revealed its emotional power even more effectively than would an explicit statement. From the facts of his marriage and of his friendships, at least the outer form of that life can be distinguished, the inner significance conjectured.

The thirteen years of his married life and the seven years following the suicide of his wife are omitted from the *Education*. Adams claims that his education ceased in 1871 and that he began then to put it to practical uses. In 1892 his experiment was finished and his account with society settled. He was not impressed with the result.

But there were more personal reasons for this silence. Wordsworth omitted the French romance which determined the course of his emotional life from his account of the "growth of a poet's mind." Adams omitted the years when his emotional life was both most fulfilling and most dismaying from his account of his "education." The cases are closely paralleled: in both, the events struck too close for public discussion. They would throw emphasis upon the individual actor rather than upon the general principles of organic growth.

Such reasons for suppression, however sincere, are unsound, and the historical critic must supply the deficiency from letters and other available sources. Adams met Marian Hooper (of Boston) in London in 1866 and married her on June 27, 1872, shortly after he had begun teaching. During the preparation of the greater part of the *History*, she was with him in Washington where she made of their home on H Street a haven of Boston hospitality in a sea of national politics.

His facetious account of her to his friend Gaskell at the time of his engagement cannot be taken as evidence of coldness. He describes her as possessed of "a very active and quick mind . . . fond of society and amusement," accustomed to look after herself, and a Boston "blue" in spite of her protests to the contrary. Certainly the pair was well matched in family and personality, in common interests and tastes. He professes himself "absurdly in love," and her niece Mabel La Farge recalled from summer days at Beverly Farms "an impression of oneness of life and mind, of perfect companionship." Mrs. Adams' weekly letters to her father are filled with accounts of casual teas and formal dinners, of horseback rides and the adventures of the dog Boojum, of the repartee of men but not of women. There were no children. The strain of nursing her father through his last illness threw her into a nervous depression from which loving family care could not rescue her.

At her death by her own hand on December 6, 1885, Adams was plunged into a mood of despair which made him turn to friends, to books, to travel, and to introspection as sources of relief. Once before, when his sister died of tetanus in Rome in the summer of 1870, he had resorted to blasphemy rather than stoicism. The God who indulged in such cruelty could not be a person.

Flung suddenly in his face, with the harsh brutality of chance, the terror of the blow stayed by him thenceforth for life, until repetition made it more than the will could struggle with; more than he could call on himself to bear.

When tragedy next struck even closer home, it was greeted by stoicism.

These are the few given facts and one is left with the dangerous task of reading biography from fiction. Two novels, *Democracy* (1880) and *Esther* (1884), were the anonymous by-products of his married years. The work of an inspired amateur rather than a finished artist, they deal respectively with the two most pressing problems of the day, the corruption which resulted from the grasp of business upon government and the religious doubt which resulted from the attack of science upon established dogma. They thus help to fill the twenty years of silence in Adams' account of his life and give us at least some of the links of thought and feeling between his early and his late work. The one leads to the *Education*, the other to the *Chartres*, as he himself liked to call it. . . .

To draw a close analogy between these novels and the lives of Marian and Henry Adams, as some critics have done, is to oversimplify. Although Esther has many traits in common with Mrs. Adams, Madeleine of *Democracy* is more masculine, more nearly like Adams himself. The latter's motives for coming to Washington were his:

To see with her own eyes the action of primary forces; to touch with her own hand the massive machinery of society; to measure with her own mind the capacity of the motive power.

And there is nothing in the characters of Senator Ratcliffe or Stephen Hazard, physically, mentally, or emotionally, to suggest the self-effacing scholar that Adams had become. To push identification is to strain the evidence too far. If these novels are records of their author's emotional failure, they are evidence only of a failure of the ideal. Because the union was so great, it taught the inadequacy of all such meetings.

As studies in emotional failure they have nevertheless profound significance for their author. Adams has drawn on his own sensitive and suppressed inner life to depict the conflicts which these two women suffer, and he has applied his discoveries to human nature at large. Marian Hooper taught him to know himself, to admit that the riddle of life cannot be solved by the mind alone. In both novels, the theme is the conflict of the inner demands of the individual for unity and integrity with the requirements of a world which, in its materialism and its confusion, had substituted conformity for values. Whether the framework be politics or the church, modern man must accept doubt rather than faith in order to preserve his two remaining values, self-respect and the right to speculation. This is the final stage in the progress from an authoritarian to a pragmatic morality which might be followed down from Jonathan Edwards, through Channing, Emerson, and Whitman, to the passionate skepticism of Henry Adams. But the Puritan core is still there.

Whether viewed as a personal or an objective problem, the dilemma in which Adams found himself, when in 1892 he once more took up his "education" upon completion of the *History,* is not hard to define. "It belongs to the *me* of 1870," he wrote to Elizabeth Cameron from Tahiti; "a strangely different being from the *me* of 1890. . . . I care more for one chapter, or any dozen pages of *Esther* than for the whole history, including maps and indexes." *Esther* was suppressed even though the reason given was that he wished to experiment with the public—to see whether or not an unadvertised book would sell. He had written into it too much of himself, and he had not yet achieved the larger perspective which was necessary to an expression of his discoveries. The historian and commentator who could use his scholarship and skill to investigate and to influence the course of American democratic thought had died with his wife although he had still much unfinished business to complete; the poet who must use symbols to express the deeper meanings of the inner life had still much to learn.

His first experiment in symbolism was made by proxy in an art other than that of writing: the hooded figure which he commissioned Augustus Saint-Gaudens to place over the grave of his wife—and later of himself—in Rock Creek Cemetery, Washington. It is somewhat difficult to separate that which is Saint-Gaudens from that which is Adams in this profoundly mystical conception, as the specifications were purposely indefinite. Many of Saint-Gaudens' statues have a vague poetic quality; the figure of "Silence," for example, made for the Masonic Temple in New York, has the heavily draped anonymous head and figure of the Adams monument, but lacks its massive impassivity, its sexlessness, its timelessness, its power. The stark simplicity and the deeper meanings of the statue can safely be attributed to Adams.

From the moment of giving Saint-Gaudens the commission, Adams refused for five years to approve or disapprove the progress of the work. He spent the summer of 1886 with the artist La Farge in Japan. There he met the Americans, Ernest Fenollosa and his cousin Sturgis Bigelow, both of whom had renounced their native heritage for Oriental faith. No hint of Brahman or Buddhist mysticism creeps through the skeptical and worldly tone of his letters, but the seed was planted. An early note in the sculptor's scrapbook reads: "Adams—Buddha—mental repose—calm reflection in contrast with the violence or force in nature." Photographs of Michelangelo's Sistine frescoes and other such objects were advised as inspiration, as were talks with La Farge, but no books. Hints were to be drawn from Chinese Buddhas; an early sketch shows the figure of Socrates.

Gradually the conception was transferred from the spirit of one man to that of the other. When this act had transpired, Adams left once more with La Farge for a year and a half in Honolulu,

Tahiti, Sydney, and Singapore, and home via Paris and London, bearing with him the sorrow of the loss of both father and mother. When he returned to Washington in February, 1892, the statue was cast and in its place. He was being drawn to the East by the lure of the reopening Orient, as were Lafcadio Hearn and Sturgis Bigelow.

Meanwhile, Adams had journeyed to Anuradhapura in Ceylon to meditate under the sacred bo tree of Buddha on the mysteries of two thousand years and the ruined temple of a living faith:

> Life, Time, Space, Thought, the World, the Universe
> End where they first begin, in one sole Thought
> Of Purity in Silence.

From his now deeper knowledge of Asiatic religion, he was satisfied with the work he had inspired. "He supposed its meaning to be the one commonplace about it—the oldest idea known to human thought." Later he discovered that it was "a sealed mystery to the American mind." For him it was no more than a mirror to reflect what one brought to it, and the habit of returning to learn what it had to tell him became a ritual. That his contemplation, however abstract, was not impersonal is revealed in a letter to Gilder in 1896:

> The whole meaning and feeling of the figure is in its universality and anonymity. My own name for it is "the Peace of God." La Farge would call it "Kwannon" [the Japanese Goddess of Mercy], Petrarch would say: "Siccome eterna vita è veder Dio."

This is the opening line, "As to see God is eternal life," of the sonnet which, in his novel, had brought Hazard into his first rapport with Esther, and had made him feel "that to repeat to his Laura the next two verses of the sonnet had become the destiny of his life:

> So to see you, lady, is happiness
> In this short and frail life of mine—"

He was not alone on these pilgrimages to Rock Creek Cemetery, nor did he go merely to brood over a personal sorrow. His tragedy had become his secret index to the mystery of life and death. The burden of meaning which neither history nor fiction was strong enough to bear was beginning to find expression in symbol; but adequate symbols were yet to be discovered.

V

But first, the meaning itself must be explored, and the mind alone was insufficient instrument. Forced back into himself by the death of his wife, Adams turned once more to his friends and to his books.

The capacity for making and holding close friends was one of the most pronounced traits of this presumably cold and intellectual man. No idea, feeling, or experience was complete until it had been thrown back to him from the sounding board of another's consciousness. Because no thought or emotion ever settled into a fixed pattern for him, he awakened in others something of the questing spirit which was always his. Every important facet of his versatile personality is directly reflected in at least one other person. Such friends virtually lived in his home or he in theirs; they traveled with him to every corner of the earth; they suggested books which might satisfy his cravings and then had to submit to a complete experience with him in what such books offered. There were women as well as men in the group, artists as well as statesmen and historians. The only prerequisite was that they should share with him some part of the never-answered riddle of experience.

In his English friend Charles Milnes Gaskell, Adams found the connoisseur of life who, between 1863 and 1908, shared with him an ironic perspective on its strivings and its follies. His letters to Gaskell are his best, but he depended more for the closer intimacies of friendship on the American statesman John Hay and the geologist Clarence King. These two, with Mrs. Adams and Mrs. Hay, made up the "Five of Hearts" during the Washington years, the nucleus of a larger circle. Hay understood Adams thoroughly and confesses that he depended on him "to keep me in the straight path by showing me the crooked." It was he who commissioned Saint-Gaudens to make a caricature medallion with the wings of an angel and the body of a porcupine: "Henricus Adams Porcupinus Angelicus." Doubtless the mutual friendship with the leading geologist of his day, Clarence King, was the bond which held them most firmly, but in many respects, Hay accomplished where Adams failed: he met the nineteenth century world and put it to his own uses. His private life was a model of domestic happiness; his public, a triumph of international policy. The *Education* ends with his death, leaving the last of the trio in the "depths of Hamlet's Shakespearean silence."

For King had gone before, in some ways the closest of all Adams' friends. Adams wrote:

> His only ultimate truth was the action, not the thought. To him all science and all life were in that law, which, after all, is the only result of his generation—the law of Energy. Those of us who gladly and carelessly gave ourselves up to his influence and let him swing us as he liked—those he loved.

It was largely under King's influence that Adams embarked upon his most profound exploration of human experience. While in London in the sixties, he had talked with Sir Charles Lyell and the door of scientific speculation had been opened to him. Later he reviewed the *Principles of Geology* in the *North American*. When, with this common interest already deeply rooted, he met King in Estes Park and, sharing room and bed, "talked till far towards dawn," it was "never a matter of growth or doubt." The friendship was sealed. King's pioneer work in geology was a mere starting point for a philosophy of energetic skepticism. Once more, in another's success, Adams had recognized his own failure. His mind and feeling went with his friend into the High Sierras and into the depths of emotional abandon with the defiance of personal danger, which his body could not summon. King expressed in action what Adams could experience only vicariously. But King did not stop to reason, to analyze, to explain. Adams was the historian of the adventure in books which contain scant if any reference to King by name. It was not Langley, but the spirit of inquiry awakened by King which sent him exploring the speculations of Stallo, of Karl Pearson, of William James, even though Willard Gibbs and Raphael Pumpelly helped. It was King who stood behind his shoulder when he wrote *A Letter to American Teachers of History* and who first prompted the final pages of the *Education*.

As King led Adams into the profundities of scientific speculation, so John La Farge, without benefit of passion, led him into the world of color and form and idealization which is art. Twice the historian sought the artist when the only answer to his sorrows and perplexities seemed to lie in travel. Both times they turned to the East, first to Japan, then to the South Seas and India. The diary letters which he wrote to Elizabeth Cameron from these trips merely skim the surfaces of color and form of the sea and the islands; the naïveté and spirit of the native girls dancing their native dances; the hospitality of the queens and princes of a dying race of primitives. But such experiences led Adams out from his sorrow and spread a surface gaiety over his numbness. Under La Farge's tutelage he tried painting, but only learned to see color, not to reproduce it. Through borrowed artist eyes he awoke to the beauties of the physical world at their most brilliant, the gaiety and warmth of primitive people who knew how to live in the sun even when their European oppressors were closing in upon them. Vague stirrings of response to Asiatic religions sent Adams to books on Buddha, as earlier he had read Dante in a garden at Nikko, the sacred heart of Japan, while La Farge painted the fountain below his veranda. Here were the first tentative explorations of those depths which he had sighted in *Esther* and which he was to fathom with the aid of the Virgin of Chartres. But La Farge could not accompany him on these later journeys.

With La Farge, the story of Adams' formative friendships loses its sharper outlines except for his brothers Charles and Brooks. The first early helped him shape his career, the second debated with him during the summer of 1893 the collapse of the Exchange and the theory of history which made all civilization ultimately follow the exchanges into disintegration. Like Henry in many ways, Brooks was even more a solitary, even more a concocter of historical if not cosmic theories. "The two brothers could talk to each other without atmosphere" and together they worked out the theory of history which in the one became a law of decay, in the other a dynamic entropy.

But the deeper levels of experience were still to be explored. Perhaps Adams went on these journeys alone, perhaps his reticence kept him from acknowledging his companions. "Adams owed more to the American woman," he once wrote, "than to all the American men he ever heard of," and, especially in his later years, he formed the habit of turning to women for guidance. The book upon which he expended most of himself, the *Chartres*, was written for his "nieces." In these later years Elizabeth Cameron, niece of Senator Sherman, as well as Mrs. Lodge and visiting nieces, helped with the hospitality at 1603 H Street. To Mrs. Cameron he wrote the record of his travels for the broken circle of friends in Washington; with her and her husband he traveled to London and on the continent.

The other "nieces" were actual nieces of Mrs. Adams. One of them, Mabel Hooper, later Mrs. Bancel La Farge, has spoken for them all and has given his letters to print.

To them all [she writes], he was the *generic Uncle,* the best friend —to whom they not only could confide their innermost secrets, their perplexities, hopes and aspirations, but also at whose feet they could sit endlessly, listening to the most thrilling talk they had ever heard, or were likely to hear again.

It was to them and to such foster nephews, or "nieces in wishes," as Cecil Spring-Rice that the childless and lonely old man opened his home and his heart; and it was under the tutelage and care of Aileen Tone, an adopted "niece" and a Catholic, that he discovered, after his paralytic stroke in 1912, his last great enthusiasm, the music of the old French songs of which he had known the words for so long. Mabel La Farge and Mrs. Winthrop Chanler, who knew him well in these days, have expressed the belief that he was himself virtually a member of the church in faith, but most other Catholics do not agree with them. The Virgin of his *Chartres* was at heart a pagan.

V I

On the assumption that Adams was primarily, if not wholly, a man of intellect, the majority of his critics have attempted to evaluate his final accomplishment as a logical statement of the philosophy of mechanism applied to history. With comparative ease they have pointed out fallacies in his premises, faults in his logic, and exaggeration in his conclusions and predictions. Some have argued convincingly that Brooks Adams, in his *The Law of*

Civilization and Decay (1895), has made out a better case for the application of the thought of Newton, Comte, Darwin, and Marx to the history of Western civilization than did Henry. The result has been a tendency to discount the achievement of the latter almost as effectively as he did himself.

Throughout his life Adams thought of himself as a man of letters rather than primarily as a historian, scientist, or philosopher. He never lost his eager interest in the central and tragic conflict of man and nature; but he was thwarted, as all American writers have been until very recently, by the absence of a matured and autogenous literary culture. He instinctively knew, as Cooper and Melville and Mark Twain had each discovered in his own way, that American literature must be a reinterpretation of the eternal issues in human experience in terms of life in contemporary America. Politics, economic history, science, philosophy, and art itself were means and materials only. To the man of letters, no truth is new, its expression never done.

The discovery of an authentic and adequate medium of expression was his life's quest, and the recognition that form cannot be imposed, that it must result from understanding, made "education" for him the primary good. His confession of failure is merely, in its larger implications, his version of the failure which underlies tragedy from Aeschylus to Eugene O'Neill.

For Adams was primarily a man of feeling, and his ultimate strength lay in his long delayed but overwhelming discovery of that fact. Before he could justify his choice of a career of writing in his own eyes or in ours, he had to rid himself of two assumptions that inhibited his development: that thought without action is void, and that thought without emotion is valid. He had to learn that living thought may be in itself a kind of action and that thought cannot live when divorced from emotion. His career as publicist and historian proved to him that writing could be a form of action; his personal tragedy and the release of his emotional life into friendships taught that no scientific truth could be final without imagination, no writing could be intrinsic action if it relied upon reason alone.

His transition from the man of thought to the man of feeling was, however, so gradual that the stages in the progress can readily be lost and the issue confused. In its last and crucial phase it cen-

ters on the application of the findings of science to history. But
before science could produce original art, it had to become an
instrument of the imagination rather than merely a method for
the discovery and analysis of facts; history a record of man's
whole development rather than merely a narrative of his past adventures and vicissitudes.

In the decade between the publication of the first volume of
the *History* and his address to the American Historical Association
in 1894, his view of the possible relationship between science and
history had progressed far beyond the mere use of the inductive
method and the assignment of historical evidence to man-made
law. "The situation," he told his fellow historians, "seems to call
for no opinion, unless we have some scientific theory to offer."
From this day forward his energies were devoted to the search
for that formula rather than to the writing of history itself according to established premises and rules. Although he does not
seem fully to have appreciated the fact, such a quest was as romantic as those of Ahab for Moby Dick or Parsifal for the Holy
Grail. As in those cases, it became a search for the symbol of the
life force, an effort to wrest the meaning of man from a reluctant
nature by sheer violence. The discovery of a new and scientific
basis for history would mean the creation of a new religion.

The task of Adams' generation was not the completion of that
creation. Rather they were to break down old structures by techniques which science had given them, to define issues, to set up
working hypotheses for the new synthesis. Adams took as his
particular task the discovery of an organic aesthetic form which
could give expression to the significance of his age as he saw it.
He proceeded direct from the experience to the expression because he had rejected all models. The result was the single gigantic but incompleted act of the imagination which resulted in the
Chartres and the *Education*.

The final chapters of the *Education* state briefly the "dynamic"
theory of history which Adams had adopted as his tentative instrument, a theory which is more fully expounded in *A Letter to
American Teachers of History* (1910), his last important book,
which his brother Brooks edited posthumously, adding the unpublished essay on "The Rule of Phase" and giving the whole his

own unfair but provocative title, *The Degradation of the Democratic Dogma.*

The choice of the second law of thermodynamics, the law of dissipation of energy, as the needed formula was dictated by the stage to which physical science had developed by 1910. If the attempt were made today, Adams might equally well have adopted the law of relativity and developed a science of history in quite other terms. To him the important factor was the relation of the two components, science and history, to each other, not the final truth of the findings of either one. In the later and even more daring essay on the law of phase, he allows his imagination such range as to venture by computation to fix a date for the moment of dissolution. Impatience with the rapid progress of science and the stodgy conservatism of historians provoked heroic measures.

Adams' version of the more fully developed theory of entropy which he adopted for his two major literary works may, for convenience, be stated as two related hypotheses:

(1) Accepting force as ultimate fact, two kinds of force are recognizable in experience: an inner force which makes for unity and which man has traditionally known as religion or God, and an outer force which makes for multiplicity and which has come to be known as science or nature. Absolutely considered, both these forces may be traced to a common center in a mechanistic view of the universe, as in the past both were traced to a theistic center, but in human experience they have always been and probably always will be differentiated and in opposition to each other. This is no more than a restatement in modern terms of the classic theory of metaphysical dualism.

(2) Historically considered, experience shows that man reached the peak of his development in the era of medieval Christianity because he then succeeded through the instrument of the church in attaining the highest degree of unity; but the discovery of the inductive method of reasoning and its application to physical science in modern times introduced a new "phase" of evolution in which nature supplants man as dynamic center of the universe. Unity was then mortally challenged and the universe began to move toward disintegration by a law of accelerated entropy which should by now be reaching its culmination and which should be

followed by complete dissolution or by new and unpredictable forms of life. Thus the historical framework is provided for the application of the theory of dualism.

These two hypotheses are complementary when treated in purely intellectual terms, but they present a fundamental inconsistency when viewed in the light of emotion. Adams thus also creates, perhaps unwittingly, a dichotomy between intellect and emotion which supplies the pattern for his art form, but which destroys the validity of his theory as an instrument for the logical explanation of the universe. Art alone could resolve this inconsistency because art records and evaluates rather than accounts for the evidences of experience.

Adams' creation of an arbitrary cosmology for his purposes suggests Milton's similar acceptance of the Ptolemaic system at a time when his own reason might have dictated the Copernican. Adams' acceptance of a modified Newtonian mechanism is a necessary premise to his artistic construction, and its degree of logical soundness has no bearing on its aesthetic validity. It was many years before Miltonic criticism could free itself from this difficulty and accept *Paradise Lost* as a great epic poem in spite of the fallacious cosmology upon which it is based. The criticism of Henry Adams has not yet reached that stage.

Only in the aesthetic expression of his position did he reach any degree of finality. To him the two major works of this period, the *Chartres* and the *Education*, formed a unified, albeit an imperfect, whole. The importance of their interrelationship is stressed by his quoting in his preface the key passage from Chapter XXIX of the *Education* when he finally decided that his time was up and he could bring his work no nearer to completion:

Any schoolboy could see that man as a force must be measured by motion, from a fixed point. Psychology helped here by suggesting a unit—the point of history when man held the highest idea of himself as a unit in a unified universe. Eight or ten years of study had led Adams to think he might use the century 1150–1250 expressed in Amiens Cathedral and the Works of Thomas Aquinas, as the unit from which he might measure motion down to his own time, without assuming anything as true or untrue, except relation. The movement might be studied at once in philosophy and mechanics. Setting himself to the task, he began a volume which he mentally knew as "Mont-Saint-Michel and Chartres: A Study in Thirteenth-Century Unity." From that point he proposed to fix a position for himself, which he could label: "The Education of Henry Adams: A Study in Twentieth-Century Multiplicity." With the help of these two points of relation, he hoped to project his lines forward and backward indefinitely, subject to correction from anyone who should know better.

The student who reads this passage ten times should need no further elucidation of these two books. He will not make the mistake that many critics have committed of assuming a finality in Adams' logical position; he will know that the two books in concept are one, a planned work of the imagination rather than an historical, autobiographical, or scientific record or argument; he will evaluate their timeless quality rather than their circumstanial reference.

As art, these books should therefore be approached only as companion studies in unity and multiplicity. As contributions to the philosophy of history, they may be accepted or discredited at will without invalidating his approach. Man's inner need for discovering a system of unity in his experience and his constant difficulty in reconciling this need to the multiple influences of the world outside of himself is the most persistent theme of all literature. It is the problem of Oedipus, Hamlet, and Faust, of Tom Jones, Ahab, and Ma Joad. Emerson discussed it for his age; Henry Adams did the same for an age when the conflict was infinitely more acute and the solution less apparently obvious.

We have seen at least some evidence that Adams at one time hoped to find his center of unity in Oriental art and religion and his symbol of that unity probably in Buddha. His poem "Buddha and Brahma," not published until 1915 but written earlier, reveals the failure of Buddhist quietism to make unity dynamic, of Brahmanism to achieve unity beyond action. When he turned from travels in the East to travels in France, he discovered in the arches and spires of Mont-Saint-Michel, Amiens, Coutances, Paris, and Chartres the symbol of unity which he sought, and communicated it in his only other known poem, "Prayer to the Virgin of Chartres." Not much more than adequate in technical skill, these two poems have an intensity of blended feeling and thought which gives them the dignity of art.

In exploring the nature of unity, Adams was led back to his

study of medieval history, and he added to it a wide reading in chivalric poetry, works on medieval architecture, and the writings of Christian philosophers from Abélard to Thomas Aquinas. Again he was the inspired amateur rather than the documentary scholar or the conventional man of letters. He read books only when they "helped." Slowly he formed his pattern about the symbol of the Virgin—not Mary as person or as divinity, but the Lady of Chartres as creation of the medieval imagination. The selection of the century 1150–1250 was dictated by the facts because then the conception of the Virgin had become, for one moment in history, an effective symbol of man's eternal desire for inner and outer harmony, expressed both in art and philosophy. Just how this image evolved and what significance it might have not only for medieval but for universal man became one half of his life's concern. The result has served as a study of the medieval mind; it is only now coming to be recognized for its insight into the universal mind.

The structure of the book is apparent only when this central purpose is kept in mind. Adams' facetious statement that it is merely a tour de force for the entertainment of his nieces and "nieces in wishes" is obvious screening of its profound value to him. His light bantering tone persists throughout, but the careful unfolding of his plan is not hampered by it.

The book falls into three somewhat unequal parts: the preparation of the medieval mind for its gigantic effort of synthesis just before its collapse; its achievement of emotional unity in the first half of the thirteenth century as represented in the Cathedral of Chartres; and the translation of this process into the rational terms of medieval philosophy. For the first the Archangel Michael serves as personal focus, for the second the Virgin, for the third St. Thomas. Above them all, the Virgin becomes the symbol of unity achieved. The transition from worship of a masculine to that of a feminine deity is hinted at in the *Roman de la Rose* and acknowledged in the religious chivalry of Thibaut. Poetry, history, and architecture combine, with all their intricate details, in an aesthetic synthesis which makes manifest the sovereignty of the Virgin. Abélard, Bernard de Clairvaux, St. Francis, and St. Thomas add each his philosophy to emphasize the result and to translate it back from emotion to scholastic logic, from the supreme feminine intuition to the masculine approximation of truth through reason. For once, man's inner need for harmony seemed, at least in the perspective of later centuries, to have been partially supplied.

The truth which Adams here tacitly recognizes is that unity may be achieved through emotion even when denied by reason. His Virgin is completely irrational, her power nonetheless centripetal. Mary filled her church without being disturbed by quarrels because she "concentrated in herself the whole rebellion of man against fate. . . . She was above law; she took feminine pleasure in turning hell into an ornament; she delighted in trampling on every social distinction in this world and the next." Yet she answered the prayers of her suppliants because she judged by love alone. She could put in terms of positive symbolism what the hooded figure in Rock Creek could only permit by reflection. This is what Adams had learned from the American woman, but he had to trace it back to twelfth century France to find it unembarrassed and whole. Intuition is above reason; love may triumph over logic; art can speak deeper truths than science.

With the same detachment Adams then turned immediately to the other half of his problem: the study of multiplicity. Here the age of obvious choice was the present, the person of obvious focus himself. Even at the risk of being accused of merely writing his autobiography, he undertook *The Education of Henry Adams: A Study in Twentieth-Century Multiplicity*. The detachment of the third-person pronoun is not an affectation; it is an integral part of his scheme. He might have written of someone else had he known any other experience as well as his own. As the forces which he wished to examine are universal, as well as peculiar to the age, he would do as well as another for their point of impact. For the impersonality of the Ego, he turns again to Oriental thought. In a biographical testament of friendship to George Cabot Lodge, published in 1911, he states that the poet seeks unity in "some one great tragic motive." Lodge's

was that of Schopenhauer, of Buddhism, of Oriental thought everywhere,—the idea of Will, making the universe, but existing only as subject. The Will is God; it is nature; it is all that is; but it is knowable only as ourself. Thus the sole tragic action of humanity is the Ego,— the Me,—always maddened by the necessity of self-sacrifice. . . . In order

to raise the universe in oneself to its highest power, its negative powers
must be paralyzed or destroyed. In reality, nothing was destroyed; only
the Will—or what we now call Energy—was freed and perfected.

Thus perhaps from the analysis of his own experience, Adams
might witness the action of this tragic movement in the modern
world and in harmony with the new concept of Energy which
science had supplied. This he attempts in the *Education*.

This book also falls roughly into three parts: the inadequate
and misleading preparation of a generation which reached maturity at the moment in history when the challenge of modern
science became generally felt; the effort of one individual to
adjust to this new and centrifugal world of multiplicity; and the
translation of the result into a rational formula. The problem
was more baffling because the perspective of time was lacking. On
the other hand, the material was more familiar. Nor was a central
symbol as easy to find. Frank Norris, at the same time on the
same quest, adopted the railroad as symbol in *The Octopus*.
Adams, in the high excitement of discovery, chose the dynamo
which he saw first at the Chicago Exposition in 1893, later in
Paris in 1901. Here was the outward image of his second kind of
force, almost specific enough to excite worship if worship were
due.

It would be dangerous to press the symbolic parallelism of
these two books too far, but the temptation to explore it is great.
As the power of the Virgin is humanity on the level of divinity, so
that of the dynamo is mechanism raised to the infinite. In the one
case, the power operated on an impassive and nonhuman object,
the Cathedral of Chartres, which in a sense becomes a subordi-
nate or reflective symbol; in the other, the object of the mechanistic force is human, is Henry Adams made impersonal and passive. From this perfectly balanced equation, the symbolism is developed on the one hand in terms of architecture, art, philosophy,
persons and events (stained-glass windows, figures of saints, the
rebellion of Pierre de Dreux, the poetry of Thibaut, the philosophy of Abélard); on the other in terms of politics, science, philosophy, and again persons and events (Anglo-American diplomacy,
the geology of Sir Charles Lyell, two World's Fairs, William
Henry Seward, and Lord John Russell).

Intricate and balanced as these imaginative elements are, it would be a mistake to hold that Adams had perfected a new sort of epic or symbolic form. The result gives the impression of work still in progress as Adams felt that it was. The overall form is massive and sprawling as are those of Melville or Whitman, rather than balanced and finished as one knowing the man Adams might expect. He was never satisfied with it, published the books privately, allowed them reluctantly to be offered to the public. But they are thoroughly American in that whatever order and discipline they achieve is organic. The refined inheritor of Adams' energy had allowed his feelings and his understanding to mold their own form about them.

The pen works for itself [he confesses] and acts like a hand, modelling the plastic material over and over again to a form that suits it best. The form is never arbitrary, but is a sort of growth like crystallization, as any artist knows too well.

In his style, Adams came nearer to a classic restraint, but here too he indulged in extravagance when the pen became willful. His revisions of his historical essays when he collected them show a peeling off of the superfluous phrase, a stripping down to clear and explicit statement. When he turned from direct to imaginative writing, he deliberately created an *alter ego* and from an oblique angle surveyed himself together with other phenomena, past and present. The direct style would no longer do and he deliberately cultivated, even in his personal letters, the irony which had always been his. A careful reading of Pascal, Montaigne, and Voltaire helped in this study. In his final testament of futility and affirmation, his vein was comic in spite of the tragic intensity of his feelings. Wit alone could bear the burden.

NOTE

1. *Yale Review*, n.s., V, 88 (October, 1915).

Sidney Lanier:
Ancestor of Anti-Realism

This "essay-review" appeared in the *Saturday Review of Literature* for January 10, 1948. In arranging for this reappraisal of Lanier, editor Henry S. Canby wrote, "I like your idea as far as Lanier is concerned. . . . So go to it. I can't see that there is any great haste in publication in a definitive set like this one."

SOME TIME AGO Henry Seidel Canby announced in the *Saturday Review of Literature* the obsequies of the realistic movement and named as its pall bearers those professors of our literature who have but recently discovered such up-to-the-minute writers as Theodore Dreiser. The purpose of this article is to sound a warning to at least one of the successors of realism—the as-yet unlabeled literary movement centered in the poetry and criticism of T. S. Eliot—for the academic termites are at work upon it. This movement is analytical, critical, mystical, intellectual, symbolic, decadent—in short, it is everything antirealistic. It is concerned with the extension of the human personality into pure meaning rather than with the direct communication of ideas and emotions. It is impressed by the value of the single word, the rhythm of the single phrase, the power of the simple or the complex image. It looks into a mirror to find truth. Its poets and critics and novelists support and attack and amuse each other while the book clubs pass it by and the public largely ignores or resents it. But the professors are giving courses and writing learned articles about it. Beware!

And the professors are discovering that this movement, like its antithesis, the realistic movement, is an American tradition with roots that extend well back into our literary history. We are confronted, therefore, by a paradox. On the one hand it has been demonstrated that close attention to actualities and the effort to reproduce life accurately in story and verse have created the dominant trend in American literature at least since the time of William Dean Howells. On the other, we find our leading poets and novelists of today turning away from actualities and seeking to articulate their inner experiences by systems of images and rhythms and intricate prose forms which apparently have little connection with actual experience. The dominant trend in contemporary American literature—a trend which has been growing in strength since about 1925—seems to be violently antirealistic. Sources for it have been sought—and found—in Joyce, Proust, and Freud, but little effort has been made to trace it back in our own literary history. Surely it must have, like realism, a native ancestry of its own.

The recent publication by the Johns Hopkins Press of the complete (perhaps all too nearly complete) writings of Sidney Lanier [1] provides some evidence that this antirealistic tradition is as American in its ancestry as is realism itself. And the publication of a selection of his works by his original publisher,[2] with the main emphasis placed on the later poems, shows that his experiments have added to his popularity through the years. It is only unfortunate that, with the definitive text of the poems established by Anderson, the editor of this volume of selections chose to base his text on that of 1884. But add to these evidences of interest in our nonrealistic writing of the eighties, the appearance of a new collection of the work of E. A. Poe,[3] and a revival of interest in Henry James and Henry Adams. It is obvious that some new historical backgrounds for contemporary American literature are being sketched in by the scholars. Much detailed work remains to be done on such problems as the probable connection between the symbolism of Adams and that of Eugene O'Neill, the Jamesean analysis of personality and that of Faulkner, and the mystical split between the psyche and the conscious will as found in Poe's "Ulalume" and Eliot's "Prufrock." But a few broad generalizations may be made by way of initial hypothesis. One of these is that Sidney Lanier, in the last eight years of his life (1874–81), provided by his studies and his experiments rather than by his actual poetic achievement much of the preliminary groundwork for contemporary poetry.

Lanier was a man of books and music rather than of life. With health destroyed by the Civil War, he announced in 1878, in a series of articles on "The Physics of Poetry," a break with literary fashion as emphatic as that of Walt Whitman. These lecture-essays were then revised and published as "The Science of English Verse" in 1880. Amateur and unsound as this book may be in some respects, it is the first comprehensive study of English prosody by an American poet; and it is supported and illustrated by a hand-ful of experimental poetry unlike anything previously written in our literature, even though its kinship with the ideas and experi-ments of Poe can easily be discovered. With it, at least one source for the contemporary movement in American poetry came to the surface of recognition. Behind it are four volumes of letters and several more or less skilful critical writing which reveal the form-ative stages of its central thesis.

Poetry, said Lanier, is basically sound, not sense. It is music in words and it can be comprehended only when the physical laws of sound are deliberately applied to it. It should be measured by such agencies as duration, pitch, intensity, and tone-color rather than by meter, accent, rhyme, alliteration, assonance, and stanzaic structure. It should be represented by musical notes, rests, bars, and staves rather than by feet, accents, and diacritical marks. It achieves its effects by such manipulation of words into pure rhythm and imagery as:

> To the zenith ascending, a dome of undazzling gold.
> Is builded, in shape as a bee-hive, from out of the sea:
> The hive is of gold, undazzling, but oh, the Bee,
> The star-fed Bee, the built-fire Bee,
> —Of dazzling gold is the great Sun-Bee
> That shall flash from the hive-hole over the sea.

And not by such metered ideas as are found in Longfellow's:

> Let us then be up and doing
> With a heart for any fate;
> Still achieving, still pursuing,
> Learn to labor and to wait.

In reading poetry, asserts Lanier, the eye "merely purveys for the ear. . . . The term 'verse' denotes a set of specially related sounds." Ornate and repetitious as Lanier's own sound-picture effects often are, they establish an attitude toward the technique of verse quite new in its day. Restraint and polish were to come later.

I I

New, that is, except for Poe and perhaps some lesser Southern poets like Chivers and Timrod. Poe had similarly emphasized esthetic values at the sacrifice of intellectual content as much as thirty years earlier in his "Philosophy of Composition" and in such wholly mechanical experiments in verse as "The Bells." But Lanier's challenge was nevertheless startling to an age in which Longfellow, Lowell, and Whittier were ensconced in the public taste. Whitman alone was in full revolt in the Seventies, but Whitman's challenge to the dominant British romanticism was as different from Lanier's as it was from that romanticism itself. Whitman was leading in the direction of life—of realism; Lanier, in the direction of art—of self-conscious technique. Whitman was surging outward from his personality; Lanier was turning inward with the sharp scalpel of analysis. Emerson in that day was almost alone stressing the inwardness of the poetic revelation but his ear was unfortunately not attuned to his beloved Aeolean harp and he was not widely accepted as a poet. Emily Dickinson, the most musical and "metaphysical" of them all, was to remain unheard for several decades more. Lanier's revolt may therefore well prove to be the turning point in the historical development of our poetic tradition.

So sharp a turn in direction must have well defined sources, and a few of these can here be indicated even though the problem is far too complex to be solved in so hasty a review. Whereas most American poets like Bryant, Halleck, Longfellow, and Whittier had been schooled in the English eighteenth-century nature poets like Cowper and Gray and had followed this source of inspiration down into the romantic revolt of Wordsworth, Coleridge, and Byron, Lanier, like Emerson, went back directly to the Elizabethan lyrists, from them to the seventeenth-century metaphysicals, and, jumping over the whole of eighteenth-century rationalism, to the romanticism of Keats and Shelley. Lanier's enthusiasms were Keats and Spenser, Shakespeare and Herbert, and he read deeply into the Elizabethan-Aristotelean controversies on the nature and purpose of poetry as expressed by Gosson, Sidney, and Puttenham. He was thus early imbued with the Elizabethan religion of art, and he was schooled to deal with ideas as entities of the consciousness rather than as components of systematic philosophies in the tradition of rationalism, or as servants of the emotions in the tradition of romanticism.

With the Elizabethans, he shared a love of music, and he had more than a little competence with the flute. The connections between poetry and music seemed to him, therefore, an inevitable consequence of the common origins of the two arts rather than an artificial study of analogies. The art of poetry thus became for him primarily the manifestation of sound and, through tone-color, of sight, rather than the communication of "truths."

In emphasizing Lanier's concern for the art of sound I am here, of course, deliberately by-passing an obvious kinship between him and the more conventional poets of his day, and an obvious difference between him and the moderns. This is his emphasis on moral idealism as expressed in his most-quoted line: "Music is Love in search of a word." The development of this idea would provide material for at least another essay, and as I am here attempting merely to stress one historical aspect of his work rather than to provide a well-rounded critical analysis, it is perhaps unnecessary. In any case, it is impossible.

The third source of his emphasis on art rather than on actuality lies in his interest in science. Lanier went far beyond the Elizabethan in his curiosity about the link between music and poetry and in his hope of finding its explanation in physics. When he went to Baltimore in 1873 he was immediately absorbed into the renaissance of orchestral music by playing in the Peabody Symphony Orchestra and into the renaissance of American science through his connection with President Gilman and the infant Johns Hopkins University. He was thus deeply impressed by the possibility of discovering a scientific basis for both music and poetry in mathematical physics. (Compare here Henry Adams's assertion that history must find a scientific basis or retire from the field of scholarship, and the turn, not many years later, of literary study to scientific linguistics for its authority.) In this new interest he was undoubtedly stimulated by his association with the mathematician Sylvester, the classicist Gildersleeve, the visiting physicist Hastings, and the philologist Cook. Largely as a result of these contacts, he took as his own specialized task the discovery of the physical structure of verse, and he even applied unsuccessfully for a fellowship so that he might pursue the study of physics for itself. Physics-music-poetry—here is the trilogy of elements that Lanier, the pioneer, the amateur, strove to weave together into a single fabric. Inevitably, art in itself became for him an obsession rather than merely a relaxation or a means of communication and uplift. Almost with his dying breath he stated his thesis, but he could do little more. The effort was too great for his rapidly failing health and his inadequate scholarly equipment. One challenging book of critical theory, a handful of experimental poems in illustration, and a huge store of lecture notes and personal letters alone remain. But his emphasis on the technical possibilities of the spoken word was to be handed on to others of greater scholarly training and more time and strength. T. S. Eliot and his fellows are no sports in our literary history.

One further note must be added, a note which perhaps ties this belated Elizabethan even more closely to modern trends in poetry than do the above somewhat desultory comments. Lanier differed from his rival for the Johns Hopkins professorship in English literature, Albert S. Cook, in one important respect. Both were attempting to find scientific bases for literary study, but whereas Cook was a philologist and thought of the study of literature as a branch of historical linguistics, Lanier strove toward an appreciation of the work of literature in itself by analysis of the forms and ideas to be found immediately in it. Although he attempted to master the history of English literature, he used what little knowledge he thus acquired to point up analogies and contrasts in form and theme rather than to define influences. That Cook and not Lanier received the appointment is a significant fact in the history of our university departments of English, with their emphasis on German philology rather than on French *explication de texte*. Perhaps if this true poet had held a pioneering chair of English and had lived to fill out his calling, there might not be as wide a chasm as there has been, at least until recently, between Cambridge gown and New York town.

NOTES

1. *The Centennial Edition of the Works of Sidney Lanier*, edited by Charles R. Anderson and others (Baltimore: Johns Hopkins Press, 1945), 10 vols.
2. *Selected Poems of Sidney Lanier*, with a preface by Stark Young (New York: Charles Scribner's Sons, 1947).
3. *Complete Poems and Stories of Edgar Allan Poe*, with introduction and explanatory notes by Arthur Hobson Quinn and bibliographical notes by Edward H. O'Neill (New York: Alfred A. Knopf, 1946), 2 vols.

Edmund Wilson:
The Dual Role of Criticism

This essay was solicited as one of three on "Edmund Wilson: Essays in Appreciation" by the editors of the *Nation* and was published in the special issue of February 22, 1958.

THE HIGH PLACE OF EDMUND WILSON in modern American literary criticism has been slow of recognition because he has always seemed to play the role of counselor, interpreter, and friend to his fellow writers and readers rather than that of the lawgiver or that of the chronicler.[1] Because most of his critical essays have been in the form of reviews of current books in such journals as the *Dial,* the *New Republic,* and *The New Yorker,* his philosophical depth and his historical perspective have not always been appreciated. Yet he has been, from the twenties down to the present time, the leading voice among those critics who cling to the conception of a work of art as an expression of its own creator and of the culture of which that creator is himself a product. A historical critic rather than a literary historian, he has done more that anyone else in his time to make the master works of his contemporaries intelligible to their own readers and to assign to them the values which posterity in many cases must accept. In this first of three essays in tribute to his achievement, it is my task to sketch in the outlines of the modern movement in American literary criticism so that, in his turn, Mr. Wilson may find his place in the literary hierarchy. The essays which follow will discuss his work as critic and journalist in more detail.

The late F. O. Matthiessen, speaking of the state of American poetry in the years prior to 1948, warned against the "serious cleavage" it revealed "between what we have learned to call mass civilization and minority culture." In broader terms, the same cleavage has tended to divide our critics into two principal groups: that which has made persistent efforts to read and evaluate literature as an immediate expression of life and that which has made it an object of aesthetic experience in itself. The issue is, of course, the old one between emphasis on content and emphasis on form, but it has gained a peculiar force in a time when the United States was producing a body of literary work which was at once violently critical of its own social ideals and institutions and obviously successful as works of art. Whatever his special school of thought, the critic today must choose whether for him literature is a means or an end; whether he looks closely at the novel, play, or poem in order to understand and evaluate better the life behind it and within it, or merely to understand it as an object in itself and to rise with it from the complexities of actual experience to a plane of ideal order. For T. S. Eliot and the so-called "New Critics" the role of literature is mainly the latter; to Edmund Wilson and the sociohistorical critics it is mainly the former.

The cleavage between these two groups dates back to the late nineteenth century when William Dean Howells was calling for a "truthful treatment of materials," and his close friend Henry James was admonishing, "Try to be one of the people on whom nothing is lost" so that your fiction may produce a total illusion of life rather than life itself. The facts that they remained friends and that subsequent literary historians classed them both as "realists" suggest that these early glimpses of the issue were abortive. It was not until the new literature came out in force that the voice of mass civilization in a Theodore Dreiser so dramatically challenged that of the minority culture in a Barrett Wendell. There was to be no blurring of the central problem from that time forward: American literature, and with it American literary criticism, must once more seek its roots in its own soil.

The literary radicalism of the next period was somewhat vague as to the social philosophies behind its protest, but it seemed consistent because it attacked the vested interests of nineteenth-cen-

tury gentility and called with a single voice for awareness of the
rising power of America and of the raw violence and conflict
which the new civilization revealed. Van Wyck Brooks called attention to the cleavage between the "high-brow" and the "low-
brow" in letters, Randolph Bourne saw the issue as one between
complacent age and rebellious youth, and H. L. Mencken led the
attack on the "Puritans" and the "Professors." The vague mirage
of "Socialism" promised solution to the problems thus laid bare
except when the more daring critics leaned to the then leftist extreme of "Anarchism" or to an even more sinister rightist form
of antidemocracy. The seeds of later dogmatisms were all present,
but none were defined as yet explicitly.

I I

It was at this time (1920–21) that Edmund Wilson returned from
his medical corps service in France and became managing editor
of *Vanity Fair,* and that T. S. Eliot, now permanently located in
London, became the editor of the *Criterion* (1923). The two
major critical voices of the new era of literary fulfillment had
chosen their rostrums and their philosophical angles of vision.

Edmund Wilson himself recognized the wide difference between
his own position and that of Eliot when, in his Princeton address
of 1941, "The Historical Interpretation of Literature," he summarized the essay on "Tradition and Individual Talent" and
pointed out that the relating of a work of art to its own "ideal
order" rather than to its own time, place, and authorship is a comparative rather than a historical method. He also attempted to
distinguish his own from the apparently historical but actually
chronological impressionism of Saintsbury. He then sought to find
the roots of his own thinking in the tradition (in another sense)
of Vico, Herder, Taine, Marx, and Freud. In doing so, he drew
up his own agenda. He did not plan to write a literary history,
but he did plan to use the historical method in his criticism of
individual works of art and he looked upon his task rightly as a
complex and demanding one. The critic, he concludes, is self-
elected as one who, through cultivated feeling and taste, *knows*
more about literature than do most other readers and he has an

obligation to help others give a meaning to experience. To do so, he must not only enjoy, he must *understand* the work under his review, and, to understand it fully, he must know the forces and the circumstances which have brought it into being. In thus pushing past mere form and probing into content, the critic become involved in the life issues with which the author was engaged and he must deal with the culture of which the work is an expression as well as with the work itself.

Three of Wilson's books stand out from the rest of his work as direct attempts to implement this philosophy by dealing with the culture behind a group of authors: *Axel's Castle* (1931), *To the Finland Station* (1940), and *The Wound and the Bow* (1941). The first deals with Aestheticism, the second with Marxism, and the third with Freudianism. In all, he attempts to move behind the historical context of a single work or a single author in order to discover and evaluate a cultural movement which seems to link the works under his review. In each case, he produced a book which went a long way toward giving a contemporary dogmatism its historical place and value and thus partially removing its sting.

In attempting to define Symbolism in its historical setting and to examine the work of its chief proponents, Edmund Wilson in *Axel's Castle* was, so to speak, carrying the war to the enemy; yet, in spite of a dubious linking of the movement with historical Romanticism, he pinpointed the central critical issue of the time. The symbolism of a Melville is of course romantic, but that of an Eliot or a Joyce is rather a part of the analytical reaction to the romanticism of a past era. Yet here for the first time, the intentions and techniques of an international group (Yeats, Eliot, Joyce, Proust, Stein, and Valéry) are brought under review, and the meaning of each made brilliantly clear by relating it to the common meaning, as Wilson sees it, in the movement. The final diagnosis of the alternatives open to Axel and Rimbaud, the retreat to the castle or the retreat to far lands, may not be entirely satisfactory but it helps in the historical judgments. Thus the historical method illuminates, in six cases, the critical judgment, even though the result is not quite literary history. A dogmatism is broken down and made to serve rather than master its adherents. A group of writers which, by their own principles, reject historicism, are found to have historical setting and to be what they are largely because of this fact.

To the Finland Station is a similar tour de force. While contemporaries who shared with Wilson the conviction of social responsibility in letters were being carried, during the late thirties, into various degrees of commitment to organized Communism and Fascism, Wilson reported, in *Travels in Two Democracies* (1936), on his visit to Russia and then took a Guggenheim fellowship year to study Marxism in its historical setting. The result gave the group of disillusioned spiritual exiles a reasoned analysis of this dogmatism when the Russo-German pact revealed the fallacy of identifying idealistic socialism with Russian politics. A comparison of Wilson's application of the Marxist formula to literary criticism with the literary criticism and history of Max Eastman, Granville Hicks, V. F. Calverton, Newton Arvin, and many others reveals the difference between the concepts of an ideology as servant and as master.

The third dogmatism of the times to come under Wilson's review was Freudianism. *The Wound and the Bow* follows the pattern of *Axel's Castle* in that a series of studies of individual authors is concluded by an essay which provides the clue to their common meaning. In this case, the wound of Philoloctetes provides Sophocles with a psychological reason for the myth of the unerring bow of Apollo. Again, the application of a Freudian formula is related to the larger mythical traditions of literature before being applied directly, as it was by Ludwig Lewisohn, Waldo Frank, Van Wyck Brooks, and many lesser critics to the neuroses and psychoses of authors. And again Wilson provided a historical dimension to modern American literary criticism without himself writing literary history.

The school of critics of which Wilson is thus the leader was disrupted during the thirties and forties by the conflicting strengths of these and other distracting dogmatisms. A few critics like Malcolm Cowley, Maxwell Geismar, Howard M. Jones, F. O. Matthiessen, James T. Farrell, Alfred Kazin, and Lionel Trilling have shared with him the task of keeping alive the intimate relationship between the work of art and its culture, but the group as a whole lacks the coherence and commitment of its analytical opposite. Whether the temperate liberalism of these genuine critics will survive one more dogmatism remains to be seen.

NOTE

1. In this reprinting, I have restored the few cuts that were made in the original text by the editors of the *Nation*.

III
Trans-Atlantic Perspectives

The English Literary Horizon: 1815–35

Published in a special "American" issue of *Studies in Philology*, edited by Norman Foerster, at the University of North Carolina, XXIII (January, 1926): 1-15.

"THE ATLANTIC," said Nathaniel Parker Willis, "is to us a century." In other words, he assumed that the interval of some three thousand miles was equivalent to the passage of a hundred years, and that the American of about 1830 could therefore view the English literary horizon of that day with a clearness impossible to a native English observer. If this exceedingly novel idea had even a slight basis in reason, the literary opinions of those Americans who visited England have far more significance than has been attached to them.

Irving develops the theory even further in his essay on Campbell. "The vast ocean that rolls between us," he says, "like a space of time, removes us beyond the sphere of personal favor, personal prejudice, or personal familiarity. A European work, therefore, appears before us depending simply on its intrinsic merits. We have no private friendship, no party purpose to serve, by magnifying the author's merits; and, in sober sadness, the humble state of our national literature places us far below any feeling of national rivalship." [1]

The natural place to turn for this American judgment of Eng-

lish literature would be the critical reviews of the time, but unfortunately there were none published in America which could, in
the fullest sense, be called independent. The practices of clipping
from English journals or deferring to English judgments were
still dominant in American journalism in spite of the efforts of
the *North American Review* and to some extent the *Port-Folio*
and the *Analectic*. Even the *North American* was modeled on
lines laid down by the *Edinburgh* and the *Quartely*.

The American traveler in England, however, was in a position
to judge with far greater freedom. In the first place, unlike his
English brother in America, he was a man of exceedingly broad
culture and persistent energy. England sent her fops and adven-
turers to America; America sent her leaders of thought in all lines
to England. The English traveler felt that he was descending to
a lower plane of civilization and was fully prepared with his quota
of scorn; the American traveler frankly recognized his ascent to a
higher, and for the most part took the step in order to learn rather
than to criticize.

I I

At the time when Irving and Willis wrote, many of America's
best minds had made the trip on a variety of missions, had met
and been entertained by England's most exclusive society, and had
written their impressions home in the form of letters, journals,
and travel books. Her outstanding statesmen, her leaders of industrial and religious thought, and by 1835 many of her literary
men, had become familiar with England's culture, not only from
reading her literature, but from mingling intimately in her intellectual and social life as well. Irving himself traveled over much
of Europe, including England, in 1804-5, and spent a large share
of his time from 1815 to 1832 in London and Liverpool; Cooper
took his entire establishment, including his servants, to England
in 1828 and lived in London as well as Paris; Emerson made his
first trip in 1833; and in the same year Willis obtained his entrée
to that circle of London wits and fashionables which gathered
about the brilliant Lady Blessington, a group which included
Disraeli, Tom Moore, Byron, Bulwer, and Campbell, as well as
lords and ladies of no mean rank. By 1835 also, there had been

published in America as many as thirty books of travels in England, and the distinguished American visitors who had left less formal records numbered many hundreds, among them Longfellow, Ticknor, John Quincy Adams, Edward Everett, and the artist Washington Allston. The composite picture of literary England afforded by such a group as this could scarcely fail to be significant.

George Ticknor, who was in England from 1815 to 1819 for the sole purpose of enlarging his own intellectual horizon, has expressed perhaps better than any other the primary motive which brought the cultured and ambitious Americans to British soil. "In every literature," he says, "there are many things to be learnt besides the words and the language, which can never be learnt but on the spot, because they are preserved but as a kind of tradition." His objective consisted chiefly, as he puts it, in seeing many different persons, learning their opinions, modifying his own, and, in general, collecting that undefined and indefinite feeling respecting books and authors which existed then in Europe as a kind of unwritten tradition but was almost wholly lacking in America.[2]

It was with this viewpoint that the best of the American travelers made out their lists of English literary celebrities whom they thought worthy of visit. They had read countless English books, they were familiar with English history and philosophy, and they were eager to add, by personal contact with the great, to a culture of their own which they were frank to recognize as built solidly upon English foundations.

If we were to look back now over our histories of English literature to that period so commonly labeled "The Romantic Revolt," we should probably reach the conclusion that a visitor to England during the period 1815–35 would think first of Byron, Shelley, and Keats, then of the Lake poets, Wordsworth, Coleridge, and possibly Southey, certainly of Lamb, Hazlitt, and Scott, and probably of Jane Austen, Blake, Landor, Hunt, and De Quincey. At all events, if any one of us were privileged now to make a journey to the England of that day, we should seek out our authors in some such order.

It is somewhat surprising, therefore, to turn to the estimate of this self-appointed posterity, the American in England, and to find an entirely different order of rating. Cooper makes his Mr. Howell in *Homeward Bound* name Scott (with emphasis), Southey, Coleridge, Wordsworth, Moore, Bulwer, Disraeli, Rogers, Campbell, Horace Smith, Miss Landon, and Barry Cornwall as proper subjects for a visit, and this list is similar in its surprising inequalities to that of the average traveler from America.

Whether Scotland or Walter Scott first attracted the American, certain it is that the reputation of each augmented that of the other; and, as Scott was usually first on the list of English authors, so the literary society of Edinburgh was more appealing than any other. Perhaps because so many Americans had studied at the University of Edinburgh, or because the Scottish character and country were more like his own than England, or because he had read the Waverly novels from cover to cover and loved the background against which they were written and the author who wrote them—whatever the reason, the American, high or low, literary or not, sought out the north country as the first object of his pilgrimage. There is almost more about Scott, his haunts, and the scenes of his novels and poetry than about places connected with the names of all other English authors, living or dead, put together.

The society of Edinburgh was frankly and liberally of a literary cast and interest, chiefly centering about the University. Many literary salons were held by professors and by those with literary pretensions or interests. The one most frequently mentioned is that of Mrs. Grant of Laggan, "one of the women that the world is willing to call meritorious to save themselves the trouble of making any inquiries about her." [3] With a slight literary reputation of her own and a power of conversation which attracted even though it did not hold for long, she collected about her most of the interesting people of the town, and practically all of the Americans. Hers was typical of many such coteries, and was particularly congenial to the Americans because she was uniformly cordial to them.

It was in such society as this that the real lions of literary Scotland sometimes found their way and were trapped by the curious visitor. Scott, Jeffrey, Wilson, and Sydney Smith were often met for the first time at one of these formal but hospitable gatherings.

The life of Scott from the days when he was a clerk of the

sessions in the parliament house of Edinburgh to the last days of his declining health and death at Abbotsford, as well as every foot of ground of which he wrote or on which he stepped, might be followed in these journals. A glimpse of him is caught in that "small dark room in the Court of Sessions," where he was introduced by Jeffrey to the plain American Quaker John Griscom; he is to be seen walking about the streets of Edinburgh with Ticknor, pointing out the sights which had association with the great of Scotland; in Paris the Scottish met the American lion, Cooper (in Scott's own phrase); in London he dined, together with Cooper, at Sotheby's, and afterward advanced graciously into the adjoining room, "a maze of petticoats," so that the fair one might "play with his mane." [4] At Abbotsford, with his children, Sophia and William, and his dogs and cats, he threw open his doors to Irving, Cooper, Willis, Edward Everett, and almost every American visitor who passed his house with or without introduction; and few who came to spend an hour left at the end of the second day. The education of the sport-loving and altogether unliterary William, the charms of Sophia, the beauties and associations of the surrounding country, Melrose and Dryburgh Abbeys, and the locality of what was once the Forest of Sherwood, were the chief subjects of discussion with these strangers, and when they left, it was with a promise to visit again before returning to America.

After the death of its owner, Abbotsford was second only to Stratford as a literary shrine, and the thought of standing before the desk at which the Waverly novels were in all probability written was enough to make the hurried traveler take as much as a day from his tour, and a night as well, if the moon were clear, for Scott himself had advised:

> If thou wouldst view fair Melrose aright,
> Go visit it by the pale moonlight.[5]

The Scott country too was hallowed by his touch. The barren borderland was made fertile for the imagination, the charms of the magnificent scenery of the lakes were doubled, and the owner of Ellen's Isle set up a bower after the description given in the poem as a memorial to its author and, it is safe to add, as a bait to these tourists. Derbyshire, Kenilworth, Tantallon Castle near Yester,

and other spots scattered over the entire island called forth memories of this or that novel or poem, while the people who furnished the originals for some of the characters were visited as
though they had something of greatness in them thereby.

The extent of this attitude of reverence may be estimated by
the remark of Dr. Valentine Mott that, upon visiting Edinburgh
in 1834, he was not unmindful of "breathing within the atmosphere that had been enchanted by her own *Great Wizard of the
North*." [6] It was with the man more than with the novels and
poems that these travelers were concerned. The most frequent
picture of Scott which they present is that of a warm-hearted
country gentleman, and the popularity of the Waverly novels
seems to have established their excellences and to have precluded
even a thought of criticism.

None equals Scott in the fullness of his place in the heart of
the American visitor, but the kindness of Professor Wilson, the
"Christopher North" of *Blackwood's,* of Francis Jeffrey, and of
Sydney Smith added to the pleasure of a visit to Edinburgh.
Henry B. McLellan, a young American student of theology, describes "a fine burst of eloquence from Professor Wilson on the
loud whispering of the students in the lecture room." [7] Later, he
says, he called on Wilson and was ushered into his study, where
among a chaotic mass of books and papers, he found him reclining
on an easy elbow chair, and Wilson told him of the time when
De Quincey had stayed with him and spent most of his day in
bed drinking coffee.

Jeffrey was always interesting, but did not create a uniformly
favorable impression. The American naturalist, Audubon, describes him as he entered the room with his wife as a "small (not
to say tiny) being, with a woman under one arm and a hat under
the other," but "fully aware of his weight in society" and with a
shrewd, not to say cunning, eye.[8] But to Dr. Gibson, who saw
him several years later, he appeared thoroughly engaging, of a
"light, slender figure, florid complexion, round, sparkling, prominent, black, eye, animated and rapid elocution, and stylish
dress." [9]

It was Sydney Smith, however, who was most famed for his
talk. Ticknor exclaims that he "never saw a man so formed to
float down the stream of conversation, and, without seeming to

have any direct influence upon it, to give it his own hue and charm." [10] A corpulent gentleman of fifty he was at the time (1819), yet a man of brilliant wit and sound judgment. Later, from Smith's own pew in St. Paul's, Ticknor heard him preach a moral sermon of "great condensation of thought and purity of style," by far the best, he asserts, that he had ever heard in Great Britain.

In Liverpool the man who was most cordial to the Americans was the banker, William Roscoe, who was likewise an historian, a philanthropist and something of a literary man. As Liverpool was the commonest port of entry, few Americans missed a visit to this hospitable Englishman; while in London Sir James Mackintosh occupied a like position, going out of his way to discover the American visitors and invite them to his table.

I I I

This sort of welcome of course colored the American travelers' estimates of their hosts, but not so far as to rank them second to Scott in literary interest. It was Wordsworth who was accorded this honor. To many, however, the motive for the visit to Cumberland was one of sceptical curiosity rather than of reverence. Southey was almost equally worthy of a visit in the American estimation, and very often the two were seen together at the house of one or the other. To some the trip to the lakes was primarily for the scenery, and a visit to the poets was most incidental. The picture of Wordsworth most frequently drawn is that of a quiet, rather old man, living among the lakes in philosophic calm and interesting himself in America, although not believing in the ultimate success of her experiment in democracy or in the practicality of reform in his own country. When the subject of conversation was religion, he usually took his guest for a walk at sundown to a high place where they sat for a time in devout silence; and when it was politics and Southey was present, they sat in the well furnished library or walked about the garden. Dorothy was often present with her welcome, but neither Coleridge nor any of the other frequent English visitors to Grasmere appeared. Of the two, Wordsworth and Southey, the former left the more favorable impression upon those of a devout turn of mind; while the latter was invariably recalled for his facility of conversation and his wide knowledge.

Coleridge was, in these later days, resident at Highgate under constant medical supervision. Nevertheless, he became a close friend of Allston, Irving, Samuel F. B. Morse, and C. R. Leslie, and was accorded the honor of a reverential visit by many another. It was into the studio of the two last-named artists that he once came in one of those fits of deep despondency so frequent with him at that time. His friends, however, had planned a means of attack. Morse saw that diplomacy was needed and immediately greeted Coleridge with the statement that he and Leslie had just been discussing the nature of beauty and wanted his opinion. Leslie sensed the situation and took up the argument, as it were, in the midst. Coleridge soon became interested and launched forth on one of those floods of eloquence which were at once the joy and the dismay of his friends.[11] White haired and dignified, with a mind absorbed in his own vague thought, he presented a somewhat formidable though cordial aspect to his less intimate visitors.

Of the other poets, Keats and Shelley are scarcely ever mentioned, while the scandal connected with Byron made him more an object of gossip than of visit. Their absence in Italy for so much of the time may likewise have had something to do with this oversight. Ticknor called on Byron, however, and discussed many things, among them the prospects of a visit to America. Willis followed his footsteps through Greece and discussed him with the Countess Guiccioli, whom he met in the Tuileries. Irving and many others visited Newstead Abbey, where the memories of his destructive actions were softened by a visit to Annesley Hall, the former home of Mary Chaworth, enriched by the romantic associations with Byron's early love and disappointment. There was reason for staying at Newstead also; for its new master, Colonel Wildman, was among the most cordial of country-house gentlemen in England. Fourteen years after Byron had so despoiled it of its timber that not a tree remained and had allowed the abbey to deteriorate until hardly a room was habitable, C. S. Stewart, another American, spent some time there and found that the new owner had surrounded the estate with six miles of high and substantial brick wall, planted thousands of young trees, and built new dwellings and outhouses. He was assigned to the top of the tower adjoining the old ivy-covered arch and accessible only by a winding stone staircase, up which Byron had retreated after the rest of the building had almost fallen in ruins.[12]

It is curious to note, after this neglect of those poets whom we have since numbered among the great, the large number of Americans who stopped off in Sheffield long enough to see the melancholy James Montgomery, writer of hymns and editor of a local paper, "no less respected for his mild virtues as a man, than admired for his excellence as a poet." [13] He was one of those men who are popular in their day because they express with facility the respectable emotions of the average man. And it was this same feeling for propriety in literature and life which made Hannah More the most visited of all English literary women. In a quiet cottage at Barleywood on the Bristol road, she was to be found with her sister. Visitors had become so numerous by 1828 that she was obliged to admit them only three times a week, when she made up in cordiality for the seeming lack of hospitality in the restriction. Often she sent them on their way with inscribed copies of her works, and always with a "sensation of awe and pleasure." [14] Page after page of the American records is filled with accounts of these visits. Similarly Maria Edgeworth was, among novelists, second only to Scott in the homage paid to her. Her correspondence with the latter had materially added to her fame; but above all it was her elderly modesty, coupled with an entertaining vivacity, which made the visit to her family one of special pleasure.

This was the average list of English literary celebrities whom the American traveler thought worthy of visit. Carlyle does not seem to have been noticed except by Emerson and Longfellow, and the latter was not particularly impressed. The warm and immediate kinship between the Scotsman and Emerson, however, is one of the most notable examples of all literary friendships. Emerson felt that Wordsworth, Coleridge, and Carlyle were the only literary masters of any great note in England, and he found Wordsworth "not prepossessing" and Coleridge unable to "bend to a new companion and think with him." [15] He had discovered Carlyle in the reviews and the two men warmed to each other immediately. They went out together, says Emerson, to "walk over long hills," and finally "sat down and talked of the immortality of the soul," [16] while Carlyle testifies that the only American who had sought him out at dreary Craigenputtock had talked and heard talk to his heart's content, and left them all really sad to part with him.[17]

Similarly Ticknor and Willis were among the few who looked upon Charles Lamb and his friends as people of any real distinction, and neither of them shows any too great a degree of reverence or admiration. Ticknor visited Hazlitt in the room which had been previously occupied by Milton and found its walls whitewashed and scribbled over with short scraps of poetry and brilliant thoughts in the nature of a commonplace book. Later he met "these people" at a dinner at Godwin's and makes notes of "Lamb's gentle humor, Hunt's passion, and Curran's volubility, Hazlitt's sharpness and point, and Godwin's great head full of cold brains, all coming into contact and conflict, and agreeing in nothing but their common hatred of everything that has been more successful than their own works." [18]

The picture which Willis draws is more sympathetic. At breakfast with a lawyer friend in the Temple, he was introduced to Elia and Bridget a short time before Lamb's death. "There was a rap on the door at last," he says, "and enter a gentleman in black small-clothes and gaiters, short and very slight in his person, his head set on his shoulders with a thoughtful, forward bent, his hair just sprinkled with gray, a beautiful deepset eye, aquiline nose, and a very indescribable mouth. Whether it expressed most humor or feeling, good nature or a kind of whimsical peevishness, or twenty other things which passed over it by turns, I can not in the least be certain." He was followed by the "small, bent figure" of his sister. The subsequent conversation was full of trifles, although in it Lamb answered the famous question, "Who reads an American book?" by confessing that Mary devoured Cooper's novels with a ravenous appetite and that Woolman's *Journal* was the only American book he had ever read twice.[19]

But most of Willis' time was spent in the brilliant circle of Lady Blessington, where he met literary notables who were socially inaccessible to the average American. His *Pencillings* are crowded with anecdotes of Bulwer, Disraeli, Procter, Tom Moore, and Campbell, as well as many others. For Moore and Campbell he had great sympathy, although he was not uncritical. On one occasion he breakfasted with Procter, and then the latter was out of the room, he copied from an edition of his poems some comments scribbled on the fly-leaf by Coleridge, inscribed "a map of the road to Paradise drawn in Purgatory on the confines of Hell, by S. T. C. July 30, 1819." The note began, "Barry Cornwall is a poet, *me saltem judice,* and in that sense of the word in which I apply it to Charles Lamb and W. Wordsworth," and it proceeded with some admonitions to the author and to authors in general on the subject of writing poetry.[20]

Much of Willis' most entertaining gossip concerns Tom Moore. One of his best pictures is of a group around the piano after a dinner at Lady Blessington's when the poet played and sang his own songs "with a pathos that beggars description," and then rose and disappeared from the room before his hearers could collect their feelings enough for speech.[21]

Like Willis, Cooper met only a restricted group of British litterati and hence had opportunities not open to the average American for forming a judgment of English literary society. There was some confusion as to just who he was, and both Godwin and Samuel Rogers called on him shortly after his settlement in London under the impression that he was the son of a former friend. He was strongly impressed with Godwin's sincerity in his philosophy but scornful of his ignorance of America, while in Rogers he found a sympathetic friend and later a cordial host. He took dinner with him a number of times and attended many of his *petits déjeûners,* which then had "deservedly a reputation in London." It was principally through Rogers, a certain Mr. Sotheby, and Sir James Mackintosh that he met those literary and political figures who so cordially entertained him during his stay and from whom he derived that impression of the English character which later formed the basis of his adverse criticism in his *Gleanings in Europe* and elsewhere.

I V

Irving had one very important point in common with Willis and Cooper. After the publication of the *Sketch Book* in 1820 he was recognized as a literary man himself and was welcomed to exclusive circles which were closed to others. One of the most remarkable facts about the visits of these three Americans is the British lionizing of them at a time when the sting of a second military defeat at the hands of the United States was still fresh. It only proves what a slight effect the American wars had upon English society. Cooper's novels were being read almost as widely as Scott's, Willis was well armed with letters which told of his native importance in no uncertain terms, and Irving wrote two books on England which flattered and idealized her in irresistible terms. In circles where Byron was mentioned with horror and Lamb ignored, these three Americans found themselves altogether at home.

Irving's shyness before he became famous and his later willingness to accept what favors were extended to him make his literary judgment of England entirely different from that of the average American. He was never a traveler in England in the ordinary sense. He was a stranger until he became practically a native. His first visit to Europe in 1804 was planned by his brothers, who feared for his health; and he reached London only after a tour of the Continent, in which, he confesses, he shifted from city to city and laid countries aside like books after giving them a hasty perusal.[22]

His visit of 1815 was with similarly unliterary intentions. He arrived in Liverpool as the agent of a company which was trembling on the verge of bankruptcy, and his closest associations were with his brother, Peter, then an invalid, and with his sister, Sarah Van Wart, and her family at Birmingham. His chief concerns, apart from his business cares, were in touring places of historical interest and in attending the theaters, always of first importance with him.

Little by little, however, and without previous intention, he gained a foothold in literary England. He called upon Campbell at Sydenham, only to find him away; but a conversation with Mrs. Campbell laid the foundations for one of his major literary associations.[23] On another excursion he visited Scott at Abbotsford and was urged to extend his stay to several days. Through the publisher, Murray, he met the elder Disraeli, but his contacts extended no further at the time. Later he became more or less intimate with Moore, Rogers, and some others; still his closest friendships were with the American artists Allston, Morse, Leslie, Stuart Newton, and their associates.

The reason for this was that Irving's literary mind lived in an England of the past, an England that never was. He sought out the places made famous by literary and historical associations. He would go far to see Stratford, but experienced no unusual excitement at a first meeting with Coleridge. It was this quality which made him so valuable in uniting the feelings of the two countries, but of little worth as a judge of contemporary literature or literary people.

Of Scott and Campbell he has written at some length. His account of Abbotsford and its owner is full of personal admiration and kindly remembrance of the time spent there; while in his estimate of Campbell, he merely voices the opinion so generally held at the time that the poet was sacrificing a delicate but undoubted genius in critical work because of his despair of ever sustaining his early reputation.

Irving's literary interest in England's past was, however, shared by many of his fellow visitors from America. The most universally appealing association was, of course, that of Stratford and Shakespeare. On the high road to London, not a traveler failed to pay it a visit, and its honors were almost equally shared by the English poet born there and the American essayist who had immortalized it. Irving was not the first to visit the Red Lion, but the charm of his essay in the *Sketch Book* cast a glamour over places and sights already sacred and started that reverence for old world shrines which has ever since been the dominant interest of the American abroad. The old landlady showed Willis the poker on which she had inscribed the words "Geoffrey Crayon's Sceptre" and recounted the story of the evening when she had tried to persuade the American to wake from his reveries by the fire and go to bed. The house where Shakespeare was born, Ann Hathaway's cottage, the site of the once famous mulberry tree, the little church and the tomb of the poet, as well as the forbidding estate of Sir Thomas Lucy, were all the objects of pilgrimages. The traveler scrawled his name on the visitor's books and took coach again on his way to London.

Next to those of Shakespeare, the former haunts of Samuel

Johnson were principal objects for the tourist. Litchfield is mentioned many times; few stopped to visit it, although the very name suggested to Dewey a "sort of home." Many, however, shone in the reflected glory of the memory of their contacts with the old doctor, and Dr. Parr, that curious and ponderous replica of the literary dictator, was the object of a visit from Ticknor chiefly for this reason.

The picture of literary England thus afforded by the records of American travelers is curious in its inequalities and its eccentricities. Irving and Willis were right in their assumption that three thousand miles of water would make for a different perspective, but they were wrong in their hope that this perspective would coincide with the judgments of posterity. Rather it coincided more nearly with those of the age immediately preceding. The English authors most sought after by the Americans were those of established reputation, either gentlemen and ladies who were enjoying in their latter years the results of their previous work, or writers who had won contemporary favor, as did Scott, by producing exactly what the public wanted. The American observer had learned his English literature from the same sources as the average Englishman. His own magazines copied generously from those of England, and his own publishers found greater profit in reprinting the novels of Disraeli or Scott without copyright royalties than in venturing to put forth the work of native Americans. His literary fads had, therefore, a marked tendency to follow those of England, and if he was free of one prejudice, he usually substituted another for it. Where he was uninfluenced by the curse of domestic politics, which so controlled the criticism of the *Quarterly* and the *Edinburgh,* and by the social dominance of literature which ostracised Shelley and lionized Disraeli, he suffered instead from political jealousy and hurt pride on the one hand, and from too great a reverence for old England on the other. He gives us a different and altogether interesting picture of literary England, but his limited perspective, in spite of his basic intelligence and his eagerness to learn, is somewhat disappointing.

In his appreciation of the human aspects of those authors he visited, however, his comments have greater value. It is hard to believe that Scott and Cooper belonged to two separate nations which, for almost forty years, had been in a state of actual or near hostility. In the realm of literature the bonds of humanity and a common language so far counter-balanced political hostilities and national rivalries as to make harmony inevitable. The Americans were not jealous because, as Irving admitted, they had nothing with which to rival England's supremacy; and the English were uniformly cordial because their guests were their admirers. As long as the American visitors were willing to sit at their feet, the English literary celebrities were not immune to the flattery implied and spoken; the Americans were wise enough to accept the situation and to profit by the rich culture of the older country. The result was that they were afforded an unexampled opportunity of surveying the accepted English literary world from a fresh viewpoint and of recounting its human and personal aspects in records that vary from hurried letters to formal travel books to be printed and read at home.

NOTES

1. *Biographies and Miscellanies* (New York, 1866), pp. 142-143.
2. *Life, Letters and Journals* (Boston, 1877), I, 274-276.
3. Letter to W. P. from Edinburgh, in 1814 *North American Review*, I (July, 1815): 193-194.
4. *Gleanings in Europe: England* (Philadelphia, 1837), I, 219.
5. *Lay of the Last Minstrel*, Canto II.
6. *Travels in Europe and the East* (New York, 1842), p. 26.
7. *Journal of a Residence in Scotland, etc.* (Boston, 1834), pp. 204ff.
8. Maria R. Audubon, *Audubon and His Journals* (New York, 1897), I, 200-201.
9. *Rambles in Europe in 1839* (Philadelphia, 1844), pp. 180ff.
10. *Life, Letters and Journals* (Boston, 1876), I, 265-266.
11. *Letters and Journals* (Boston, 1914), I, 95.
12. *Sketches of Society in Great Britain and Ireland* (Philadelphia, 1834), I, 235ff.
13. Zachariah Allen, *The Practical Tourist* (Boston, 1832), I, 293.
14. Jacob Green, *Notes of a Traveller* (Philadelphia, 1830), II, 98ff.
15. R. W. Emerson, *Works* (Boston: Houghton, Mifflin Co., 1903-4), I, 14.
16. *Ibid.*, I, 18.
17. J. A. Froude, *Thomas Carlyle* (London, 1882), II, 290-291.
18. *Life, Letters and Journals* (Boston, 1876), I, 24.
19. *Pencillings by the Way* (New York, 1844), pp. 184-185.
20. *Ibid.*, p. 189.
21. *Ibid.*, p. 193.
22. *Life and Letters* (London, 1864), I, 120.
23. *Ibid.*, p. 253.

The American in Europe:
Then and Now

Address at the farewell banquet of the second triannual conference of the Nordic Association for American Studies on June 26, 1964, held under the sponsorship of the Amerikansk Institutt of the Universitetet I Oslo, Norway. From *USA in Focus: Recent Re-Interpretations*, edited by Sigmund Skard (Oslo: Universitetsforlaget, 1966), pp. 174-188.

IN BEING AN INVITED AMERICAN VISITOR among Europeans who are making a serious study of the history and culture of the United States, I cannot help recalling the very different feeling of Mark Twain when, almost exactly a century ago, he read in the newspapers an announcement of a proposed "Pleasure Excursion to Europe and the Holy Land" on which his Innocents Abroad were to "see the ships of twenty navies—the customs and costumes of twenty curious people—the great cities of half a world—they were to hob-nob with nobility and hold friendly converse with kings and princes."

These innocents were Americans and the countries they were to visit were European and romantic and different, as these Nordic lands are but there would seem to be very little in common between them and those of us who are now traveling and anticipating what sights and experiences travel would bring. The stereotypes associated with the "Overseas American" as he is sometimes called, and the peoples of his visits have basically changed in these years and the relationships between the American traveler and the distant lands of his visit are no longer what they were when the "half-man and half-allegator" of Davy Crockett set out for the "forbidden seas" and the "barbarous coasts" that lured Melville's Redburn to run away from home. As Americans in Europe we have lost much of the romance that comes from distances and differences. We are interested in Europeans and you are interested in our culture, not so much because of strangeness and variety as because we recognize that we are at bottom one people inhabiting one shrinking and overcrowded planet. Our primary motive for visit and study is an effort to understand each other better so that we may live together in cooperative endeavor.

But it was not always so. There are and always have been differences between us, stemming not so much from our basic common human nature as from the circumstances of our different experiences of the past three hundred years.

It is probably very difficult for Europeans who have lived on the same land for a thousand years or more to realize what it means to an American to come to Europe. For there is always in his experience more or less of the element of the prodigal, and he expects a taste of the fatted calf. His attitude toward his parents is inevitably mixed, confused, and ambivalent, for he is no ordinary traveler visiting a foreign country; he is a native coming home after a long—oh, so long, absence.

I am not, as far as I know—and unhappily for me—a Scandinavian, but my name probably derives from the Anglo-Saxon verb "spillan" (to murder), my family on both sides came from midland England, and I am neither Celt nor Norman. I must therefore be a Saxon emigrant who went to the United States two or three centuries ago after a brief stop-over of some thousand years in the British Isles. So this evening I am in fact as well as in sentiment, a prodigal son. And to bring my point down to the more immediate, let me add that my uncle, whose forbears emigrated to New Jersey in 1685 and became succesful farmers and businessmen, owning large tracts of arable soil and comfortable country and city homes, returned in 1890 to the Sheffield farm of his family origin and found the inhabitants of the same name still renting from an absentee landlord. This is, in a nutshell, the American success story of the local boy who went to the big city to make his fortune and now returns, with or without that fortune made, to the scenes of his origin. And this is the story, in essence, of the American in Europe, both then and even now. He is a traveler in only a very limited and special sense and his attitude, as well as the attitudes of the Europeans toward him, is colored by these filial implications.

Oscar Handlin and others have attempted to reduce this experience of the emigrant-immigrant to a sociological formula, but I do not find that easy to do. I would rather think of it as a human and historical process, as a basic American condition of life, persistent always in the national character, but altered through the years by circumstance. And I would look to the writings of Americans who, like myself, have repeatedly felt the lure of Europe, with its divisive East–West tug of war, for its ultimate expression.

II

Americans have traditionally had two basic reactions to these circumstances. These are best expressed, I think, by our two first national men of letters, the essayist Washington Irving and the novelist James Fenimore Cooper. I have heard these described as the "Oh, Mother, is it really you?" attitude; and the "What makes you think you're better than I am?"

Washington Irving has been called our first "Ambassador at large from the New World to the Old," and no better phrase could be invented to describe the role which he played and which many another American before or since has played. To him there were two worlds—an Old and a New—and they were both, but in different ways, his home. Essentially a warm and friendly person, he wandered through England, Germany, and Spain during the best parts of his life, seeking out the quaint relics of the past and the kindlier human traits of the present in the people and places he encountered. "I am always fond of visiting new scenes and observing strange characters and manners," wrote Geoffrey Crayon, Gent., the imaginary author of *The Sketch Book*. "My native country was full of youthful promise; Europe was rich in the accumulated treasures of age. Her very ruins told the history of times gone by. . . . I longed to wander over the scenes of renouned achievement—to tread, as it were, in the footsteps of antiquity . . . and lose myself among the shadowy grandeurs of the

past." So Irving created an England that never was from the fig-
ments of his fancy and peopled his native Hudson valley with
ghosts from the Rhineland and from Granada. At the same time
he was immersed in the gaiety of the present. I have been, he confesses, "at the levee and drawing room, been at routs, and balls,
and dinners; been hand-and-glove with nobility and mobility,
until like Trim, I have satisfied the sentiment, and am now preparing to make my escape."

There is something of the provincial in all this. No native lover
of England—no Lamb or Dickens—would write of ruins and routs
with such wide-eyed wonder. And this is Irving's charm; he is the
spokesman for the naïve American confronting things vaguely
familiar but forever new and fresh, things which the native would
take for granted but which for him are objects of fancy and
wonder. He is the prototype of the innocent American abroad.

Fenimore Cooper will model for the second kind of early
American traveler, the skeptic and critic who shows his provincialism by resenting the very things Irving so happily accepts. At the
end of his visit to England, he took leave of "a country that I
would fain like, but whose prejudices and national antipathies
throw a chill over all my affections; . . . a country that all respect
but few love." He had had much the same social acceptance as
had Irving, for his early novels were already well known, but
when he saw his first ruins, he remarked, "Had we seen Netley
Abbey, just as far advanced toward completion as it was, in fact,
advanced toward decay, our speculations would have been limited
by a few conjectures on its probable appearance." And he traveled
from Canton to Canton in Switzerland observing at firsthand in
this laboratory of political change all the variations from democracy to aristocracy which were crowded, like the snow-capped
mountains, into this tiny nation.

This was another kind of Ambassador from the New World to
the Old, the critic who constantly observes men and manners
wherever he goes and who uses his ambivalence to provide perspective for analysis and comment. Equally with Irving a traveler
of divided loyalties who is returning from his new home to his old
one, he recognizes the importance of American ideas—fresh and
crude and dynamic—as they apply to the problems and prejudices of
European facts—mellow and warm and stagnant and corrupt—but

perhaps mainly because of a difference of temperament, his reactions are in almost every case the opposite of those of the genial
essayist. Here then is the pattern of the American in Europe, at
least for the first century of independence, the pattern of the
prodigal returning from his wanderings, sobered, soured, sad, or
sentimental, to the home of his youth. He came from a New
World; he was returning to an Old one.

Mark Twain was therefore right when he defined the traditional role of the American traveler as that of an innocent abroad.
Americans today are inclined to flatter themselves on their out-
growing of this innocence and to write books about their "coming
of age" and of the end of what may be called their prolonged
adolescence, a state from which some of the authors of these books
do not seem even yet to have fully recovered. But the record
would substantiate a conclusion that a whole people devoted some
three hundred years—from 1600 to 1900—to the process of growing up on a new continent. The American immediately feels himself a new man in a new world when he steps off his ship at
Roanoke Island in 1585 or at Ellis Island in 1885. This is a New
World with new resources and opportunities, and the immigrant
immediately recasts his life in terms of a New World–Old World
dichotomy. Cushing Strout in his recent book[1] attributes to Jefferson "the mythical conception of a Europe whose every charm is
the vicious opposite of an American virtue. . . . His rhetoric trans-
formed Americans into a group of idealized sculptured figures. On
the one side stand Liberty, Happiness, Innocence, and Simplicity,
pointing toward the Future, while separated by a pool of water
and facing them with menacing mien stand Despotism, Misery,
Corruption, Sophistication, wrapped in the shrouds of the Past.
. . . It was a set piece easily and frequently envisaged by the nineteenth-century American imagination."

This is at least one way of seeing the myth, but a reverse image
may also be visible in the mirror across the hall of our gallery.
Here the naïve untutored American with his awkwardnesses and
his social crudities, his pragmatic and materialistic concerns, and
his cultural poverty, is counterpoised to the rich and secure culture of the tradition-drenched Europe. This is the image presented
by the early European travelers in America—by Trollope and
Dickens—and fixed for all time in the art of fiction by Henry

James. In describing the reactions of the fifty year old Hawthorne to England and Rome, James carves for us our other set-piece: "I know nothing more remarkable, more touching, than the sight of this odd youthful-elderly mind, contending so late in the day with new opportunities for learning old things, and on the whole profiting by them so freely and gracefully. The Note-Books are provincial, and so, in a greatly modified degree, are the sketches of England in *Our Old Home*," but they succeed in giving "the whole thing the appearance of a triumph, not of initiation." Here is the Christopher Newman, the Isabel Archer, the Milly Theale of the novels; here the oft-repeated story of the initiation of the novice, or the eating of the apple, depending upon one's reading of the values concerned.

Up to the very recent past, the relationship of the American and the European, of the United States and the rest of the Western world, can only be described as a four-way complex, based on the New World–Old World dichotomy. The American of the American dream was also the overgrown and gangling American adolescent and the Europe of a rich cultural tradition was also the sink of corruption and the den of thieves. One could draw this complex of distorted images as a square and then write in diagonal and straight lines to indicate how the American innocent interacted with the corrupt Europe, the sophisticated European with the America of the dream, the crass American materialist with the Europe of culture and tradition, and so forth. By doing so, one might not learn much truth in history, but one could discover many a truth of the human heart and imagination. For however unreal and misleading all these images and stereotypes may be, there is no doubt that they have shaped and directed America's cultural relations with Europe from the start. The dichotomy of the Old World vs. the New has formed the basic structure within which we have framed our generalizations about each other as persons and as peoples for three hundred years. From the sentimental Old-World-lover Washington Irving and the irascible New-World-defender and critic Fenimore Cooper to the Henry Adams of *Mont St. Michel and Chartres* and the Woodrow Wilson of *The New Freedom*, the East and the West, the Past and the Future, have supplied the American with an uneasy love-hate attitude toward both his own world of actuality and the world of his racial and cultural memory.

I I I

Just when did the New World become sufficiently old and the Old World sufficiently new to blur the lines dividing them and make all these traditions and stereotypes suspect? And how did this happen?

It would be easy enough to turn to the events of history to explain these slow changes and to start, as Sigmund Skard does, with the aftermath of the Civil War. That war, he says, "was to give the United States a completely new position in the world. . . . The territory of the republic increased and its population soared. Its economic and industrial growth was explosive; almost overnight its display of strength gave the United States a voice in world politics. . . . This new America, which thus arose behind the morning fogs, was bound to scare the Old World." [2] This picture in its main lines is accurate, but it may be somewhat foreshortened. Perhaps it was not until the Spanish War in 1898 that the United States became in any real sense an imperial power and a sympathetic partner with Great Britain in world politics. It was rather the defeat of the agrarian-minded populists by McKinley that united the nation from coast to coast in a single industrial economy that required world expansion. The first Roosevelt's aggressive foreign and domestic policies and the crusade of Woodrow Wilson to "make the world safe for democracy" in 1917–18 were but further evidences of national maturity, and the latter's policy of self-determination for emerging nations helped to bring about the crack-up of the Europe-dominated world empires of the nineteenth century. History alone would give us a date about 1920 when the United States could be declared a power of the Western world on a par with the great powers of Europe, and the events of the following years but strengthened and expanded this position.

But I am always somewhat suspicious of depending upon political and economic facts to explain historical change. I would rather turn to what people say about their feelings in seeking for

causes, and the comments of European commentators on America
and of American commentators on Europe would seem to suggest
that during this period Europe gradually became "Americanized"
and the American traveler "Europeanized," much to the fear and
even disgust of both. The New World–Old World dichotomy has
been eroded away and the images based upon it are happily in
danger of disappearing entirely. The American traveler from
Philadelphia may actually now feel more at home in Oslo than in
Omaha, in Tokyo than in Toledo.

A closer look at the American traveler of the 1880's and 1890's,
at Henry James, his brother William, Henry Adams, or William
Dean Howells, will reveal that the process of Europeanization was
by then already well started. I mean Henry James himself and
not the characters in his novels, none of whom, with the possible
exception of Lambert Strether in *The Ambassadors*, attained to
the cosmopolitan perspective of their author. In speaking of
Turgenev's "minutely psychological attitude" as a "dweller in
many cities and a frequenter of many societies," [3] James is really
describing himself. Of American travelers in Europe, he was
perhaps the first to accept into himself the modes and codes of
Old World society without loosing the feel of his own roots
clinging to native American soil. Van Wyck Brooks has called him
a man without a country and has pictured him as a wanderer between two worlds, but it would perhaps be more accurate to call
him a man of many countries. Most of the transplanted Americans
who people his novels are imperfect cosmopolitans, too naïve like
Caspar Goodwood to become identified, or too completely identified like Gilbert Osmond with the corruptions of Old World culture. But neither of these extremes portrays Henry James. In devoting himself to the misty midregions of international society,
he at least made a move away from the provincialism of earlier
Americans abroad, even though the dichotomy of the two worlds
is still at the root of all his cosmopolitanism.

Not so with Henry Adams whose American of the *Education* is
saturated with international politics and whose Europe of the
Mont St. Michel is born of the twelfth rather than the nineteenth
century. Adams would seem to be doing little more with his creation of a dream world of the Middle Ages than Irving did with
his synthetic Old England, but there is a difference, for now the

cathedral of Chartres is lifted out of time and place to become a symbol and a universal shrine to the Virgin created by and for the American traveler of the mind and spirit. In Henry Adams' blending of philosophy, art, religion, and politics, there is a cosmopolitanism on a deeper level than that of Henry James. The fact has become symbol, and the world is more nearly one.

This in a sense is what the exiles of the 1920's were attempting to achieve in their more organized flights from an intolerably mechanized America to a Europe of imagined riches of art and feeling. In the first impulse of their expatriation they were no less provincial than their predecessors of a century earlier but, as Malcolm Cowley has pointed out, they quickly learned their lesson and in them we perhaps can see the breakthrough of the new point of view. "Later," says Cowley, "after discounting the effects of the war, they decided that all nations were fairly equal, some excelling in one quality, some in another—the Germans in mechanical efficiency, the French in self-assurance, the English in political acumen; the Americans . . . were simply a nation among other capitalist West European nations." [4]

If the expatriate Americans for the most part returned after a few years thus disillusioned and cosmopolitanized it was as much because they had discovered an "Americanized" Europe as for any deep-seated change in themselves. "The whole world," wrote George Santayana in 1922, "is being Americanized by the telephone, . . . the department store, and the advertizing press. Americanism, apart from the genteel tradition, is simply modernism—purer in America than elsewhere because less impeded and qualified by survivals of the past." [5] And Edmund Wilson has more recently summed up the change: "Industrially, politically and socially," he says, "Europe . . . is becoming more and more like America every day. . . . It is up to American writers to try to make some sense of their American world—for their world is now everybody's world." [6]

But, like the Europeanizing of the American traveler, this process of Americanizing of Europe did not occur overnight. It was well back in the nineteenth century that the immigrant dream of a city with streets paved in gold began to seem more like the nightmare of a mechanized dollar-grabbing civilization. Even Tocqueville had warned of the levelling action of de-

mocracy, but it was an Englishman, George W. Stevens, who gave
overt expression to the European stereotyped image of a mechanized and materialistic America. "Materialistic in the sense of
being avaricious, I do not think they are;" he charitably allowed,
"they make money, as I have said, because they must make
something and there is nothing else to make. But materialistic, in
the sense that they must have all their ideas put in material form,
they unquestionably are." [7] Hamsun expresses the same idea with
less charity in describing Walt Whitman as "born in America,
that backwoods of the world, where everything shouts hurrah
and whose people's sole acknowledged talent is for making
money." [8] And if Hamsun rightly is rejected as a spokesman for
the Scandinavian view, essentially the same idea is found in a
more thoroughly and judiciously developed form in Veblen's
doctrine of conspicuous waste. But be it said for the latter that
he at no point limits his theory to the American character as
such; he speaks rather of the qualities and values and dangers of
modern industrialized capitalism.

Others have not been so kind. It is these very qualities and
values that many other European critics, particularly the French,
have narrowly assigned to the American character with the warning to beware. *"Qui sera le maître, Europe ou Amérique?"* cried
Lucien Romier in 1927 and André Siegfried in the same year
made an exhaustive analysis of the frightful consequences of
America's threatened conquest of Europe. "The American people," he writes in *America Comes of Age,* "are now creating on
a vast scale an entirely original social structure which bears only
a superficial resemblance to the European." [9] "If the aim of society
is to produce the greatest amount of comfort and luxury for
the greatest number of people, then the United States of America
is in a fair way to succeed." "Big profits overshadow liberty in all
its forms." "So the discussion broadens until it becomes a dialogue,
as it were, between Ford and Gandhi." Thus speaks the modern
voice of the Old World, forgetting perhaps that it was Thoreau
rather than Voltaire to whom Gandhi turned for strength and
solace.

The dollar sign has done America more harm in the eyes of the
world than can ever be balanced by the ideals of the founding
fathers who brought liberty and equality from Europe and would

today attempt to return those riches with interest. But there is no symbol for this kind of influence. Fortunately not all Europeans feel as did Siegfried, but, whether we call it Americanization or merely the common advance of modern man into a world in which material forces threaten human values, it is obvious that American civilization, although easily distinguished in detail, must now be dealt with at least on a par with and as a part of the civilizations of Western Europe. As nations, we today speak a common language, man to man, television set to television set, one world to another, not as a New World to an Old or an Old World to a New. The Europeanizing of the American traveler and the Americanization of European culture have brought an end to the traditional dichotomy of the Old World vs. the New.

I V

Is there a similar formula that would furnish the American abroad today with an equation to symbolize his new position? Certainly not a good one that is generally accepted, but we might experiment and offer an image drawn from science, or rather from the teaching of science. I remember a lecturer on the nature and structure of matter representing a molecule by a cluster of small wooden balls connected with each other in a fixed pattern by small wooden sticks. This is perhaps a little like the human universe. Any of the small balls, as atoms, or perhaps neutrons or even smaller subdivisions of matter, is the nation of which we are a part. The network of small connecting sticks is the complex of relationships which binds us together into a meaningful whole. Similar arrangements of smaller units into larger units can be found in the galaxies. Unless my science is hopelessly out of date, there would seem to be a kind of common pattern to the macrocosm and the microcosm which our poor middle region of a human universe might share. Only thus can the cosmopolitan traveler find himself at home in a mechanized universe.

The ideal of this cosmopolitan in a modern mechanized Europe is perhaps realized best in T. S. Eliot. Born in St. Louis, Missouri, of New England parents, educated at Harvard and Oxford, he lived most of his life in London. In an address delivered in St. Louis in 1953, he identified his own work with that of the modern movement in poetry which rose simultaneously in England and America as a revolt against the nineteenth century, but of which the pioneers were "more conspicuously the Americans than the English." These Americans, he says, "assembled a *body* of American poetry which has made its total impression in England and in Europe," of which he considers himself to have a share. But he adds ruefully of the leading British representative of the revolt, "I do not know whether Auden is an English or is an American poet; his career has been useful to me in providing me with an answer to the same question when asked about myself, for I can say: 'Whichever Auden is, I suppose I must be the other.' " [10] "Here," he says in the fourth of his *Four Quartets,* "The intersection of the timeless moment / Is England and nowhere." The universal is discovered only in the intense realization of the time and the place. The cosmic poet which Whitman hoped to be, Eliot has become; but restraint and sophistication have taken the place of buoyancy and abandon.

One could hardly pursue the doctrine of the universal in culture much further, and the recognition of American literature and philosophy and science abroad in recent years would suggest that, in theory at least, the New World has at last outgrown its adolescence. But when we turn from such ideal considerations to the practical circumstances of international cultural relations, a much more modest attitude is called for. If the American abroad has any tendency to gloat over his new role as cosmopolitan, he need only read such books as Graham Greene's *The Quiet American* or Eugene Burdick's *The Ugly American* to have his wings clipped. And a recent Fulbright visiting professor in an Austrian university is even more pessimistic when he reports that "the prevailing image of the United States is that of a materialistically driven and technologically enslaved society which is pathetically confused by its new responsibilities for world leadership."

I am not personally inclined to so dark a view even though I realize that the role of the American abroad today is not entirely easy; nor is his reception easy for his hosts. I have myself attempted the role often enough—not only in the Scandinavian countries, but in England, in Continental Europe, and even briefly in India and Japan—to realize its difficulties as well as its rewards. For the role is neither that of the student, the missionary, the statesman, nor the sight-seer, even though it seems to partake of all of these, and the opportunity is great for those of us who have come to Europe as participants in the effort of the Americans, through their foundations and their government, to improve international cultural relations. After more than a quarter of a century that effort may now be ready for some sort of inventory and appraisal, and I would like to conclude by touching on a few of the things that such an appraisal might expect to uncover.

The initiative taken by the Rockefeller Foundation immediately after World War II in forwarding the cause of American Studies abroad is perhaps the first to be noted. Its support initiated or made possible the Salzburg Seminar, the pioneer American Institute at Munich, the Tokyo seminar (out of which grew the Japanese American Literature Associations and, more recently, the American Studies Foundation), and the Cambridge and Oxford seminars (out of which grew the British Association for American Studies). In addition, early grants to people like Sigmund Skard, Max Beloff, and Maurice LeBreton for visits to the United States and grants for the buying of American books by such universities as Manchester, Copenhagen, Ghent, Oslo, Cambridge, London, Groningen, Leiden, Pisa, and Rome established policies which other American foundations and the Government have followed since. Seldom has there been a more impressive record of the effects from small grants at the right time and place.

As far as I know, the Rockefeller theory was never formulated in so many words, but it seems to have been, first to meet people abroad who had an initial interest in things American, and then through them to plant seeds of future development. The Institute at Oslo is surely one of the finest fruits of this Johnny Appleseed technique, and our genial host the author of Johnny Appleseed's own book.

The effort grew and expanded in the following years. The United States government came into the picture early through Senator Fulbright's 1946 amendment to the Surplus Property Act (P.L.584) and the Smith-Mundt Act of two years later (P.L.402) under which semiofficial educational foundations and commissions were set up in such countries as had a favorable debit relationship with the United States. The American State Department at about the same time joined in helping to develop cultural agencies like USIS and UNESCO, in sending qualified (and sometimes not so well qualified) students, teachers, and scholars to former military friends and enemies alike, and in supplying books and documents for foreign universities and research centers.

It would seem that between 1949 and 1963, nearly 53,000 visitors from overseas went to the United States and over 21,000 Americans went abroad under State Department auspices. While recognizing the weaknesses of the program—chief among which are the scarcity of really top-quality American scholars who can afford long periods of time away from their homes and work and the failure of some of the countries of visit to prepare for and to use their visitors to full advantage—the 1963 so-called Gardner Report sums up its objectives in a way that helps to make clearer the new role of the American abroad:

> When viewed as an aspect of a great nation's foreign relations, the program has four rather remarkable characteristics impressed upon it by the American people who gave it shape: First, it is based on a strong, perhaps typically American faith in direct exposure and personal face-to-face experience between peoples as a means of dispelling misconceptions and developing understanding. Second, it uses education as the principal bridge of contact—the exchange of students, professors and scholars, and also of non-academic visitors on "study tours." In essence it is a program of international education. Further, it asserts the strong American commitment toward freedom of inquiry; exchange visitors are free to look and listen and to draw their own conclusions (a privilege, I might add, which they ask for and often receive when they in turn go abroad). Finally, it relies in very large part on private participation and initiative.

One of the controlling features of the program is therefore that it is a "two-way street" for cultural exchange. The establishment last year of a center for Indian studies at Poona with a matching center for American studies established more recently at Hyderabad is a case in point. And such mutual exchange is especially desirable and possible with the nations of Europe where there is approximate equality of value in the cultural and human factors involved. This is the philosophy behind the new Ford Foundation–American Council of Learned Societies program which provides both chairs and book subsidies for the teaching of American Studies in Europe and fellowships to bring young European scholars to the United States to prepare themselves for these new opportunities. If successful, this program would ultimately create and staff all the needed American Studies centers in Europe with Europeans trained at least in part in the United States, and would make the Fulbright visiting professor a less frequent and more carefully selected guest. And more attention could be paid to the building up of Scandinavian and central European study centers in the United States by the reverse of this process.

All of which sounds very complicated but at the same time very possible and very necessary if we are to destroy the false and prejudiced stereotypes which have so largely controlled our ideas about each other in the past and to substitute first-hand knowledge in their places. Things have surely changed since the days of innocence abroad from Irving to Mark Twain. American history and literature are accepted today in most European universities as legitimate fields of higher study, and American scholars are no longer uneasy about their own culture among the other cultures of the world. It hardly seems possible that, a half century ago when I was choosing a career, American literature was considered an unacceptable field for higher academic research for the student of literature in English. And it was not until I met such people as Charles Cestre, Sigmund Skard, Carl Bodelsen, Lars Åhnebrink, and Tauno Mustanoja that, for me at least, our growing confidence in our own cultural maturity was reflected in the serious scholarship of those who viewed it from across the seas. If the American in Europe has lost some of his ambivalence of attitude toward the Old World because he now knows that it is no longer old, it is largely because the scholars of that Old World have learned that the New World is no longer new. The mutual exchange of scholarly interests between America and Europe is but one way to study the complex cultures that the human animal has thrown around itself in various forms at various times and places like the shells of the multiform denizens of the sea.

2. *The American Myth and the European Mind* (Philadelphia: University of Pennsylvania Press, 1961), p. 34.

3. Leon Edel, *Henry James, The Conquest of London* (Philadelphia: J. B. Lippincott Co., 1962), p. 167.

4. Malcolm Cowley, *Exile's Return* (New York: Viking Press, 1934), pp. 95-96.

5. *Dial*, LXXII (June, 1922): 555.

6. Edmund Wilson, *The Shores of Light* (New York: Farrar, Straus and Young, 1952), p. 440.

7. H. C. Commager, *America in Perspective* (New York: Random House, 1947), p. 163.

8. *Fra det moderne Amerikas Aandsliv*, quoted in G. W. Allen, *Walt Whitman Abroad* (Syracuse, N.Y.: Syracuse University Press, 1955), p. 76.

9. André Siegfried, *America's Coming of Age* (New York: Harcourt, Brace and Co., 1927), pp. 34, 348-349, 350, 353.

10. T. S. Eliot, *American Literature and the American Language* (St. Louis, Mo.: Washington University, 1953), pp. 22-23.

IV
Postscript

Those Early Days: A Personal Memoir

An informal talk at the luncheon of the American Literature Section of the Modern Language Association and the American Studies Association, New York, December 27, 1966.

IT MAY COME as something of a surprise to learn that systematic historical scholarship in American literature dates from the year 1921 and that my invitation to speak was addressed to "the last surviving *active* member from the old days when the Group numbered only a dozen or so." No wonder that I felt like the Ancient Mariner who was impelled to hold the wedding guest with his skinny hand and his glittering eye in order to tell him of that fearsome voyage which he alone had survived. But when I got down to reviewing the vital statistics of the situation, I found that, unlike Ishmael, I had with me other survivors clinging to Queequeg's coffin. So if you think you are listening to a voice from the grave, it will be only the wee small voice of the Acting Secretary of the American Literature Group at its third meeting, in Ann Arbor in 1923, when neither the elected Chairman Percy H. Boynton of Chicago nor the elected Secretary Francis A. Litz, then of Johns Hopkins, were present, and that old war-horse of the pioneer days, Arthur Hobson Quinn, took the chair for the second of three consecutive years and asked his graduate student to take notes.

May I read you those notes? because this is where I came in

and because they contain most of what I would like to say today, forty-three years later:

(English XII) American Literature. *Chairman,* Professor Percy H. Boynton. In the absence of Professor Boynton, Professor Arthur H. Quinn served as Chairman.

Professor Pattee read a paper giving in retrospect the introduction of American Literature in the College curriculum. The discussion that followed favored presenting American Literature as expression of national (historical) consciousness and not as aesthetic offshoot of English Literature.

In reporting on Problems under Investigation, Professor Leisy called attention to a list of articles to date in scholarly journals, to theses now in progress, and to a number of possible subjects for investigation. Professor Pattee suggested rewriting official biographies because of their prejudiced matter; Professor Hubbell told of teaching literature by backgrounds; Dr. Mabbott recommended biographical and bibliographical studies of local authors.

A committee, consisting of Professors Hubbell, Mabbott, and Leisy (Chairman) is to report what theses are completed, what ones are under investigation, and what special collections are available for research in various libraries.

About twenty-five persons were present.

Professor F. L. Pattee was elected Chairman and Dr. E. E. Leisy, Secretary.

R. E. Spiller, Acting Secretary

The striking thing about these notes is, I think, that they represent so vigorous and ambitious a response to the presidential challenge of John Mathews Manly of two years before. Manly, as chairman of a committee to study and reorganize the diffuse and boring paper-reading sessions of the Association, had recommended a breakdown into small research groups. "The general impression produced by a survey of our work," he had charged, "is that it has been individual, casual, scrappy, scattering," but, he continued, "this age is increasingly one of specialization and of organization for the accomplishment of purposes too large for a single investigator." [1] The solution he proposed was for scholars in the modern languages to group themselves for cooperative research and specialized meetings; and American literature was obviously one of the subdivisions of the English language segment—specifically English XII.

Up to this time an American specialization was hardly respectable; in fact, it was close to professional suicide. Quinn had spent many years studying the American drama; Cairns had devoted his attention to British criticisms of American writing, and Boynton and Pattee chiefly to the more recent local colorists of the West. Even the *Cambridge History* editors, to whom everything in print was literature, were predominantly apologetic in tone. It was a ragged army of minutemen who assembled that day to take stock of the state of scholarship in the American field and to plan the future.

I I

It is not surprising, therefore, that the first years of group history, in spite of Quinn's devotion, were still somewhat scattered and scrappy. Rather it was to the committee of which Leisy was chairman that we came to look for the thrust that put us, so to speak, on the road. Leisy's surveys, which were subsequently carried on by Gregory Paine, Lewis Leary, James Woodress, and others, have provided us with an essential focus which was lacking in the activities of most of the other early MLA groups, a bibliographical backbone. From that day, we have always known where we stood at any one time in scholarly achievement and have therefore always been ready for the next cooperative move, whereas it was not until 1934 that the Association as a whole had a committee on research activities. Most of the other groups, with the possible exception of that on Chaucer, which was already organized and committed to the Manly-Rickert project, kept on their happy-go-lucky way of collecting audiences of drifters, different from year to year, and then electing officers from the floor from among those who hadn't been too bored to last out the meeting.

But the American literature group had a vitality of its own. It was a combination of the philosophical perspective of Norman Foerster and the tactical generalship of J. B. Hubbell which finally gave it the sense of direction and purpose which rescued us from being merely gentlemen-scholars, like so many of our colleagues, with an overdeveloped taste for the hotel bar and an underdeveloped will to get things done. The elements of organization first appeared in 1925 when Chairman Hubbell and Secretary Leisy were elected to second terms and the critic-historian Foerster, who had just read his classic paper on "The Present State of American Literary History," was made chairman of a newly created executive committee, the body which later became the Advisory Council. This, I think, was the first time a Modern Language Association research group had organized itself as virtually an independent cell within the larger organism and had created the means of continuing activity between meetings and from meeting to meeting over the years. From then on, American literature as a scholarly discipline was on the offensive and the note of apology began to fade.

III

Before looking more closely at Foerster's program, however, I would like to turn to another factor in our history. When the scholars in English literature back in the 1890's broke away from their dependence on Classical philology for the disciplinary core of their studies, they substituted Anglo-Saxon and comparative Teutonic philology for Greek and Latin on the grounds that the teutonic tradition was more relevant to their subject and that it provided an equally good discipline because it was equally hard. But when the American scholars in their turn attempted to break away from this Old English philological tradition, now become the establishment, and to declare their independence, there was no separate American philological discipline for them to turn to in spite of the efforts of Louise Pound to make American Speech academically respectable and of Stith Thompson, John Lomax, and others to substitute American Indians and cowboys for Beowulf and Grendel's Dam. Without an American language with a history and a literature of its own (this was before Mencken became respectable) it is not surprising that they turned to intellectual, social, and cultural history as a way to cut the umbilical cord with Mother England and to relate the American literary tradition more vitally to the tradition of all Western Europe, the tradition which had come down unbroken from the Renaissance and had been imported to the New World by Spanish Cavaliers, French priests, Irish farmers, and German

Protestant refugees as well as by British immigrants. Foerster's paper became the introduction to the first cooperative effort of the group, the *Reinterpretation* volume of 1928, the year in which the journal *American Literature,* as Hubbell has told you,[2] was initiated.

"The central fact," Foerster claimed, "is that American literature has had its own special conditions of development and its own special tendencies arising from these conditions. Among the literatures of the modern world, its case is unique. The culture out of which it first issued was not a native growth but a highly elaborate culture transplanted to a wilderness that receded slowly as the frontier pushed westward. . . . The three broad problems with which the student of American literary history is concerned are: (1) In what sense is our literature distinctively American? (2) In what ways does it resemble the literature of Europe? and (3) What are the local conditions of life and thought in America that produce these results?"[3] Foerster's basic approach to the problem as one of the interaction of European (not merely English) culture (not merely literature) and the American environment, and his identification of indigenous romantic and realistic movements in its development were generally accepted at that time as the structural frame for our literary history, from which no later historians have wished to depart to any significant degree.

I wish I could recreate the excitement aroused in some of us by such words as these. Was it really possible for American literary history to make a clean break with historical philology and to share in the vital concerns of the "New History" which was creating such a stir at the other end of the hall in most of the "Old Mains" of the country's universities? For this was the day of James Harvey Robinson, Arthur Schlesinger, Sr., Carl Becker, E. P. Cheyney, Charles A. Beard, and Samuel Eliot Morison. Turner's collected frontier essays had been published in 1920 and Harry Elmer Barnes' *The New History and the Social Sciences* in 1925. These daring new social sciences were apparently developing interdisciplinary concepts and methods which might draw all the traditional disciplines to a new center! Was this the approach we were looking for?

As John Higham has recently pointed out,[4] the revolt of the New History was rather *against* the old order than in favor of a new and consistent one. Provoked mainly by restlessness with the objective reliance on fact and document and by the antiquarianism of the older historians, these radical few turned to the emerging social sciences for help in dealing with the history of modern man in the living terms of ideas and culture. Vigorously present-minded and speculative, they seemed on the verge of developing a new discipline in economic, intellectual, and cultural history which might fit the facts of American literary development as well. At about this time, the American literature group seriously debated the desirability of seceding from the Modern Language Association and joining the American Historical Association, or perhaps the then emergent Society of American Historians, which has survived as one of the sponsors of *American Heritage*. Fortunately it remained within the fold, for by 1933, John Livingston Lowes was demanding in his presidential address that the Modern Language Association as a whole cease trying to learn "more and more about less and less" and turn to vital and immediate concerns and methods.

Thus when I became chairman of the group in 1930, I found it already virtually committed to the gigantic task of restudying the American past from the point of view of a literary history which was nationalistic without being chauvinistic and which attempted to discover the relationships between the literature actually produced in America and its immediate sources in cultural evolution; while the shift of emphasis from historical philology to intellectual and cultural history opened the way for studies of its indebtedness to the tradition of all of Western Europe rather than exclusively to that of England. There was even a proposal for a new Ph.D. in American literature along these lines, first formulated by Foerster and endorsed by the group under Murdock and Bradley. Meanwhile attendance at its meetings had increased from 25 to 149 and was soon to rise to three or four hundred and more, while its internal organization became increasingly firm, purposive, and effective within the larger association. The masthead of its new journal announced a concern for "Literary History, Criticism, and Bibliography," without reference to "Language," and the early papers which were read to the group or published in the journal followed this program.

I V

Focus for major researches had early been set by Pattee on the restudy of individual biographies with the aid of the new psychological and sociologicals insights and by Hubbell on the redefinition of the special characteristics of regions with the help of frontier and ethnological discoveries. Murdock had reexamined Increase Mather, and with him the whole history of European and American Puritanism; Williams was at work on the definitive biography of Washington Irving with special reference to his Spanish sources; Melville had been exhumed from oblivion by Weaver, Thorp, and others; Rusk was beginning to collect the letters of Emerson in preparation for his masterly biography; Quinn and Mabbott were putting the elusive Poe into a believable world from which the Rev. Rufus Griswold had been finally exorcised; and McDowell was discovering a very American Bryant, while Randall Stewart was at work, with Norman Pearson, on the task of eliminating the gentle Sophia from the notebooks of Hawthorne in preparation for a three-dimensional story of his life; Bradley had resurrected Boker, not only as a respectable playwright but as a love-sonneteer honest enough to make Longfellow shudder; Harry Clark was dividing his time between the radical Paine and the genteel Professor Lowell of Harvard, while I was at work taking James Fenimore Cooper and his Indians away from the kiddies.

There were more general studies also. Howard Mumford Jones was discovering that the Europeans, particularly the French, brought deviltry as well as divinity in their baggage when they emigrated to this continent, while Pochmann was doing much the same thing for German culture; Hubbell was reassessing the special features of the literary culture of the Old South, Rusk of the Middle West, Quinn of the Middle Atlantic States with special reference to the theater, and Murdock, Jones, and later Perry Miller, of colonial New England in a plan to rewrite Moses Coit Tyler in three volumes. Walter Blair was taking American humor as his province, Clark and Hornberger American science, and Arthur Christy the Oriental influences; but the most emphatic as well as the least expected revisionist document of them all came out of the West in 1927 when V. L. Parrington launched the first two volumes of his *Main Currents in American Thought,* which Murdock reviewed for the group at an animated meeting and which left many of us wondering whether we had gone too far in our flirtation with the historians and social scientists and had become outright political economists ourselves.

There were also many studies undertaken to determine the exact conditions under which the American writer worked. Magazines and newspapers were reexamined by Frank Luther Mott, gift-books and annuals, publishers and bookshops, libraries, literary clubs and theaters all had their histories written, and contemporary reviews were scanned for evidence of reader-reception of American works.

V

My own chief concern during all this time was moving toward the problem of the philosophy and structure of American literary history taken as a whole, toward accepting the challenge of Foerster and Pattee to attempt a single and total synthesis along new lines, but the way was not yet clear. Chairing that 1930 meeting was a task like that of the old woman who lived in a shoe. The business of the group had moved forward on all fronts and we had so many projects that we did not know what to do. Reports were heard on the progress of the journal, now two years old, and on the Columbia-based Facsimile Text Society, on the committee on manuscript resources, on the historical *Dictionary of American English* and the *Linguistic Atlas of the United States,* and on the *Dictionary of American Biography.* That was the first year of a double session, with a luncheon and business meeting between, and a letter was drafted to the executive council of the association asking for more autonomy as well as more direct representation of the group in its higher echelons of power. Even a sharp slap on the wrist at the council's meeting of 1932 (and as I *now* read the record, probably a deserved one) did little to curtail the brash energy of this prodigious infant!

By 1939 at the New Orleans meeting, the group's committee on a cooperative literary history and bibliography, which had been appointed at Columbia the year before, was authorized to sign a contract for a multi-volume work and to set up the machinery for its execution. I have often wondered what would have happened if we had taken that charge literally, but caution intervened and action was postponed. Instead, at the 1940 meeting at Cambridge this committee's revised and more specific recommendations were withdrawn in the face of mounting resistance from those who felt that the time was not ripe for such a group undertaking. The papers prepublished in *American Literature* and then discussed made clear the general conviction that there was so much "spade-work" still to be done that any attempt at an authorized synthesis would be premature. The solution of the issue—that the group as such should continue this spade-work by undertaking a nationwide survey of manuscript and other resources, leaving the field open for individual and unsponsored attempts at synthesis—was unquestionably a wise one. It established a policy of sponsored research for factual compilations and symposia while encouraging individual initiative in works of interpretation and synthesis. The recent launching of a five-volume short history of American literature under the general editorship of Quentin Anderson, without group sponsorship, tends to confirm the continuing soundness of that policy, while the group itself has officially authorized the symposia on *Transitions,* edited by Clark; and that on *Criticism,* edited by Stovall; the bibliography *Eight American Authors*; the checklist volume on *American Literary Manuscripts,* edited by Joseph Jones and others; Leary's lists of articles on American literature; the *Bibilographical Guide,* edited by Gohdes; the several dissertation lists; and now the annual volume on *American Literary Scholarship*; to say nothing of the Center for Editions of American Authors, which was initiated by the group and is still informally controlled by it.

This last stupendous project, which has for the first time attracted major financial support from outside sources, is the greatest test to which the American literature Group—or rather, now Section—of the Modern Language Association has been submitted. Have we the cooperative energy and vision to carry it through, even with the help of the parent Association? And have we the perspective which will allow us to sponsor a cooperative project without infringing on the prerogatives of the individual scholars involved? This review of our past experience, I hope, will help us to move ahead confidently with the guidance of our accumulated experience and a working sense of what *can* be done in the world of humanistic scholarship by cooperative effort and what must be left as always to the vision and energy of the individual scholar. Let us not merely imitate the scientists and learn to depend too heavily on government foundations for the support of cooperative research. For as humanists we must always remain a free society of scholars rather than a committee of management, or even worse, a computer. The Center, so far, has been true to this ideal under the wise leadership of its director and executive committee; may it continue to be so and may the American Literature Section move on to the initiation of further and even more ambitious projects of both individual and cooperative scholarship.

V I

Before I close, I would like to add a word to the members of the American Studies Association who may have wondered where they fit into this history. I was tempted to broaden my range today to include you, but I decided to respect the limits of your patience. Suffice it to say that, when the group about 1950 began to move with the fashions of the times to an increasing emphasis on analytical and textual criticism and away from literary and cultural history, its old concern for the relationship between literature and culture was largely taken over and developed by the new Association, to the benefit of both. But as that is in itself a complicated story, which others are perhaps better qualified than I to tell, I will conclude as I started, as one of the few surviving of the ancient sages who can cull from the past what he believes to be the wisdom of hard-earned experience, but which may well be little more than fragments of memory. Take it for what it is worth, and let's get to work on the next chapter in the history of American studies, literary and otherwise.

NOTES

1. *Publications of the Modern Language Association,* LXXIII (December, 1958): 35.

2. Jay B. Hubbell, *South and Southwest* (Durham, N.C.: Duke University Press, 1965), pp. 22-48.
3. *The Reinterpretation of American Literature,* edited by Norman Foerster (New York: Harcourt Brace and Co., 1928), pp. xi-xii.
4. *History,* edited by John Higham and others (Englewood Cliffs, N.J.: Prentice-Hall, 1965), pp. 104-116.

Index